A Practical Guide
to Federal
Special Education Law

A Practical Guide to Federal Special Education Law

Understanding and Implementing PL 94–142

Philip R. Jones

Virginia Polytechnic Institute and State University

Holt, Rinehart and Winston
New York   Chicago   San Francisco   Philadelphia
Montreal   Toronto   London   Sydney   Tokyo
Mexico City   Rio de Janeiro   Madrid

Library of Congress Cataloging in Publication Data

Jones, Philip R.
  A practical guide to federal special education law.

  Includes bibliographies and index.
  1. Handicapped children—Education—Law and legislation—United States. I. Title.
KF4210•J67   344.73'0791   81–6212
ISBN 0–03–055551–5   347.304791   AACR2

CBS COLLEGE PUBLISHING
Holt, Rinehart and Winston
The Dryden Press
Saunders College Publishing

"May He who has chosen to limit some of His children, be merciful enough to guide the hands of us entrusted with their care."

R. Wayne Mooers

Preface

This book is written primarily for educational administrators and provides information to assist in understanding and implementing federal special education statutes. It will also be of use to advocates, parents, physicians, attorneys, and others who need information on special education law—specifically The Education for All Handicapped Children Act of 1975 (PL 94–142).

A straightforward, nontechnical approach to the overall federal requirements is presented throughout the text. Historical information and philosophical background material are provided for a better understanding of the "why" questions regarding implementation of special education programs. Such understanding should allow the reader to analyze requirements and determine best practices as opposed to merely meeting the letter of the law.

Major sections of the book focus on:

1. Historical background of PL 94–142 and why Congress passed the statute
2. Description of the reactions of educators, parents, and policy-makers when the law was passed, and what progress and changes have taken place since 1975
3. Practical material on important aspects of the law and suggestions on implementation strategies.

Individual chapters address the following topics: (a) funding; (b) least restrictive environment; (c) individualized education programs; (d) due-process procedures; (e) personnel development; (f) organizing to get the job done; (g) other issues and concerns; and (h) future implementation challenges.

This book is not intended to be a step-by-step guide or "recipe" approach to providing special education programs and services. Such a book would be impossible to prepare because there is such a wide variation between each state's laws and regulations. However, after reading this book, administrators and others should become aware of the complexities involved in the provision of special education and related services, and should develop a philosophical and logical approach to resolving the majority of these problems. This book also stresses the fact that successful program development and maintenance in special education can only come about through the joint efforts of administrators, teachers, and parents, and necessary ingredients for the development of this needed cooperation are provided.

If one major purpose is sought by the author, it is to provide a more complete understanding of federal involvement in special education programs that guarantee the rights of *all* handicapped individuals. Without such understanding, it is doubtful that effective implementation of PL 94–142 and similar laws will be achieved.

Acknowledgments

Many individuals and groups have contributed formally and informally to the development of this manuscript. Public school, state education agency, and higher education colleagues over the last 25 years provided the experiential base necessary to undertake this project.

Doctoral advisees explored many new areas which caught the continuing interest of the author. Problems encountered by former doctoral students as they assumed their professional roles also assisted in developing an initial outline for this book. Special mention goes to Dr. M. Angele Thomas for reacting to drafts of the manuscript.

The Council for Exceptional Children is hereby acknowledged for providing the author with an opportunity for continued professional development.

Thanks to Valerie and Diana for their willingness to share the time and energy of their father with this project. And last, but not least, the typing, comments, assistance, and encouragement of my wife really made the book possible. Dorothy, thank you! I promise to restore the areas of the house used for this project to their original uncluttered condition.

Contents

CHAPTER 3   A View of Progress since Passage of PL 94–142   27

CHAPTER 4   Special Education Costs More— More Than What?   45

CHAPTER 5   Least Restrictive Environment   61

CHAPTER 6 Individualized Education Programs 77

CHAPTER 7 Due-Process Procedures 89

CHAPTER 11   Future Implementation Challenges   125

APPENDIX A   Text of Public Law 94–142,
The Education for All Handicapped Children Act of 1975   129

APPENDIX B   Sample Formats of Basic Multi-Year
Individual Education Program (IEP)   153

APPENDIX C   Office of Special Education Policy Paper,
Individualized Education Programs (IEPs)   163

APPENDIX D   State Education Agency Special
Education Units   198

APPENDIX E   National Centers for Information
on Education of the Handicapped   207

APPENDIX F   Newsletters Containing Current Information
on Programs for Handicapped Individuals   209

APPENDIX G   Legal Advocacy Organizations   210

Index   213

A Practical Guide
to Federal
Special Education Law

Introduction

PL 94–142: An Educator's Lament

*by Thomas J. Goodman, Ed.D. (1976)**

Why such a law as this comes about,
    Is a question frequently wailed.
And why so specific, so terribly tight
    So demanding, so greatly detailed?

Due process, it would seem to some,
    Is methodic, condoned insurrection,
Not a tool for handicapped kids
    To provide their rights to protection.

We want you to know our hackles are raised
    When sanctions are frequently mentioned.
Everyone knows that schools do their job
    And people are all well-intentioned.

Oh, maybe a few handicapped kids slipped by
    While we busily taught to the norm.
But face it, my friend, great resources are needed
    To weather the parental storm.

To give all those kids what the others have had
    Is a simple statement to make.
But where will we get the dollars we need
    To allow all kids to partake?

Can't we delay for five years or so
    Until the economy rises?
Maybe the Feds will send us the cash
    To begin realistic compromises.

Oh what's the use complaining like this?
    I guess the law says it best.
Educate all of the handicapped kids
    Just as well as you do all the rest.

*Reprinted by permission of Dr. Thomas J. Goodman.

The passage of The Education for All Handicapped Children Act of 1975 (PL 94–142) was greeted with widely divergent reactions from various groups. Some educators expressed alarm and dismay. Other educators, as well as parents of handicapped children, looked to the future with renewed hope for equal educational opportunities for handicapped children and youth. Administrators and policy-makers were deeply concerned about the fiscal requirements of the statute. The general public expressed fear that funds would be diverted from regular education programs to initiate and expand special education programs. And special educators themselves were split. Some expressed hope for the future and others feared changing past practices. Confusion and concern seemed to prevail in all groups.

Now that initial clamor has subsided, it is time to step back and reflect on the overall impact PL 94–142 has made on education in general and on special education in particular. Full implementation of the statute has not yet been achieved. It will take some additional time before the lines of the poem, "Educate all of the handicapped kids, Just as well as you do all the rest," ring true. How long it will take may well be related to how soon educators, parents, advocates, policy-makers, and bureaucrats develop a more complete understanding of the statute.

The main purpose of this book is to foster understanding of the law and hopefully speed up its full implementation. Practical suggestions for successful program implementation and maintenance are presented along with background information.

The purpose of this chapter is to:

1. Review briefly the provisions of the law
2. Describe general reactions to its passage
3. Examine some results since its passage
4. Review the organization of this book.

BASIC PROVISIONS OF THE LAW

The Education for All Handicapped Children Act of 1975 guarantees the availability of a free, appropriate, publicly supported education for all handicapped children. PL 94–142, Section 4, defines handicapped children as:

mentally retarded, hard of hearing, deaf, orthopedically impaired, other health-impaired, speech-impaired, visually handicapped, seriously emotionally disturbed, or children with specific learning disabilities who, by reason thereof, require special education and related services.

Section 4(a.)(16) defines special education as:

Specially designed instruction, at no cost to parents or guardians, to meet the unique needs of a handicapped child, including classroom instruction, instruction in physical education, home instruction, and instruction in hospitals and institutions.

Section 4(a.)(17) defines related services as:

transportation, and such developmental, corrective, and other supportive services (including speech pathology and audiology, psychological services, physical and occupational therapy, recreation, and medical and counseling services, except that such medical services shall be for diagnostic and evaluation purposes only) as may be required to assist a handicapped child to benefit from special education, and includes the early identification and assessment of handicapping conditions in children.

These definitions clearly indicate that a child with a disability is covered by provisions of the law only when the disability is sufficiently intense as to require special education. Many children with disabilities can, and should, attend school without program modification.

The definitions further indicate that program modifications, when required, must indeed be specially designed to meet the unique needs of the individual child. Truly individualized instruction is required; the handicapped child should not merely be assigned to a preexisting program.

Finally, related services are necessary when they will help the child to benefit from the specially designed program.

REACTIONS TO THE LAW

Initial reactions to the law could be grouped into four major categories: (a) hope for the future; (b) concern for the education of the handicapped child in the regular classroom; (c) fiscal concerns; and (d) federal intrusion on state's rights.

Hope for the Future

The primary reaction of parents of handicapped children and advocacy groups was one of optimism. State mandates in special education, which had been passed prior to PL 94–142, had not resulted in full-service special education programs. Many handicapped children were still denied entry to public educational programs, which resulted in those families having to bear the cost of private education. And as far as public facilities were concerned, many substandard or inappropriate programs existed. Little coordination existed between day and residential or public and private programs.

PL 94–142 set a national standard for the education of handicapped children. Consequently, parents no longer had to relocate from one community to another just to find a suitable special education program for their child.

Education of the Handicapped Child in the Regular Classroom

As mentioned before, the possibility of placement of a handicapped child in the regular class generated fear and concern among parents and teachers alike. Parents of nonhandicapped children feared that instructional time would be diverted from their children when a handicapped child was in the regular classroom. Regular education teachers feared the unknown and maintained they had not been trained to work with special education students.

Many parents and teachers of handicapped children feared the movement of children from segregated classes and buildings to the less restrictive regular class environment. Such seemingly overprotective feelings are understandable and stem from the fact that in former years it was often thought that segregation was required to provide special education for these children, and both parents and teachers were convinced of this necessity.

Fiscal Concerns

At a time when inflation was rampant, school enrollments were declining, and taxpayers were defeating school referenda, the primary concern of school administrators was necessarily fiscal in nature. While PL 94–142 held the possibility of additional new funds, administrators had seen other federal programs fall behind in actual appropriations, and they envisioned a further drain on dwindling resources. Indeed the signing statement released by the President expressed doubt that the government could meet the authorized funding levels.

Regular classroom teachers and parents of nonhandicapped children had already seen the effects of local budget cutting as evidenced by the reduced number of teachers, the increased class size, and the provision of fewer extracurricular activities. Implementation or expansion of special education programs and services were seen as a potential cause of further cuts in regular programs.

Loss of State's Rights

State-level policy-makers argued that the passage of federally mandated special education further eroded the constitutionally provided rights of the states.

In reality, the majority of the content of PL 94–142 was already present in existing state and federal statutes, although programs had not yet been developed to meet the intent of the state mandates. Thus there were fears of federal monitoring of states' implementation of programs. The statute does, however, leave many areas, such as age ranges to be served and operational definitions, to existing state standards.

RESULTS OF THE LAW

Prior to the enactment of PL 94–142, special education had been the subject of much state and federal litigation. While many individuals and groups predicted that the federal statute would further increase the amount of litigation, such has not been the case.

Many issues which had formerly gone to court could now be decided by the statutory language of PL 94–142 or, more importantly, be resolved through local and state-level administrative due-process procedures established by the Act.

The primary litigation since passage of PL 94–142 has been more substantive in content and seeks clarification and interpretation from judicial authorities where the law is either silent or not sufficiently specific.

While Congressional appropriations have not kept pace with the fiscal authorizations included in the law, appropriations have increased significantly from 100 million dollars in 1975 to over one billion dollars today. The number of handicapped children served has increased by over one-half million since 1975. It is also true that state and local special education budgets have increased dramatically without significant reductions in regular education programs.

The creation of the Department of Education in May 1980 replaced the US Office of Education (USOE) as it was designated previously under the Department of Health, Education, and Welfare. Under the new arrangement, the former Bureau of Education for the Handicapped (BEH) and the Rehabilitation Services Administration (RSA) are combined under an Assistant Secretary, Office of Special Education and Rehabilitation Services (OSERS). While there is not a cause and effect relationship between the new department and PL 94–142, the combining of the two units should result in improved coordination of services for handicapped individuals. Both agencies have been elevated to higher levels of the federal government.

In summary, we have witnessed a flurry of activity since the passage of The Education for All Handicapped Children Act of 1975. Public awareness of the problems of handicapped citizens has increased dramatically. Federal, state, and local authorities have taken many steps to equalize opportunities for handicapped individuals. Many of the steps taken have been focused on short-term solutions and, in some cases, additional forethought may have been advisable. School administrators, special educators, and parents have learned many experiential lessons from these early efforts at implementation. This book will provide practical suggestions and guidance for the long-term provisions our society makes for handicapped children.

ORGANIZATION OF THE BOOK

This book provides the reader with: (a) a greater understanding of why Congress passed PL 94–142 and a review of progress since 1975; (b) an analysis of the more relevant features of the law, with suggested implementation strategies at the local and state level; (c) and finally, a look to future challenges in implementation.

Understanding and History (Chapters 2 and 3)

Chapter 2 provides an historical sketch of the "why" questions leading up to the enactment of PL 94–142 as well as a further delineation of provisions and procedures contained in the statute. Chapter 3 amplifies the progress that has been made since 1975. The primary purpose of these two chapters is to develop the rationale for federal action to foster the education of handicapped children and examine the fiscal support offered to states and local school districts. Understanding that state-level policy to provide equal educational opportunities for handicapped learners had resulted in wide discrepancies on an inter- and intra-state basis is fundamental to developing awareness or appreciation of the need for PL 94–142.

Relevant Features (Chapters 4-10)

Chapters 4 through 10 analyze and discuss provisions and procedures contained in PL 94–142 that have an impact on every state (SEA) and local educational agency (LEA) in the United States. These chapters focus on the most frequently expressed concerns of school administrators, teachers, and parents since passage of the act.

Major concern for financing special education has been expressed by local and state-level groups of policy-makers, educators, and parents. Chapter 4 acknowledges that there are many high-cost programs in the schools, only one of which is special education. In addition to reviewing the various methods states utilize to offset the differential costs of special education, this chapter examines the creative use of federal revenues generated under the PL 94–142 formulas. A review of other funding sources for special education is also provided.

Chapter 5 focuses on providing educational programs for handicapped learners in the least restrictive environment (LRE). The least restrictive environment (LRE) includes a continuum of service options from highly restrictive, segregated classes or buildings to primary placement in regular education programs. Decisions based on the individual needs of the child are the key to determining the least restrictive and most productive environment. Practical tips on implementation are included.

The individualized education program (IEP) required by PL 94–142 has been the source of confusion, criticism, and concern. Possible reasons for these varied reactions to the IEP are provided in Chapter 6. The chapter also suggests how the IEP may be able to replace other forms and paperwork. Key points to remember in developing IEPs are suggested, and the idea that the IEP is probably beneficial to all children, not just handicapped children, is expressed.

While due-process procedures and hearings as embodied in the statute are seen as time-consuming and costly, Chapter 7 suggests that in reality there are now rules and guidelines which protect the school as well as the parent and child. Suggestions for preparing for the due-process hearing are offered for utilization by educators, but they apply equally to parents. Finally, the chapter makes it clear that the school may wish to implement the hearing process when parental consent is not provided.

The issue of training regular education staff to assist in meeting the needs of handicapped children in regular classes is discussed in Chapter 8. Sources of in-service education funds and topics are considered in a review of a comprehensive system of personnel development required by PL 94–142. This chapter should assist the schools in developing an on-going in-service program, which is necessary for full acceptance and implementation of special education.

The need for qualified leadership staff to achieve effective implementation is addressed in Chapter 9. A discussion of the need for administrative *and* supervisory personnel is expanded into the concept of developing a leadership plan for special education. Cooperative programs and preparation of special education leadership staff conclude this chapter.

Chapter 10 addresses many other concerns expressed about the statutes and offers implementation strategies to assist in resolving problems. The concerns cover the general areas of personnel, evaluation, and service.

The Future (Chapter 11)

The final chapter suggests what challenges lie ahead in the implementation of full-service programs for handicapped children and youth. What legal challenges will appear? The threat of a backlash by parents of nonhandicapped children is examined. Such factors are critical to consider when striving for the goal expressed by The Education for All Handicapped Children Act.

SPECIAL FEATURES OF THIS TEXT

Preceding each chapter of the book is a list of some of the most commonly asked questions about provisions of the law. Reasonably brief and concise answers are provided for these questions. More in-depth coverage of these questions is found in the chapter. This feature may also serve as an outline to help the reader recall the more detailed analysis of the issue provided in the specific chapter. For information the reader should not rely on the questions and answers alone, but should use them only after having read the entire chapter.

The Appendices contain not only a copy of the law (PL 94–142) and a federal policy paper on IEPs, but also the addresses of various information sources. The list of the special education unit in each state education agency (SEA) is provided to assist in contacting your state for requirements which may exceed or differ slightly from the federal requirements contained in the book. Other lists provide addresses of organizations, agencies, and advocacy groups which respond to inquiries or publish newsletters.

CHAPTER 2 QUESTIONS

Q: Should every handicapped child be placed in special education?

A: No. The individual needs of the child must be considered in making special education placements. A child who is confined to a wheel chair would not necessarily require special education or related services, so long as he or she could participate in the regular program. In such a case, Section 504 of The Rehabilitation Act of 1973 would apply as to program accessibility.

Q: What is the minimum length of the school day for students in special education?

A: In many communities the length of the school day for handicapped children has been shorter than that for nonhandicapped children, due to multiple trips of available transportation equipment. This practice may be open to question by parents since the individual states usually define the minimum length of day for any child. Since PL 94-142 implementation is based on standards of each state education agency, it appears that the length of day standard must be met for the handicapped child unless a specific waiver is received from the state.

Q: Is every school district required to have a special education advisory council?

A: PL 94-142 requires a state advisory panel composed of the following types of individuals:

1. Handicapped individuals
2. Teachers of handicapped children
3. Parents of handicapped children
4. State and local education officials
5. Special education program administrators

The federal statute does not require such a group for each district. Various state laws do, however, have a local advisory panel or committee requirement. Such a local requirement may apply to an individual district, county, or region. Whether required or not, good practice would appear to dictate the need for such a group, the composition of which could parallel the federal requirement for a state panel.

Q: Can a school district expel a handicapped child?

A: While a school-aged handicapped child may be formally expelled from school attendance, the district is not relieved of its responsibility to provide a free appropriate public education for the child.

Historical Perspectives on Education of the Handicapped

2

The passage of The Education for All Handicapped Children Act of 1975 caused nation-wide confusion and alarm, due to the fact that many aspects of the law were not understood and were thus misinterpreted.

This chapter is divided into three major sections: (a) first, a discussion of the passage of the law and initial reactions to it; (b) second, an analysis of the simplistic nature of the law; and (c) third, a review of a series of events that led to passage of the law.

The purpose of this chapter is to provide a rationale for PL 94-142 and to explain the true meaning of its provisions, in the hope of overcoming the misunderstandings that have surfaced and, in some cases, continue to exist.

PASSAGE OF PL 94-142

On June 18, 1975, after four years of legislative development, with hearings conducted by the House and Senate in Washington, DC and all across the country, the Senate approved S.6 (the Senate version of the bill that ultimately became PL 94-142) by a vote of 83 to 10. On July 29, the House version (H.R. 7217) received a vote of 375 to 44. The House accepted the joint conference committee report on S.6 on November 18 by an even greater margin of 404 to 7. The Senate followed suit the next day by a vote of 87 to 7 (Weintraub, et al., 1976).

President Gerald R. Ford affixed his signature to S.6 on November 29, 1975 and thus was born The Education for All Handicapped Children Act of 1975

(PL 94-142). Over the previous four years, in numerous hearings, critics had voiced objections to a federal mandate for special education. President Ford's statement upon the signing of the bill echoed some of these concerns:

> I have approved S.6, the "Education for All Handicapped Children Act of 1975."
> Unfortunately, this bill promises more than the Federal Government can deliver and its good intentions could be thwarted by the many unwise provisions it contains. Everyone can agree with the objective stated in the title of this bill—educating all handicapped children in our nation. The key question is whether the bill will really accomplish that objective.
> Even the strongest supporters of this measure know as well as I that they are falsely raising the expectations of the groups affected by claiming authorization levels which are excessive and unrealistic.
> Despite my strong support for full educational opportunities for our handicapped children, the funding levels proposed in this bill will simply not be possible if Federal expenditures are to be brought under control and a balanced budget achieved over the next few years.
> There are other features in the bill which I believe to be objectionable, and which should be changed. It contains a vast array of detailed, complex and costly administrative requirements which would unnecessarily assert Federal control over traditional State and local Government functions. It establishes complex requirements under which tax dollars would be used to support administrative paperwork and not educational programs. Unfortunately, these requirements will remain in effect even though the Congress appropriates far less than the amounts contemplated in S.6.
> Fortunately, since the provisions of this bill will not become fully effective until fiscal year 1978, there is time to revise the legislation and come up with a program that is effective and realistic. I will work with the Congress to use this time to design a program which will recognize the proper Federal role in helping States and localities fulfill their responsibilities in educating handicapped children. The Administration will send amendments to the Congress that will accomplish this purpose. (Office of the White House Press Secretary, 1975)

During his Conference on Inflation (1974), convened shortly after his taking office, President Ford had pledged to veto any bills that contained significant new funding authorizations. The President explained that by curtailing federal expenditures he hoped to curb inflation. He vetoed politically popular legislation dealing with such areas as day care for young children and school lunch programs. It is difficult to assess just why he did sign The Education for All Handicapped Children Act into law, since it contained authorization increases from one hundred million dollars to over three billion dollars. During the concluding statement at the Conference, however, President Ford did acknowledge that the effects of inflation bore more heavily on the elderly, the poor, and the handicapped (Conference on Inflation, 1974). It should also be noted that the votes by Congress on the S.6 conference report seem to indicate that a veto override could probably have been accomplished, had this been necessary.

INITIAL REACTIONS

Advocacy groups and professional educators of handicapped children applauded the enactment of PL 94–142, which provides a guarantee of a free appropriate public education for *all* children. Jones (1975), as President of The Council for Exceptional Children, released the following statement upon the enactment of PL 94–142:

> The staff and 71,000 members of The Council for Exceptional Children are delighted the Education for All Handicapped Children Act was signed into law. The Council extends its thanks to President Ford for signing this significant act which assures the right to education for all children. The four years of legislative work on this act are a tribute to the members of Congress and specifically Senator Harrison Williams of New Jersey and Congressman John Brademas of Indiana, chief sponsors of the bill in the Senate and House.
>
> This major piece of legislation is indeed a Declaration of Independence or Bill of Rights for the handicapped and a most appropriate breakthrough during our nation's bicentennial observance. In addition to firmly establishing the education of the handicapped as a national priority, this act provides a strict due-process guarantee to the handicapped child and his parents as they seek their true right to an education. The act further provides incentives to local school districts and states to provide preschool services to the handicapped.
>
> Significant new funding formulae provide for funding under this act to flow not only to state education agencies as under previous legislation but also directly to local school districts on an entitlement basis.
>
> The Council recognizes the current efforts of President Ford to keep the federal budget at the lowest possible level during these unstable economic times. The Council acknowledges the difficulty the President will have in signing appropriation bills to realize the full fiscal goals of this act until he feels economic conditions have improved and stabilized. The need for federal funds, however, is not diminished as states and local school districts attempt to implement educational programs for all handicapped children at the same time local school budgets are constricting and property tax levies are frozen in many states. Funds provided by this act may be used as start up or seed monies in primarily serving the one million or more handicapped children currently receiving no educational program.
>
> Education remains a responsibility of the 50 state governments and the local school districts. The impact of this act in assisting the educational programs in the states to meet the challenge of serving all children should in no way be interpreted as the states allowing or the federal government attempting to impose federal responsibility for the educational program for all or any part of our society.
>
> The gratitude of the Council on behalf of the eight million handicapped children and young adults is expressed to President Ford and Congress.

TEACHERS EXPRESS ALARM

Teachers of nonhandicapped children expressed concerns about having to teach handicapped children in the regular classroom. At the 1975 National Education Association Convention President Harris (1975) contended, "The pending bill requires integration of handicapped children into standard classrooms."

Not only was Harris' statement misleading, but the *NEA Reporter* further indicated the least restrictive environment concept (mainstreaming) as embodied in S.6 was an innovation in federal education statutes. In reality, however, the concept was contained in PL 93–380, the Education Amendments of 1974.

Comments such as those by Harris ran rampant through teacher organizations in the schools. Apparently teachers of nonhandicapped children envisioned severely handicapped children being placed in regular classrooms, even though the law acknowledges that separate classes and schooling will still be required, depending on the nature and severity of the handicap.

FEDERAL INTRUSION CLAIMED

Federal involvement in the education and care of handicapped citizens is not new! Public Law 19–8 was enacted January 29, 1827; its title read: "An Act to provide for the location of the two townships of land reserved for a seminary of learning in the territory of Florida, and to complete the location of the grant to the Deaf and Dumb Asylum of Kentucky" (La Vor, 1976). From 1827 to 1927, handicapped citizens received attention in twenty-eight federal acts; from 1927 to 1949, 32 acts; from 1950 to 1959, 18 acts; from 1960 to 1969, 54 acts; from 1970 to 1975, 71 acts. La Vor (1976) suggests that the 1970s, which saw the passage of The Education for All Handicapped Children Act of 1975, witnessed dramatic Congressional activity on behalf of the nation's handicapped citizens. Congressional activity for the handicapped focused on health, education, welfare, housing, transportation, volunteer programs, training, and nutrition.

Special education in and of itself is not new, and neither is mandated special education at the state level new. Typically, public education has been viewed as a function of the fifty states. The Education for All Handicapped Children Act has been perceived as a federal intrusion on the rights of states. The federal government has, however, been active in public education programs for many years through vocational education, National Defense Education Act, The Elementary and Secondary Education Act (ESEA), and other programs. These programs were not mandates; participation in funding of such programs required procedural and administrative changes at the state and local level. And likewise PL 94–142 is only a mandate when a given state agrees to participate in the receipt of federal funds authorized by the Act. In reality forty-eight states had mandatory special education statutes at the time PL 94–142 became law.

Opposition to passage of the act and criticism of the act following its passage came also from the Council of Chief State School Officers, the membership of which is limited to the various state superintendents and commissioners of education.

Cronin (1976), state superintendent of education in Illinois, used PL 94–142 as the basis of an article entitled, "The Federal Takeover: Should the Junior Partner Run the Firm?" Cronin suggested that PL 94–142 was one more intrusion on state obligations, and that two of four possibilities to slow down a federal takeover of education were federal program consolidation and refusal to submit certain questionable reports. He further suggested that states and localities could " ... press harder for local and state resolution of the many problems that face us ... in order to make federal initiative redundant" (p. 500). It should be noted that Illinois' mandate was passed in 1965, to be fully implemented in 1969.

Daniel B. Taylor, West Virginia state superintendent of schools, shared with chief state school officers his 1977 letter to Senator Jennings Randolph. After stating how difficult it would be to implement PL 94–142 in West Virginia, Taylor (1977) indicated:

> PL 94–142 appears to be an invasion of the constitutional and statutory rights of State and local government for the control and direction of education. I call your attention to Section 432 of the General Education Provisions Act which states, ... shall be construed to authorize any department, agency, officer, or employee of the United States to exercise any direction, supervision or control over the curriculum, program of instruction, administration, or personnel of any educational institution, school, or school system, or over the selection of library resources, textbooks or other printed or published instructional materials by any educational institution or school system, or to require the assignment or transportation of students or teachers in order to overcome racial imbalance.
>
> I close with the thought that handicapped people living in West Virginia ought to have a right, as people of the United States, to receive their fair share of federal funds provided by the US Treasury ... for helping handicapped citizens, and that this right ought not to depend upon whether their State will also provide financial assistance to them. For the US Government to place a State Government in the position of having to spend money out of its own treasury on a federally assisted program—particularly the lion's share of the money—in order for its people to enjoy a benefit of US citizenship is questionable.

Taylor addresses the federal intrusion and fiscal problems and his letter is representative of other formal and informal reactions of chief state school officers. West Virginia passed a special education mandate in 1974 which called for implementation the same year. He, like Cronin, actually had a state mandate in existence prior to the passage of the federal mandate.

A SIMPLE LAW

To clear up misunderstandings about the law, this section will describe its nature, its relationship to state and federal statutes and case law already in existence, and some of its unique features. Public Law 94–142 is not a new law. It is actually an amendment or overhaul of Part B of the Education of the Handicapped Act (EHA), originally passed as an amendment to the Elementary and Secondary Education Act (ESEA) in 1966 (PL 89–750).

Part B, EHA, created a state grant program with an initial appropriation of 2.5 million dollars in 1967. This appropriation grew to 34 million dollars by 1971. The state education agencies (SEAs) received their allocations on a state population basis. These funds were primarily discretionary and were allocated to a variety of projects selected through SEA plans and state competition. To trigger the release of funds, SEAs submitted state plans—which were primarily projected activities—documents designating the targeted areas of need in the education of handicapped children.

The Education Amendments of 1974 (PL 93–380) increased the authorization levels of the basic state grant program to 660 million dollars. While increased authorized funding levels were important since the previous authorized levels had been achieved through appropriations, the guarantee of educational rights of exceptional children and their parents contained in PL 93–380 was even more important. The 1974 amendment to Part B, EHA, included assurance of due-process procedures and education in the least restrictive environment (LRE). Each state was also required to establish a goal of providing full educational opportunities for all handicapped children within the state and to develop a timetable to achieve the specified goal.

In 1973 Congress passed PL 93–112, The Rehabilitation Act of 1973. Section 504 of that act is very brief in language, but has far-reaching implications for the education of handicapped individuals. While not directly related to the state grant program, Section 504 certainly provides the same essential guarantees as were contained in the Education Amendments of 1974. Section 504 of The Rehabilitation Act of 1973 provides that:

> no otherwise qualified handicapped individual in the United States, as defined in section 7(6), shall, solely by reason of his handicap, be excluded from the participation in, be denied the benefit of, or be subjected to discrimination under any program or activity receiving federal financial assistance.

Section 504 guarantees the civil rights of the handicapped population and prohibits discrimination against the handicapped, not only in education but also in employment. Regulations implementing Section 504 were published on May 4, 1977 in the *Federal Register* and contain "Subpart D—Preschool, Elementary and Secondary Education."

The Education for All Handicapped Children Act of 1975 reiterates many of the previously passed educational provisions for handicapped persons, such as due-process procedures and least restrictive environment alternatives. It also states dates when the provision of free appropriate public education is to go into effect for all handicapped children, aged 3 to 18, and subsequently aged 3–21.

Unique features of PL 94–142 include the following:

1. It is permanent legislation and does not require periodic reauthorization
2. It is based primarily on existing state and federal statutes and case law
3. It has a funding formula which permits every state, Congressional district, and school district to qualify for funds

Ballard (1977) summarizes the four major purposes of PL 94–142:

Guarantee the availability of special education programing to handicapped children and youth who require it.

Assure fairness and appropriateness in decision making about providing special education to handicapped children and youth.

Establish clear management and auditing requirements and procedures regarding special education at all levels of government.

Financially assist the efforts of state and local government through the use of federal funds. (p. 2)

Ballard's (1977) booklet entitled *Public Law 94–142 and Section 504—Understanding What They Are and Are Not* is a very practical question-and-answer approach written in layman's terms. It is a useful document for parents, teachers, school administrators, and others interested in basic factual information. It helps clarify some misinformation about PL 94–142 and Section 504, and may also be used as a guide for studying the statute.

PL 94–142 has been discussed by many individuals since its enactment. Readers are encouraged to review the entire law (reproduced in the Appendix) before continuing to read the following chapters. The regulations implementing PL 94–142 are not reproduced in this publication since they are more subject to change. The current regulations for most aspects of the law were published in the *Federal Register*, on August 23, 1977. Procedures for evaluating children with specific learning disabilities were published in the *Federal Register*, on December 29, 1977.

While PL 94–142 is basically a simple law, it is also very detailed. In many instances the regulations revert to statutory language precisely because of this detail. Such is not the case with Section 504 of the Rehabilitation Act of 1973, due to its lack of detail. Readers of this book are encouraged to become familiar with relevant regulations implementing these laws.

State laws and regulations should also be carefully reviewed. Many state codes have been amended since 1975 to make them more consistent or parallel with the federal statutes.

EVENTS LEADING TO PASSAGE

Why was the Education for All Handicapped Children Act enacted in 1975? Why were four years necessary to develop a law with such a humanistic purpose?

In order to fully understand the need and reason for this law, one needs to know the conditions that brought it about. No one event could be said to have been singularly influential in getting Congressional passage of PL 94–142. Instead, a culmination of events over the previous two decades led up to its passage. These events may best be summarized by examining activities of advocacy groups, changes in state laws, and decisions in the courts. Congressional findings from hearings held in Washington and other locations around the country also led to the enactment of PL 94–142. And finally, political considerations may have prompted passage.

Advocacy Groups

Parent advocate groups were organized formally and informally in local communities and states, as well as on a nation-wide basis during the period between 1940 and 1960. Denial of educational programs for handicapped children appears to have been a major unifying factor for parent groups.

The role of advocacy groups for the twenty years following World War II was primarily focused upon local school districts. Some school districts elected to offer programs for limited numbers of handicapped children, while others did not. Even in the districts where some programs were located, waiting lists for services developed when capacity enrollments were reached.

Groups of parents who had been told, "We do not have a program for your handicapped child," or "It looks like we will not have a vacancy in the special education class for a year or two," converged on school board meetings and school administrators. Their basic request was simple: "Please develop programs for our children." Schools typically absolved themselves of any responsibility with responses such as:

1. We do not have space in our schools to serve the handicapped
2. We cannot find specially trained teachers
3. We do not have enough handicapped children in our district to start a program
4. We do not have enough money to begin programs

It should be noted that most parents of handicapped children were not militant in their requests and often accepted the excuses given by the schools for not providing programs. Parents of mentally retarded children frequently banded together to operate their own schools. Facilities ranged from homes and churches to generally low-rent facilities available in the community.

Teaching staff often consisted of one or more of the parents, or other members of the community who worked voluntarily or for relatively little pay. Not uncommonly, such parent-operated programs were financed through fund-raising events and donations. Easter Seal societies provided similar programs and clinics for orthopedically handicapped children. Parents operating such programs generally took great pride in their efforts, possibly because the only other alternatives were keeping the handicapped child at home or placing the child in a public or private residential facility.

Parents eventually began to question why, as taxpayers who were entitled to send their nonhandicapped children to school, they could not send their handicapped children to school. Questions gradually shifted away from the local schools and were directed instead toward state legislatures.

The National Association for Retarded Citizens (NARC), originally the National Association for Retarded Children, was chartered in 1950 and is probably the best known of the parent advocacy groups. State and local units of NARC were formed to assist in mustering a formal approach to the various governmental bodies. While originally concerned only with mentally retarded youngsters, NARC groups shifted their efforts toward those individuals with developmental disabilities, a more encompassing term.

State Law

State legislatures in the 1950s and early 1960s were usually first approached for mandates to serve mentally retarded children. Such selective mandates for one disability area were passed in a few states, but more often such bills did not pass in the first session or two, when they were introduced. Usually a more comprehensive mandate was passed.

Abeson and Ballard (1976) report that Hawaii passed a full program mandate in 1949 for handicapped children aged 5 through 20. In 1954 New Jersey passed a mandate that was subsequently amended to include all handicapped children aged 5 through 20. Pennsylvania passed a full planning and programing mandate in 1956. Nine states followed suit during the decade of the 1960s: Connecticut, 1966; Georgia, 1968; Idaho, 1963 (all except trainable mentally retarded); Illinois, 1965; Indiana, 1969; Kentucky, 1962 (trainable mentally retarded only); Texas, 1969; Utah, 1969; and Wyoming, 1969. Kentucky and Idaho amended their statutes to full programing in 1970 and 1972, respectively.

By July 1, 1975, forty-eight states had varying forms of special education mandates (Abeson and Ballard, 1976). With the exception of Ohio and Mississippi, all were under mandates by statute or court order.

Unfortunately, parents of handicapped children who had worked so diligently for passage of state laws often found that the school districts still were not developing programs for the handicapped. This was particularly true in those states which passed mandates prior to 1970.

Reasons given by school districts for not developing programs continued to focus on lack of trained personnel, lack of adequate facilities, and lack of financial resources. The financial resources appropriated by state government often did not match the funding formula required by the mandate. In these instances, local school districts often shifted the lack of funds issue from the local district to the state.

Michigan's mandate passed the legislature in 1971, and called for full implementation by September, 1973. The age range covered, birth through age 25, is the widest specified age range in the United States. The Michigan legislature had adopted a mandate for planning comprehensive programs for handicapped children in 1970, as a prelude to the mandate passed in 1971. Michigan legislators apparently had data available as to the potential numbers of children needing programs, as well as fiscal projections for the program. This may have influenced the inclusion of a broad age range. When most other states passed mandates, they included a two- to four-year planning and implementation period. The age ranges included in many states tended to establish ages 3 or 5 as the lower limit and 18 as the upper limit. Legislators in states where the planning and mandate were included in the same law would often claim they had not realized the full implications of the law, especially when appropriation requests were not fully funded by the state legislatures. Many of the original mandates passed by states have been amended to include disability groups not previously covered, or to change the age range of children served.

Advocacy groups felt they had won major victories in the state legislatures only to find few additional programs developing in the schools. Parents contacted state education agency personnel for assistance without too much success, for such personnel exerted little pressure on local school districts to implement state laws. The failure of the state to appropriate funds and adverse political pressures appear to have been two major causes for lack of enforcement. State education agency personnel preferred to function in a consulting or technical assistance role rather than in a regulatory or supervisory role.

In defense of school districts, it must be acknowledged that they were going through a period of increasing enrollment due to the postwar baby boom. The period from 1950 to the late 1960s did find many overcrowded school facilities with some districts forced to operate double shifts to accommodate increased enrollments. Near the end of the 1960s, enrollment declines became evident and still continue today.

Taxpayers also began protest movements which resulted in the defeat of school district referenda, which was often the only way taxpayers could make their voice heard. They felt they had little success in voicing opinions to state and federal legislative bodies. Parents continued to become frustrated in their efforts and eventually adopted more militant tactics: They began to take their problems to the judicial system at the state and federal level.

The Courts

A 1919 ruling of the Wisconsin Supreme Court allowed the exclusion of a cerebral palsied child from school because his handicap caused a "depressing and nauseating effect on the teachers and school children and that he required an undue portion of the teacher's time" (Beattie v. State Board of Education, 1919). While the Wisconsin decision has since been reversed, similar decisions in other states reinforced exclusion of handicapped children.

Establishing statutory rights to education of handicapped children did not solve the problems faced by parents. Help was then sought through the court system. While many isolated cases appeared in state courts, cases in the federal court system yielded the major precedents. Between 1970 and 1975, this age of litigation on behalf of handicapped individuals spurred the action of state legislatures to pass mandates in thirty-seven states.

As parent groups turned to the court systems, they were joined in their efforts by various professional groups. Organizations such as The Council for Exceptional Children (CEC) and its state and local affiliate federations and chapters joined the advocacy groups by helping to prepare and present testimony, and by serving in an *amicus* capacity. The Council and its affiliates also assisted these groups in varying degrees with the passage of state statutes. CEC had developed model state statutes by 1971 (Weintraub, et al., 1971).

Parent groups utilized the 1954 landmark Supreme Court decision in Brown v. Board of Education, which stated:

> In these days it is doubtful that any child may reasonably be expected to succeed in life if he is denied the opportunity of an education. Such an opportunity, where the state has undertaken to provide it, is a right which must be available to all on equal terms.

A reading of the Brown decision suggests that a guarantee of the right to education of handicapped persons should never even have been an issue needing separate state or federal statutes or litigation.

The first precedent case in federal district courts was filed by the Pennsylvania Association for Retarded Citizens (PARC) on January 7, 1971. This class action suit against the Commonwealth of Pennsylvania was filed "on behalf of all mentally retarded persons, residents of the Commonwealth of Pennsylvania, who have been, are being, or may be denied access to a free public program of education and training while they are, or were, less than twenty-one years of age" (PARC, 1971).

The right to education and training of all retarded children in Pennsylvania, whether the child was situated in a local school or state residential facility, was clearly established. The final agreement in the PARC case came sixteen years after the Commonwealth of Pennsylvania had passed a full program special education mandate. It is significant in that education and training were to be provided to *all* mentally retarded children—regardless of severity—as opposed to the typical provision of programs for mild (educable) and moderate (trainable) mentally retarded students.

On August 1, 1972, Judge Joseph C. Waddy issued a decree in Mills v. Board of Education of the District of Columbia. Named plaintiffs in the Mills case represented the class of all handicapped children whereas PARC (1971) dealt only with mentally retarded students.

In answering the complaint in Mills (1972), the District schools included the following:

> These defendants say that it is impossible to afford the plaintiffs the relief they request unless:
>
> (a) The Congress of the United States appropriates millions of dollars to improve special education services in the District of Columbia; or
> (b) These defendants divert millions of dollars from funds already specifically appropriated for other educational services in order to improve special educational services. These defendants suggest that to do so would violate an Act of Congress and would be inequitable to children outside the alleged plaintiff class. (Mills v. District of Columbia, 1972)

Judge Waddy's decision appears to have put to rest this long heard excuse, not just from the District of Columbia, but from other school districts as well, that inadequate fiscal resources prevented the provision of special education and related services. The decision's language in response to the lack of fiscal resources reads:

> This Court is not persuaded by that contention.
>
> The defendants are required by the Constitution of the United States, the District of Columbia Code, and their own regulations to provide a publicly-supported education for these "exceptional" children. Their failure to fulfill this clear duty to include and retain these children in the public school system, or otherwise provide them with publicly-supported education, and their failure to afford them due-process hearing and periodical review, cannot be excused by the claim that there are insufficient funds.
>
> . . . the District of Columbia's interest in educating the excluded children clearly must outweigh its interest in preserving its financial resources. If sufficient funds are not available to finance all of the programs and services that are needed and desirable in the system then the available funds must be expended equitably in such a manner that no child is entirely excluded from a publicly-supported education consistent with his needs and ability to benefit therefrom. The inadequacies of the District of Columbia Public School System, whether occasioned by insufficient funding or administrative inefficiency, certainly cannot be permitted to bear more heavily on the "exceptional" or handicapped child than on the normal child.

Thus, the Mills case assured the right to education for all handicapped children. Mills (1972) and PARC (1971) also assured nondiscriminatory evaluation, least restrictive environment, timely notice and free public education for the handicapped population.

Congressional Findings

The flurry of activity by advocacy groups, state legislatures, and the courts in the early 1970s did not go unnoticed by Congress.

The US Congress, as noted previously, considered the concepts and guarantees found in The Education for All Handicapped Children Act of 1975 for four years prior to final passage. Through an extensive hearing process, both in Washington and in various regions of the nation, through testimony given by many individuals and organizations, and through Congressional staff studies and reports, the US Congress found many significant and determining facts which ultimately led to passage of the law.

The Education for All Handicapped Children Act enumerates nine findings. In the "Statement of Findings and Purpose," PL 94–142 reads:

(b) The Congress finds that—
  (1) there are more than eight million handicapped children in the United States today;
  (2) the special educational needs of such children are not being fully met;
  (3) more than half of the handicapped children in the United States do not receive appropriate educational services which would enable them to have full equality of opportunity;
  (4) one million of the handicapped children in the United States are excluded entirely from the public school system and will not go through the educational process with their peers;
  (5) there are many handicapped children throughout the United States participating in regular school programs whose handicaps prevent them from having a successful educational experience because their handicaps are undetected;
  (6) because of the lack of adequate services within the public school system, families are often forced to find services outside the public school system, often at great distance from their residence and at their own expense;
  (7) developments in the training of teachers and in diagnostic and instructional procedures and methods have advanced to the point that, given appropriate funding, State and local educational agencies can and will provide effective special education and related services to meet the needs of handicapped children;
  (8) State and local educational agencies have a responsibility to provide education for all handicapped children, but present financial resources are inadequate to meet the special educational needs of handicapped children; and
  (9) it is in the national interest that the Federal Government assist State and local efforts to provide programs to meet the educational needs of handicapped children in order to assure equal protection of the law. (PL 94–142, Sec. 3(b), pp. 2–3)

The findings cited by Congress undoubtedly called for federal involvement in solutions to the complexities of educating handicapped children and youth.

Political Considerations

The final area of consideration which led to the passage of PL 94–142 is political in nature. While all of the testimony, reports, and studies certainly appear to be convincing evidence of the need for a federal mandate, political reasons may actually have been a central focus when it came to voting. If this were not the case, why didn't Congress act four years earlier? The statistics on numbers of handicapped children served in 1971 indicated that the need was even greater then than it was in 1975, when some additional programs were developed. The Education for All Handicapped Children Act of 1975 contains some unique and politically attractive sections that early versions of the law did not contain.

First, a somewhat unique aspect of the law is that it is permanent legislation. There is no expiration date as is found in most federal legislation, in particular the various sections of the Elementary and Secondary Education Act (ESEA). For example, Title I of ESEA must periodically be reauthorized and extended by Congress for an additional period of time, generally four years. Such reauthorization and extension allows Congress to rethink the need for continuation of a particular program. This is not the case with PL 94–142. Unless Congress repeals the law by amendment, PL 94–142 is authorized forever.

Second, PL 94–142 is not a new law. It is primarily based on existing state and federal statutes and judicial decisions, and is a revision of Part B (State Grant Program) of the Education of the Handicapped Act (EHA). While some features are new in the federal statute, most of the rights and guarantees can be found throughout the forty-eight state mandates in effect at the time, in PL 93–380 (Education Amendments of 1974), or in case law established by the federal courts.

Third, and quite probably the most politically popular feature of PL 94–142, every state and every Congressional district could share in the fiscal resources of the bill. This feature results from the flow-through entitlement of federal funds for the local school districts' count of handicapped children served. It is similar to federal impact aid, which is provided to school districts containing a concentration of federal employees. Most Congressional districts also receive some funding from this program. Frequent attempts by the administration to dissolve the impact aid program have thus far been defeated by Congress.

Political considerations played a part when Congress overwhelmingly voted in favor of The Education for All Handicapped Children Act of 1975. Whatever the motivation of advocates, legislators, judges, or Congress, the enactment of PL 94–142 offered a brighter future for handicapped children in the United States.

REFERENCES

Abeson, A., and J. Ballard. "State and Federal Policy for Exceptional Children." In F. J. Weintraub, A. Abeson, J. Ballard, and M. L. LaVor, eds., *Public Policy and the Education of Exceptional Children.* Reston, VA: The Council for Exceptional Children, 1976.

Ballard, J. *Public Law 94–142 and Section 504—Understanding What They Are and Are Not* (rev. ed.). Reston, VA: The Council for Exceptional Children, 1977.

Beattie *v.* State Board of Education, 172 NW 153 (1919).

Brown *v.* Board of Education, 347 US 483 (1954).

Cronin, J. M. "The Federal Takeover: Should the Junior Partner Run the Firm?" *Phi Delta Kappan* (April 1976): 499–501.

Federal Register, Part IV, Nondiscrimination on basis of handicap; Programs and activities receiving or benefiting from federal financial assistance, May 4, 1977, pp. 22676–22702.

Federal Register, Part II, Education of Handicapped Children; Implementation of Part B of the Education of the Handicapped Act, August 23, 1977, pp. 42474–42518.

Federal Register, Part III, Assistance to States for Education of Handicapped Children; Procedures for Evaluating Specific Learning Disabilities, December 29, 1977, pp. 65082–65085.

Harris, J. "Los Angeles Convention Summary." *NEA Reporter,* (September 1975).

Jones, P. R. "Statement on Signing PL 94–142." *Insight,* (Winter 1975).

LaVor, M. L., "Federal Legislation for Exceptional Persons: A History." In F. J. Weintraub, A. Abeson, J. Ballard and M. L. LaVor, eds., *Public Policy and the Education of Exceptional Children.* Reston, VA: The Council for Exceptional Children, 1976.

Mills *v.* Board of Education of the District of Columbia, 348 F. Supp. 866 (DDC, 1972).

Office of the White House Press Secretary, Statement by the President. Washington, DC, December 2, 1975.

Pennsylvania Association for Retarded Children *v.* Commonwealth of Pennsylvania, 334 F. Supp. 1257 (ED Pa., 1971).

Pennsylvania Association for Retarded Children *v.* Commonwealth of Pennsylvania, 343 F. Supp. 279 (ED, Pa., 1972), Consent Agreement.

Public Law 94–142, 94th Congress, S.6, November 29, 1975.

Taylor, D. B. Letter to Senator Jennings Randolph, June 17, 1977.

The Conference on Inflation, September 27–28, 1974. Washington, DC: US Government Printing Office.

Weintraub, F., A. Abeson, and D. Braddock. *State Law and Education of Handicapped Children: Issues and Recommendations.* Reston, VA: The Council for Exceptional Children, 1971.

Weintraub, F. J., A. Abeson, J. Ballard and M. L. LaVor, eds., *Public Policy and the Education of Exceptional Children.* Reston, VA: The Council for Exceptional Children, 1976.

CHAPTER 3 QUESTIONS

Q: The school district has been criticized for our child-find efforts. In August of each year we place ads in the paper and have radio and television announcements about the right to education for all handicapped children. Are we in compliance with PL 94–142?

A: You may be in "paper compliance" with your once-a-year efforts, but child-find should be a continuous effort throughout the year. In addition to the media approaches you mention, posters in stores, fliers in supermarket bags, and frequent contacts with physicians and service agencies are some other possible efforts. It is true that concentrated efforts may be needed shortly before school opens in the fall, but other efforts should continue on a year-round basis.

Q: Since PL 94–142 funding is limited to 12 percent of a state's school-age children, does this mean we only need to serve a maximum of 12 percent?

A: No. All handicapped children must be served. The 12 percent is a limitation on funding only and does not relieve schools of the responsibility of serving more than 12 percent, if indeed that many handicapped children are identified.

Q: An educable mentally retarded child in our school also receives speech therapy. Can he be counted twice for PL 94–142 funding?

A: No. Under PL 94–142, a handicapped child may only be counted once, regardless of the number of different services he or she receives.

Q: A child in our district is enrolled in a program for the hearing-impaired in an adjacent district. Under PL 94–142, who should count the child?

A: Generally speaking, your district would be paying tuition to the adjacent district for this child's educational program. Your state education agency can provide the best answer to your question, but, in most states, the district paying the cost of education would count the child.

Q: Our district experienced many referrals for special education this fall. While most of these referrals have been processed, thirty referrals were made after October 20 and are in various stages of the process. Can we count these children in our December 1 count, since most, if not all of them, appear to be eligible for service?

A: No. The December 1 count can include only those children enrolled in special education by that date. This in effect means that the identification, evaluation, IEP, and placement process have all been completed.

A View
of Progress
since Passage
of PL 94-142

3

What has happened since the passage of The Education for All Handicapped Children Act of 1975? This chapter will provide a quantitative review of the progress made and some related issues. The chapter focuses on the number of handicapped children served and the amount of money Congress has appropriated to pay for required programs. The data are presented both in the aggregate and on a state-by-state basis.

HANDICAPPED CHILDREN SERVED

Mackie (1965) reported that special education programs were provided for 442,000 children in 1948, and that by 1963 the number enrolled had increased to 1,666,000. In 1971–1972 the Bureau of Education for the Handicapped (BEH) estimated that 2,857,551 handicapped children had received special education services.

A problem may exist with the statistics regarding the number of handicapped children who were served prior to the official counts set up under PL 94–142. States typically counted the number of services provided to children, as opposed to the number of handicapped children receiving the services. For example, a mentally retarded child enrolled in a special education program might also be receiving speech therapy and/or physical therapy. In such a case the child might have been counted two or more times—once in each area of service. This practice was particularly beneficial to state education agencies (SEA) seeking appropriations from state legislatures.

The regulations of Part B of the Education of the Handicapped Act, as published in the *Federal Register* (August 23, 1977), clearly state that a handicapped child may be counted only once, regardless of the number of programs or related services provided to him or her. Section 121a.751 entitled, "Annual report of children served—information required in the report," reads, in part:

(c) The State educational agency may not report a child under more than one disability category.
(d) If a handicapped child has more than one disability, the State educational agency shall report that child in accordance with the following procedure:
(1) A child who is both deaf and blind must be reported as "deaf-blind."
(2) A child who has more than one disability (other than a deaf-blind child) must be reported as "multihandicapped." (*Federal Register*, August 23, 1977, p. 42503)

The early counts taken after passage of PL 94–142 may have been hampered by administrative errors in counting. Some handicapped children who were served in a program operated by a district other than the district of residence either may not have been counted at all or may have been counted by both districts.

An additional element to consider regarding the counts reported under PL 94–142 is that the law originally called for a count of handicapped children served October 1 and February 1 of each school year. Allocation of funds for the following school year was based upon the average of the two counts. The first two years of utilizing this method revealed that October 1 fell too early in the school year for a child to proceed through the referral, diagnosis, IEP development, and placement process. Also, two count dates required additional time and reports.

Recognition of these problems resulted in the first amendment of PL 94–142. Senator Harrison Williams, original Senate sponsor of S.6, offered to amend the Education of the Handicapped Act by deleting October 1 and February 1 from the law and inserting the single count date of December 1. His amendment also deleted the reference to averaging the two counts. Senator Williams said, in part:

The net effect of the current provision is that the average of the two counts does not adequately reflect the enrollment of handicapped children and deprives local schools of the support they might receive. Further, the second count is time-consuming, costly and duplicative.
... By counting the children in December, rather than October 1, time will be provided to include children newly enrolled in the fall, individual education programs can be developed, and an accurate single count can be transmitted to Washington in time for Congress and the executive branch to make accurate budget and appropriations decisions. (*Congressional Record*, August 23, 1978).

This technical amendment, as part of the Elementary and Secondary Education Act (ESEA) Reauthorization Bill, became law (PL 95–561) when President Carter signed it on November 1, 1978. It reduced paper work and time requirements, and is an example of Congress' attempt to make a law less difficult to administer.

Since the first count (taken on October 1, 1976) through the count taken on December 1, 1979, the number of handicapped children served has increased from 3,382,495 to 3,802,511. This increase, while significant, is not as great as some observers had expected. The state-by-state report of handicapped children served from October 1, 1976 through December 1, 1979 is shown in Table 3.1

It should be noted that, in some states, the December 1, 1978 national total was higher than the February, 1978 national total, while the February, 1977 count was higher than the October, 1977 count. Presumably this indicates that the December 1, count date did allow enough time from the beginning of the school year to the count date for newly referred children to complete the process from identification through placement, while the October 1 count date did not. In fact, the October 1977 count reflects a loss from the February 1977 which may be partially explained by children leaving special education programs to return to regular education programs. Based on the first year's experience, the amendment of PL 94–142 to move to a single count on December 1 appears to have achieved the desired result.

While progress has been made in the number of handicapped children served, the 3.8 million served in December 1979 is less than half of the 8,000,000 handicapped children noted in Congressional findings for PL 94–142. Where are the handicapped childred referred to by Congress? A variety of explanations is possible in deciphering the apparent discrepency.

TITLE I

First, many handicapped children meet the criteria for service under Title I, ESEA (Elementary Secondary Education Act) programs for the disadvantaged. Title I programs, which are typically supported *in toto* by federal funds, are for remedial services only. Therefore, school districts may be hesitant to identify a child in a local Title I program as handicapped, for such identification might result in the child's removal from a fully funded program to a program requiring local and state support, in addition to federal support, under PL 94–142. Children who might be identified as handicapped if they were not enrolled in a Title I program, may or may not be receiving an appropriate education as required by PL 94–142.

STATE-OPERATED PROGRAMS

A second possible explanation relates to the handicapped children served in state-operated programs. An amendment to Title I, ESEA (PL 89–313) calls for provision of federal funds for handicapped children in state-operated facilities.

TABLE 3.1 Counts of Handicapped Children Served under PL 94–142, October 1976 to December 1979

	October 1976	February 1977	October 1977	February 1978	December 1978	December 1979
NATIONAL TOTALS	3,382,495	3,613,550	3,424,217	3,684,167	3,709,716	3,802,511
1. Alabama	51,193	54,398	55,711	62,158	68,420	71,124
2. Alaska	7,110	7,658	6,992	7,629	6,995	7,999
3. Arizona	39,092	44,642	36,004	44,950	44,313	47,202
4. Arkansas	23,776	25,645	29,364	32,406	36,508	40,138
5. California	313,299	339,113	307,235	332,013	330,021	351,111
6. Colorado	40,387	48,215	39,133	43,691	43,049	43,635
7. Connecticut	55,699	63,130	56,330	59,446	58,932	59,506
8. Delaware	12,427	12,478	11,963	12,370	11,164	11,910
9. Florida	108,289	114,793	114,560	123,573	121,368	129,552
10. Georgia	77,368	88,346	77,273	91,330	95,338	99,229
11. Hawaii	9,556	9,918	10,120	10,234	10,063	10,501
12. Idaho	10,490	17,649	16,067	17,639	16,995	17,491
13. Illinois	204,635	212,526	208,677	221,441	215,679	219,103
14. Indiana	82,126	81,152	76,748	81,411	90,442	92,072
15. Iowa	48,193	51,353	50,795	51,966	55,559	58,010
16. Kansas	34,103	37,506	32,075	34,811	35,605	36,784
17. Kentucky	53,118	55,674	55,946	57,491	60,375	64,448
18. Louisiana	78,653	85,203	80,448	83,673	87,392	79,452
19. Maine	21,124	23,142	18,995	20,641	22,729	22,818
20. Maryland	72,773	87,804	80,171	86,648	84,421	90,039
21. Massachusetts	110,170	125,877	116,717	128,048	126,820	128,009
22. Michigan	135,684	146,011	139,289	144,961	144,516	143,913
23. Minnesota	66,624	75,001	70,517	75,307	77,944	81,442
24. Mississippi	26,768	28,507	29,571	32,398	37,875	41,117
25. Missouri	89,043	91,697	84,193	89,347	96,104	94,820
26. Montana	5,717	10,470	8,486	11,416	12,017	12,284
27. Nebraska	23,580	25,918	25,642	28,074	30,664	29,836
28. Nevada	10,960	9,356	9,903	10,411	10,624	10,830

	State						
29.	New Hampshire	8,373	8,975	9,066	9,011	9,409	8,957
30.	New Jersey	136,813	138,235	144,516	139,726	144,424	141,994
31.	New Mexico	13,034	15,962	14,711	17,512	18,694	19,974
32.	New York	214,110	227,160	213,274	217,101	189,827	197,863
33.	North Carolina	87,026	95,260	86,201	96,772	102,413	109,651
34.	North Dakota	8,593	8,351	8,334	9,004	9,262	9,219
35.	Ohio	150,234	158,806	159,142	166,691	177,779	188,393
36.	Oklahoma	41,228	44,091	45,420	51,040	55,874	59,113
37.	Oregon	33,698	33,350	26,951	38,016	37,014	39,464
38.	Pennsylvania	194,099	191,938	163,320	173,684	171,609	174,931
39.	Rhode Island	14,252	15,741	11,659	14,538	13,454	15,322
40.	South Carolina	67,244	71,651	67,045	70,924	68,502	69,758
41.	South Dakota	8,663	9,721	7,659	9,176	8,915	9,272
42.	Tennessee	96,106	98,223	89,186	100,030	107,287	91,394
43.	Texas	211,475	222,529	251,421	281,975	257,576	252,893
44.	Utah	34,828	37,297	33,874	36,415	34,157	34,847
45.	Vermont	3,670	4,497	4,847	5,974	9,879	10,139
46.	Virginia	70,111	77,984	77,011	79,024	83,841	87,694
47.	Washington	72,768	63,321	46,426	49,904	49,040	51,166
48.	West Virginia	27,447	30,663	27,731	30,040	30,297	32,868
49.	Wisconsin	51,780	56,398	55,112	57,283	57,813	63,317
50.	Wyoming	5,955	7,598	6,594	7,574	8,726	8,849
51.	District of Columbia	6,546	6,136	2,670	3,078	4,156	2,079
52.	Puerto Rico	9,288	10,238	13,466	14,348	18,452	19,659
53.	Bureau of Indian Affairs	—		4,220	3,776	4,550	4,839
54.	Guam	954	3,689	3,679	3,781	2,248	1,509
55.	American Samoa	166	111	115	300	240	167
56.	Trust Territories	950	1,289	1,207	1,278	1,480	1,742
57.	Virgin Islands	1,127	1,154	435	675	866	1,005
58.	Northern Marianas*	—		0	34	0	58

*Northern Marianas applies separately for a Part B grant but child count is included with Trust Territories

Source: Division of Assistance to States, Bureau of Education for the Handicapped (USOE)

Such facilities are typically, but not exclusively, residential in nature. The Bureau of Education for the Handicapped (BEH) reported that, in fiscal year 1979, allocations to serve 222,732 children were appropriated to the states. A handicapped child cannot be counted under both PL 89–313 and PL 94–142.

PREVALENCE ESTIMATES

The 8,000,000 handicapped children noted by Congress was based on the generally accepted 12 percent estimated prevalence rate used by BEH. It may be argued that this is a cumulative percent as opposed to a point-in-time incidence. That is, a number less than 12 percent of school children (aged 5–17) would be served on any given day, while approximately 12 percent would require some special education service during the span of twelve years of school.

Despite the above explanations, it does appear that large numbers of handicapped children remain unidentified and unserved today.

In its first report to Congress on the implementation of PL 94–142 (USOE, 1979), the Bureau of Education for the Handicapped indicated that an average of 7.4 percent of the school-aged population were served in programs for the handicapped during the 1977–1978 school year. States ranged from 5.2 percent to 11.5 percent. The December 1, 1979 counts report an overall average of 7.78 percent, with a range (excluding outlying areas and District of Columbia) from 4.54 percent to 10.79 percent. The 4.54 percent seems quite low, while the 11 percent seems quite high. These wide variations suggest differing levels of child-find efforts or child identification programs. How is one state able to locate so many children needing services? What approaches do some child-find programs use to better identify children? Are some states and localities performing only cursory attempts at finding handicapped children who must subsequently be served?

CHILD-FIND EFFORTS

Child-find activities that consist of an annual summer notice through local media hardly meet the statutory responsibility for an on-going or continuous child identification effort. While efforts may be greater in the time preceding the opening of school, contacts with physicians, social agencies, and news media should continue throughout the year.

Table 3.2, compiled from the USOE's first report to Congress (1979) and a BEH report of handicapped children served December 1, 1979, presents a state-by-state listing of the percentage of school-aged children served in programs for the handicapped for the 1977–1978 and 1979–1980 school years. The

TABLE 3.2 Percentages of School-Aged Children Served in Programs for the Handicapped 1977–78 and 1979–80 and Potential Number of Unserved Handicapped Children School Year 1977–78

	Percent Served		Potential Unserved
	77–78	79–80	77–78
NATIONAL TOTAL	7.36	7.78	2,380,950
1. Alabama	6.84	8.30	45,456
2. Alaska	9.55	7.69	2,502
3. Arizona	7.69	8.89	23,296
4. Arkansas	7.00	8.30	24,779
5. California	6.73	7.50	254,744
6. Colorado	7.38	7.49	28,070
7. Connecticut	8.30	8.90	27,023
8. Delaware	9.97	9.15	2,867
9. Florida	7.18	7.79	84,334
10. Georgia	7.15	8.40	58,710
11. Hawaii	5.29	5.25	13,955
12. Idaho	8.57	8.63	6,964
13. Illinois	9.00	8.75	79,798
14. Indiana	6.60	7.48	69,801
15. Iowa	7.58	9.02	30,515
16. Kansas	6.83	7.49	26,797
17. Kentucky	7.35	8.21	37,611
18. Louisiana	8.85	8.20	31,286
19. Maine	8.36	9.20	9,310
20. Maryland	8.67	9.67	33,685
21. Massachusetts	10.11	10.30	25,608
22. Michigan	6.75	6.69	120,112
23. Minnesota	7.54	8.93	43,753
24. Mississippi	5.33	6.89	40,467
25. Missouri	8.26	9.10	41,060
26. Montana	5.62	6.87	11,876
27. Nebraska	7.52	8.70	16,357
28. Nevada	7.37	7.30	6,661
29. New Hampshire	5.26	4.54	13,219
30. New Jersey	8.68	8.85	57,314
31. New Mexico	5.45	6.71	20,114
32. New York	5.68	5.21	259,337
33. North Carolina	7.65	8.85	55,674
34. North Dakota	5.74	6.22	9,956
35. Ohio	6.84	7.79	133,148
36. Oklahoma	8.21	9.71	23,076
37. Oregon	7.00	7.72	25,965
38. Pennsylvania	6.80	7.06	139,960
39. Rhode Island	6.62	7.60	11,469
40. South Carolina	10.16	10.18	12,857
41. South Dakota	5.45	5.96	10,943
42. Tennessee	9.97	9.55	19,662

TABLE 3.2 *(Cont.)*

	Percent Served		Potential Unserved
	77–78	79–80	77–78
NATIONAL TOTAL	7.36	7.78	2,380,950
43. Texas	9.50	8.51	73,972
44. Utah	11.52	10.79	1,512
45. Vermont	6.58	9.09	6,289
46. Virginia	6.92	7.79	59,792
47. Washington	6.09	6.26	49,592
48. West Virginia	7.32	8.18	19,087
49. Wisconsin	5.18	5.95	77,965
50. Wyoming	8.67	9.39	3,031
51. District of Columbia	3.89	1.53	11,918
52. Puerto Rico	1.79	2.85	87,510
53. Bureau of Indian Affairs	—	11.05	−3,998
54. Guam	14.87	3.87	−776
55. American Samoa	2.07	1.19	993
56. Trust Territories	3.45	4.37	3,078
57. Virgin Islands	6.66	3.93	908

Source: US Office of Education, *Progress Toward a Free Appropriate Public Education* (first report to Congress on the implementation of PL 94–142), pp. 162 and 163, and Bureau of Education for the Handicapped Report of December 1, 1979, "Count of Handicapped Children Served."

table also includes the Bureau's estimate of the potential number of unserved handicapped children in 1977–1978.

The categorical area of emotional disturbance seems to be the furthest from full implementation. According to BEH prevalence estimates, 2 percent of the school-aged population need programs for the emotionally disturbed. Yet BEH statistics indicated that only .56 percent of school-aged children were receiving services in the area of emotional disturbance in 1977–1978. The 1979 report to Congress listed the potential number of unserved emotionally disturbed children as 737,714, or about one-third of the 2,380,950 total potential number of unserved children. The figure for emotional disturbance (737,714) as compared to other areas breaks down as follows: speech-impaired (569,138); learning disabled (570,142); mentally retarded (235,385); and other categories such as health impaired, orthopedically impaired, deaf and hard of hearing, and visually handicapped categories (268,570).

BEH statistics suggest that the areas of mental retardation and speech impairment appear to be nearest a full-service delivery concept. Such a fact would not be unexpected since these two programs tended to be the first programs developed in the nation's schools.

It is important to note that although the BHE prevalence estimates may be open to question, they should not be totally disregarded either. (The handicapped children yet to be identified and served may be more costly to serve, given the traditional state-established lower pupil–teacher ratio and the need for more costly equipment. This topic will be discussed more thoroughly in Chapter 4.)

IMPLEMENTATION OF LEAST RESTRICTIVE ENVIRONMENT (LRE)

Limited data have been presented relative to what extent the concept of least restrictive environment (commonly called mainstreaming) has been implemented. PL 94–142 and the regulations indicate that handicapped children are to be educated with children who are not handicapped to the "maximum extent appropriate."

Available statistics are of little value in determining the extent to which this concept has been implemented. The data present no indication of the percentage of time or the portions of the school day education with nonhandicapped children takes place. In reality, education in the regular program could occur for only fifteen minutes per day or for 90 percent of the day, as might be the case with speech-impaired students.

While the Bureau of Education for the Handicapped (USOE, 1979) suggests the predominant placement of handicapped pupils was in the regular classroom with auxiliary services, it also acknowledges the need for school districts to develop more placement options for handicapped children. For 1977–1978, 1,226,957 of the handicapped children served (32.5 percent of the total number of children served) were those listed as speech impaired. Children receiving speech therapy usually leave the regular program for relatively short periods of time during the day to participate in special programs for the speech-impaired. If almost one-third of the children being served in 1977–78 (32.5 percent) were counted as speech-impaired, then it would appear that large numbers of all other handicapped children were not necessarily in the regular program. However, the intent of the law with regard to the concept of least restrictive environment appears to have been focused on children with learning, behavioral, or physical handicaps—not speech impairments.

FUNDING HISTORY

The Education for All Handicapped Children Act of 1975 not only established a national policy calling for free appropriate public education of the handicapped, but also pledged substantially increasing federal financial assistance to implement the policy. But to what extent has the federal government lived up to its pledge?

The funding formulae contained in PL 94–142 consist of two separate programs: the basic state grant program, which is a major revision of Title VI-B, Education of the Handicapped Act (EHA), and the preschool incentive grants, which represent a new program.

State Grant Program

The state grant program under Title VI-B of the Education of the Handicapped Act (EHA), was initially funded in 1967 with a 2.5 million dollar appropriation. Allotments to state education agencies for discretionary programs were made on the basis of state population. PL 94–142 amended this program in several ways.

First, funds are generated for each state based on the national average per pupil expenditure during the second fiscal year preceding the fiscal year for which the computation is made. In other words, 1978–1979 costs are the basis for average expenditure to compute 1980–1981 allocations. This expenditure figure is for all children enrolled in elementary and secondary education in the United States. The utilization of an average figure provides an inflation-proof base for Part B funding. As the costs of education escalate, so will the base dollar figure used in the computation.

Second, an escalating percentage of the above average expenditure figure becomes the unit per child. The formula figure for each year was established as follows:

Fiscal 1978 (school year 1977–78)   5%
Fiscal 1979 (school year 1978–79)   10%
Fiscal 1980 (school year 1979–80)   20%
Fiscal 1981 (school year 1980–81)   30%
Fiscal 1982 (school year 1981–82)   40%

The 40 percent level becomes permanent after fiscal year 1982 and will be a formula feature for each year thereafter.

Third, funds will be allocated to each state based on the number of handicapped children served in free appropriate special education programs on December 1 of the year preceding the fiscal year for the calculation.

Utilization of the three factors above result in a formula to determine a particular state's allocation. The formula which results is:

National Average Expenditure ×———% × Handicapped Children Served = State Allocation

The above formula does not guarantee the amount of funds appropriated to states; it merely sets the ceiling for authorizations for the program, and Congress must appropriate amounts annually to actually fund the program. This fact caused many individuals to criticize PL 94–142, because prior experiences with other federal programs had generally resulted in appropriations well below the authorized ceilings. PL 94–142 still applies, even if Congress fails to appropriate enough funds to fully implement the formula. In such cases, "ratable reductions" (Section 121a.703, *Federal Register*, August 23, 1979, p. 42502) or proration is applied to the funds appropriated, and states will be required to make up the difference. A "hold-harmless" provision contained in PL 94–142 guaranteed that no state would receive less than the dollar amount received for fiscal year 1977 (school year 1976–1977).

Congressional Appropriations

For the first two years of the program (school years 1977–1978 and 1978–1979), Congress fully funded the formula (at the 5 percent and 10 percent levels). For fiscal year 1979 it was necessary for Congress to pass a supplemental appropriation of 37.8 million dollars to allow funding at the 10 percent level (PL 95–355). For fiscal year 1980 (school year 1979–1980), proration was applied for the first time. While the authorized level was 20 percent, the amounts actually appropriated were equal to 13 percent of the national average expenditure. This same approximate level was maintained for fiscal year 1981. The inflationary period and passage of tax relief legislation, best illustrated by California's Proposition 13, obviously had an effect on Congress. Several attempts to pass supplemental appropriation bills in both the House and Senate were unsuccessful. (It should be noted that one of the few line items of the California State budget which was not reduced following passage of Proposition 13 was the funding for education of handicapped children. PL 94–142 requires that state and local effort not be reduced. Had California reduced the state appropriation for education of handicapped children, the state would have lost over 70 million dollars of Part B funds in fiscal years 1980 and 1981.)

State Allocations

Table 3.3 summarizes the actual state allocation of Part B funding for each state from fiscal year 1972 through fiscal year 1981 (school year 1980–1981). Several observations should be made about Table 3.3. PL 94–142 was signed by President Ford on November 29, 1975, which fell in fiscal year 1976. The appropriation for fiscal year 1976 was 100 million dollars. The hold-harmless feature of the law applied to the next fiscal year (fiscal 1977), during which the appropriations doubled to 200 million dollars. The actual appropriation for fiscal year 1978 was 315 million dollars. The count of handicapped children served when utilizing the formula did not require the full 315 million dollars, but actually required the nearly 253 million dollars shown in the table. The unused funds were carried over to fiscal 1979, to be added to the basic appropriation and supplemental appropriation to reach the full 10 percent level.

The national average expenditure figures rose per child from 1430 dollars in fiscal 1978 to 1561 dollars in fiscal 1979 and about 1650 dollars in fiscal 1980. On a per child basis, 5 percent of the national average expenditure for fiscal 1978 amounted to approximately $71.50. The 10 percent for fiscal 1979

TABLE 3.3 Fiscal Year Allocation Part B (EHA) State Grants 1972–1981

	FY 1972	FY 1973	FY 1974	FY 1975	FY 1976*	FY 1977**	FY 1978	FY 1979	FY 1980	FY 1981
NATIONAL TOTALS	$37,500,000	$37,500,000	$47,492,173	$99,984,194	$100,000,000	$200,000,000	$252,878,716	$563,874,752	$804,000,000	$874,500,000
1. Alabama	714,722	623,197	802,862	1,689,600	1,688,191	3,365,542	3,776,498	9,199,597	14,638,340	16,142,271
2. Alaska	200,000	200,000	200,000	297,224	300,000	490,567	490,567	1,141,091	1,496,568	1,815,449
3. Arizona	281,316	292,683	377,063	900,418	996,374	1,921,124	2,537,384	6,318,460	9,480,689	10,712,944
4. Arkansas	372,783	330,113	425,283	907,955	918,922	1,829,462	1,829,462	4,821,148	7,810,823	9,109,702
5. California	3,000,969	3,385,395	4,361,391	9,279,132	9,362,505	18,609,066	23,333,515	49,893,306	70,607,420	79,687,993
6. Colorado	357,041	401,127	516,770	1,142,175	1,190,661	2,335,174	2,845,535	6,464,413	9,210,259	9,903,380
7. Connecticut	462,435	508,420	654,995	1,387,278	1,394,136	2,763,013	3,922,276	9,036,317	12,608,399	13,505,455
8. Delaware	200,000	200,000	200,000	345,491	300,000	622,204	778,246	1,899,113	2,388,518	2,703,088
9. Florida	921,515	1,071,232	1,380,063	3,068,037	3,213,602	6,380,764	7,978,528	18,586,203	25,966,473	29,403,063
10. Georgia	854,178	832,051	1,071,928	2,292,399	2,323,561	4,618,356	5,926,761	13,159,542	20,397,400	22,520,969
11. Hawaii	200,000	200,000	200,000	418,582	416,141	836,262	836,262	1,588,630	2,152,961	2,383,302
12. Idaho	200,000	200,000	200,000	399,275	379,384	781,714	895,985	2,630,753	3,636,051	3,969,749
13. Illinois	1,863,550	1,901,098	2,449,176	5,148,004	5,138,089	10,221,515	14,912,002	33,570,710	46,144,147	49,727,517
14. Indiana	932,742	926,786	1,193,974	2,517,875	2,520,472	5,010,905	5,839,638	12,344,388	19,349,909	20,896,619
15. Iowa	541,816	492,895	634,995	1,332,112	1,327,186	2,634,753	3,293,313	8,020,418	11,886,752	13,165,923
16. Kansas	423,897	388,245	500,175	1,042,837	1,033,131	2,060,933	2,561,060	5,220,452	7,617,628	8,348,480
17. Kentucky	638,302	572,173	737,128	1,553,534	1,554,291	3,098,951	3,890,946	8,853,680	12,917,126	14,627,089
18. Louisiana	714,466	696,632	897,468	1,895,910	1,900,856	3,775,472	5,860,310	12,809,566	18,697,367	18,032,390
19. Maine	200,000	200,000	223,595	477,343	483,091	960,286	1,430,099	3,093,590	4,862,830	5,178,763
20. Maryland	618,153	691,156	890,413	1,910,231	1,941,551	3,835,476	5,108,386	13,020,301	18,061,726	20,435,211
21. Massachusetts	939,707	958,174	1,234,411	2,614,164	2,626,805	5,212,919	8,442,257	19,103,830	27,132,919	29,052,864
22. Michigan	1,587,955	1,624,522	2,085,038	4,399,160	4,435,769	8,817,578	10,074,857	22,185,712	30,918,947	32,662,429
23. Minnesota	691,697	693,438	893,353	1,889,037	1,895,605	3,758,157	4,935,284	11,381,563	16,675,983	18,484,039
24. Mississippi	500,272	423,539	545,643	1,157,947	1,165,719	2,317,010	2,317,010	4,836,602	8,103,290	9,331,896
25. Missouri	803,303	789,238	1,016,772	2,145,536	2,148,965	4,267,874	6,398,215	13,544,797	20,561,284	21,520,304
26. Montana	200,000	200,000	200,000	385,484	353,129	735,291	735,291	1,553,351	2,571,016	2,787,971
27. Nebraska	272,180	248,063	319,579	693,305	711,508	1,398,141	1,770,296	4,192,534	6,560,510	6,771,565
28. Nevada	200,000	200,000	200,000	334,459	300,000	599,425	599,425	1,585,508	2,272,986	2,457,972
29. New Hampshire	200,000	200,000	200,000	392,379	366,256	760,460	760,460	1,410,832	2,013,039	2,032,877

No.	State/Area										
30.	New Jersey	1,084,951	1,180,056	1,520,261	3,235,127	3,264,800	6,457,792	9,837,092	22,185,088	30,899,264	32,226,894
31.	New Mexico	220,142	200,000	249,853	551,868	574,983	1,128,789	1,128,789	2,515,083	3,989,549	4,533,290
32.	New York	2,917,989	2,934,166	3,780,074	7,940,709	7,921,110	15,738,278	15,782,022	33,590,847	40,613,157	44,906,897
33.	North Carolina	1,007,815	916,643	1,180,908	2,495,845	2,503,407	4,992,790	6,519,459	14,280,965	21,911,083	24,886,341
34.	North Dakota	200,000	200,000	200,000	364,798	313,746	671,532	671,532	1,353,231	1,981,589	2,092,340
35.	Ohio	1,902,397	1,875,154	2,415,753	5,067,693	5,048,822	10,057,668	11,052,816	25,431,188	38,035,508	42,757,590
36.	Oklahoma	459,249	430,532	554,652	1,177,989	1,186,722	2,354,020	2,848,682	7,528,703	11,954,145	13,416,260
37.	Oregon	349,280	355,386	457,842	981,197	996,374	1,975,798	2,343,180	5,070,752	7,919,081	8,956,732
38.	Pennsylvania	2,092,856	1,946,284	2,507,390	5,247,590	5,216,853	10,378,532	13,806,578	26,303,162	36,715,448	39,702,260
39.	Rhode Island	200,000	200,000	203,971	430,827	431,893	843,286	1,046,913	2,044,598	2,878,480	3,477,474
40.	South Carolina	561,765	494,334	636,848	1,350,514	1,358,692	2,710,586	4,967,615	10,768,402	14,655,884	15,832,244
41.	South Dakota	200,000	200,000	200,000	373,762	330,812	698,770	698,770	1,314,050	1,907,349	2,104,369
42.	Tennessee	741,666	678,849	874,558	1,850,935	1,858,848	3,707,002	5,812,671	14,768,309	22,953,867	20,742,741
43.	Texas	2,001,270	2,020,909	2,603,529	5,578,170	5,663,187	11,265,148	15,522,153	41,631,558	55,107,938	57,396,480
44.	Utah	207,289	210,893	271,693	593,015	611,740	1,213,009	2,057,060	5,485,978	7,307,831	7,908,859
45.	Vermont	200,000	200,000	200,000	317,220	300,000	539,113	539,113	844,501	2,113,595	2,301,143
46.	Virginia	826,445	822,173	1,059,202	2,264,504	2,294,680	4,561,746	5,296,653	12,178,610	17,937,636	19,902,990
47.	Washington	565,723	595,157	766,739	1,602,452	1,591,048	3,201,385	3,918,270	7,518,556	10,492,023	11,612,612
48.	West Virginia	393,108	296,941	382,548	796,267	787,648	1,567,670	2,078,304	4,509,105	6,481,991	7,459,706
49.	Wisconsin	782,823	800,113	1,030,782	2,181,611	2,190,873	4,348,328	4,348,328	8,772,508	12,368,991	14,370,398
50.	Wyoming	200,000	200,000	200,000	288,950	300,000	470,988	470,988	1,162,321	1,866,913	2,008,365
51.	District of Columbia	200,000	200,000	200,000	363,419	311,121	668,848	668,848	668,848	889,169	668,848
52.	Puerto Rico			200,000	1,341,899	1,566,542	2,899,064	2,899,064	2,899,064	3,947,773	4,461,798
53.	Bureau of Indian Affairs						1,951,207	2,483,948	5,582,918	7,960,396	8,658,415
54.	Guam				970,950	⎱	501,668	634,920	1,269,839	1,384,125	1,505,928
55.	American Samoa				150,000	⎪ 990,099	180,508	228,455	456,910	498,032	541,859
56.	Trust Territory				150,000	⎪	578,813	732,554	1,297,586	1,414,369	1,538,833
57.	Virgin Islands				150,000	⎰	319,268	404,071	808,142	880,874	958,391
58.	Northern Marianas				150,000				167,523	182,600	198,669

*PL 94–142 signed November 29, 1975.

**Hold-harmless (base funding) year under PL 94–142.

Source: Division of Assistance to States, Bureau of Education for the Handicapped (BEH).

amounted to approximately $156 per child. For fiscal 1980, 20 percent amounted to approximately $330 per child, but in reality the actual appropriation was sufficient to fund at about $214 per child (approximately 13 percent). In fiscal year 1981, the actual appropriation was sufficient to fund at about $227 per child (13%).

Will Congress reduce efforts to fund PL 94–142? Congressman Paul Simon, chairman of the House Select Education Subcommittee and member of the House Budget Committee, has indicated his priority for funding at the 20 percent level for school year 1980–1981 when the authorization was 30 percent (NASDSE, March 7, 1979, p. 5). Obviously Mr. Simon was not successful. However, programs for handicapped children survived the budget cuts of 1980, which attempted to balance the federal budget.

The hold-harmless provision was applied to thirteen states for the fiscal year 1978 allocation when the number of handicapped children counted did not generate an amount greater than the fiscal year 1977 allocation. Those states were Alaska, Arkansas, Hawaii, Mississippi, Montana, Nevada, New Hampshire, New Mexico, North Dakota, South Dakota, Vermont, Wisconsin, and Wyoming.

State Plan Process

Release of funds allocated to a state are subject to United States Office of Education (USOE) approval of the state's annual program plan or amendment thereto. Approval of state plans was a slow process for many states in fiscal year 1978 due to new procedures and requirements. It was necessary for some states to amend laws and/or regulations to meet necessary criteria for approval. Final approval in at least one instance was not completed until July of 1978. Some states, where major modification of fiscal 1979 plans was required, also received final approval late in the 1978–1979 school year. During the first two years, the Bureau of Education for the Handicapped (BEH) released one-fourth of a state's allocation when the plan reached an "essentially approvable" form, and the remainder was released upon final approval. During fiscal year 1980 (school year 1979–1980), no portion of the allocation was released without final approval of the plan (USOE, 1979). BEH initiated a multiyear plan approval process for fiscal year 1981. This process should result in more timely receipt of funds at the state and local levels.

Participation of States Not Required

A state is not required to participate in the Part B program, but must meet essentially the same requirements under Section 504 of the Rehabilitation Act of 1973 (PL 93–112). With the exception of New Mexico, all states applied for funding for fiscal 1978, 1979, and 1980. Litigation against the State of New Mexico by the New Mexico Association for Retarded Citizens may result in New Mexico's participation in future years.

State Education Agency (SEA) Discretionary Funds

State allocations under the state grant program prior to PL 94–142 were utilized on a discretionary basis by the state. Under PL 94–142, for fiscal year 1978 (school year 1977–1978), states were required to distribute 50 percent of the funds to local education agencies (LEAs). In fiscal year 1979, the local entitlement increased to 75 percent and remained at that level for all future years. Release of funds to local districts is contingent upon state approval of a local application for funds.

The portion of the allocation retained at the state level may be used for state administration costs (5 percent or $200,000, whichever is greater) and direct service programs on a discretionary basis. States have the flexibility of determining priorities within the state for such discretionary uses.

PRESCHOOL INCENTIVE GRANTS

The incentive grant provision for handicapped children aged three through five was intended to increase and enhance programs for preschool handicapped children. PL 94–142 authorizes a grant of $300 per child aged three through five, who are included in the count of handicapped children served. Incentive grants are allocated to the states to serve handicapped children in this age group who were not included in the count. In other words, the incentive grants are to be used to stimulate program growth in the area of preschool education of handicapped children. Such funds are for discretionary use by the state, subject to an annual plan approved by USOE.

Appropriations to the preschool incentive grant program of PL 94–142 have not been adequate to fully fund the program in any of the years since passage. For fiscal year 1978 (school year 1977–1978) the initial appropriations amounted to $12.5 million or $64.69 per child instead of the authorized $300 per child. Appropriations have increased $2.5 million per year to $17.5 million for fiscal year 1980. A more significant increase was seen for fiscal year 1981, when appropriations reached $25 million. The number of preschool children served has shown a steady increase, as reproduced in Table 3.4.

California, Illinois, and Texas each received grants in excess of one million dollars for the first two years of the program. In fiscal year 1980 Michigan joined the above states in surpassing the one million dollar allocation mark. By fiscal year 1981, New York and Pennsylvania joined the ranks of the states receiving over one million dollars, while California and Texas climbed over the two million dollar level.

A GOOD TRACK RECORD

Overall, the first four years of experience with PL 94–142 reveal that increasing amounts of handicapped children have been served. Congress fully funded the

TABLE 3.4   Incentive Grants for Preschool Handicapped Children for Fiscal Years 1978–1981

Fiscal Year	Children Served (Ages 3–5)	Appropriation	Per Child Amount
1978	196,277	$12,500,000	$ 64.69
1979	200,546	15,000,000	74.80
1980	215,637	17,500,000	81.15
1981	231,815	25,000,000	107.84

Source: Division of Assistance to States, Bureau of Education for the Handicapped (BEH).

basic state grant program the first two years. Appropriations for the third and fourth years of the basic state grant program and all four years of the preschool incentive grant program have required proration when appropriations did not equal authorizations.

Even when the prorations are considered, it is significant to note that substantial increases in federal funds have been received by the states. These federal funds, while targeted for implementation of a federal law (PL 94–142), have in reality assisted in implementation of state statutory requirements for the education of handicapped children.

REFERENCES

Congressional Record (Senate), August 23, 1978. UP Amendment No. 1752 (Purpose: To improve the administration of the Education of the Handicapped Act).

Federal Register, August 23, 1977, Part II, Education of Handicapped Children. "Implementation of Part B of the Education of the Handicapped Act," pp. 42474-42518.

Mackie, R. P. "Spotlighting Advances in Special Education." *Exceptional Children, 32* (1965): 77–81.

National Association of State Directors of Special Education, Inc. *Liaison Bulletin,* March 7, 1979.

U.S. Office of Education. *Progress Toward a Free Appropriate Public Education* (First report to Congress on the implementation of PL 94–142). Washington, D.C., 1979, 215 pp.

CHAPTER 4 QUESTIONS

Q: Does "no cost to parents" mean the schools must pay the total bill for education and related services?

A: Not necessarily, if available resources from other agencies are utilized.

Q: How may Part B (PL 94–142 flow-through funds) be most creatively utilized?

A: Part B funds may be best expended for items not normally reimbursed through state funds. This also tends to assure spending only in the excess cost range.

Q: Should Part B funds be utilized to employ special education teachers?

A: Since Part B funds would pay for only a limited number of special education teachers, it would probably be more advisable to employ other types of necessary personnel, such as physical therapists, occupational therapists, or teachers of adapted physical education.

Q: Must a school district pay for medical examinations or evaluations required as a part of the diagnostic process?

A: If such evaluations cannot be obtained through county health departments or other health agencies, the district is liable for payment.

Special Education Costs More – More Than What?

Special education programs and services require the expenditure of fiscal re-sources, as do all other aspects of the school program. Yet various studies of special education costs (Rossmiller, 1970; Snell, 1973; Sorensen, 1973) indicate that it costs up to two or more times as much to educate a handicapped child as it does to educate a nonhandicapped child. However, such comparisons may not be totally fair.

OTHER HIGH-COST PROGRAMS

The primary reason alleged for special education costs to appear high is the lower pupil-teacher ratio typically present. But special education programs are not the only areas of the curriculum where low pupil-teacher ratios exist. Examples of other programs with low pupil-teacher ratios include: the in-car phase of driver education; various laboratory classes; and, in smaller high schools, fourth-year foreign language, fourth-year mathematics, or other elec-tive, specialized classes.

Another point to be made is that students in elementary and secondary education do not consume fiscal resources equally. The college-bound, secon-dary-school student, who takes a full academic program (with several low-enrollment classes) and participates in most extra-curricular activities, uses a much greater share of fiscal resources than the student who takes the minimum amount of required courses for graduation and rarely participates in extra-curricular activities. The same applies to the severely multiply handicapped child as compared to the educable mentally retarded child or the child who only receives speech therapy.

45

The preceding discussion is not meant to imply that the costs of educating handicapped children are not high. It merely points out the costs of educating other segments of the school population may be equally high or even higher.

STATE AID FOR SPECIAL EDUCATION

It should also be noted that the local tax base does not bear the full burden of special education costs. In addition to each state's basic school aid program, which is generated by membership or attendance factors of handicapped and nonhandicapped children, the state's categorical (or noncategorical) aid for the education of the handicapped is also received. Federal funds under PL 94–142 are also available. Thus, nonlocal funding for education of handicapped students may come from three sources: state basic aid; state categorical aid; and federal aid under PL 94–142.

Every state has attempted to provide all or a portion of the differential costs of special education. This is accomplished by adding to or weighting either the basic state aid formula (noncategorical) or a separate categorical formula for special education. In developing such formulae, the state must make a policy decision as to the extent it wishes to assist the local education agency, and also what type of system is most appropriate to meet the state's requirements.

State Special Education Aid Methods

Thomas (1973) identified six methods states utilize to reimburse local districts for special education costs. They include:

1. Unit—a fixed sum that reimburses a school district for each unit of instruction (class), administration, or other program operation.
2. Weighted Pupil—a multiple of the regular pupil reimbursement usually with several weights depending on handicapping condition.
3. Percentage—a fixed percentage of instructional costs or personnel salaries.
4. Personnel—a fixed sum for each professional worker and often noncertified personnel.
5. Straight Sum—a fixed sum for each type of handicapped child served.
6. Excess Cost—full or partial reimbursement of costs incurred in educating handicapped students in excess of those incurred in educating the nonhandicapped.

Each of the above methods has positive and negative aspects. Methods that use the child as a unit of funding tend to continue the labeling of the handicapped child and, in addition, result in classes or programs operating with the maximum allowable numbers of children per teacher. On the other hand, methods utilizing fixed dollar amounts per child, unit, or teacher typically do not escalate as rapidly as inflationary costs. And finally, methods utilizing percentages of costs do allow for inflation but are difficult to predict for budgeting purposes.

Jones and Wilkerson (1975) cite the problem of state legislatures' failure to appropriate sufficient state funds to fully fund the state formula, regardless of the method utilized. In such cases, the local districts may have budgeted based on full payment of obligations by the state, when in reality state funds may be prorated when appropriations are not adequate to meet obligations. Jones and Wilkerson (1975) further cite lack of payment on a current basis in many states as a problem local districts encounter. They suggest that reimbursement after the fact can hamper program expansion.

Regardless of the method utilized, the various state formulae are attempts to offset the differential costs of special education in local school districts.

Various Methods Can Produce Same Result

Bernstein, et al. (1976) point out that in theory, "The choice of a funding formula is secondary to a variety of other considerations" (p. 27). In the following example, they further illustrate how identical allocations to local education agencies (LEAs) can result from any of the funding methods identified by Thomas, if certain basic policy decisions have been made by the state.

The example assumes that, by policy decisions, ten handicapped children are served by a single teacher; that costs of the program for the instructional unit are $20,000, with $15,000 representing teacher and administrative salaries; and that the state will pay 50 percent of the cost of all education including special education. Given the regular program cost of $1,000 per pupil, and the special education program cost of $2,000 per pupil, the options available as funding methods are:

1. Unit—A single unit reimbursement is $10,000.
2. Weight—A special class student is weighted at 2.0 ($2,000/$1,000), producing a reimbursement of $1,000 per pupil (2.0 X $500) or a total of $10,000 ($1,000 X 10).
3. Percentage—The state reimburses 50 percent of the total expenditure, or $10,000.
4. Personnel—Since personnel costs are $15,000, the state would choose to reimburse two-thirds of the personnel expenditures, or $10,000.
5. Straight sum—$1,000 is granted for each student, giving a total of $10,000 ($1,000 X 10).
6. Excess cost—The district is reimbursed by 50 percent of its excess cost ($2,000/$1,000 or $500 per pupil, in addition to its foundation, resulting in a total of $1,000 per pupil, or $10,000 for the program ($1,000 X 10). (Bernstein, et al. 1976, pp. 27–28)

While the example cited may illustrate the identical allocation, it must be noted that such necessary policy decisions cannot be made without knowledge of the costs incurred in delivering appropriate services in regular and special programs.

Categorical or Noncategorical State Aid

One major concern expressed in the various funding approaches utilized by the states is whether the state aid should be provided through the basic aid formula (noncategorical) or separate and distinct from the formula (categorical). The noncategorical, basic aid formula tends to use a weighted pupil approach, which has the advantages of current payment, equalization, and less paperwork. Advocates of categorical aid often cite the loss of identifiable state special education dollars flowing to the LEA as a negative feature of the formula approach.

Change from One Method to Another

Indiana represents one of several states that shifted their special education funding approach during the 1970s. Prior to 1976, Indiana used a categorical approach based on reimbursement of a percentage of personnel salaries. Since 1976, a weighted pupil basis has been utilized in funding special education through the basic aid formula. In reporting the Indiana School Finance Study, Wilkerson (1978) stated:

> Since the formula was not fully operative for most school corporations in recent years, serious questions about the utility of weighting pupils have arisen. Two of the substudies were directed toward that problem, and it was found that more money than that generated by the weights was flowing to these programs. The test of validity of the weights revealed that some were high while others were too low. The advent of PL 94–142 and its projected impact on costs suggests that the present weights should be retained until better data and experience with PL 94–142 are available. (p. 34)

Wilkerson (1978) makes further comments regarding a noncategorical, weighted pupil system versus a categorical system in concluding:

> Data on the ranges in extra costs among school corporations for the low incidence programs suggest that a future course of action might be to retain the weighted unit approach for high incidence programs and to use categorical grants for approved program areas, services and facilities for low incidence programs. (p. 34)

A combination approach of funding through the basic aid formula (noncategorical) for some programs and categorical aid for other programs, services, and facilities may result in a resolution of the issue.

Clearly Identifiable Revenues

Until the goal of free appropriate public education for all handicapped children is achieved, there are advantages to keeping special education funds identifiable for LEA policy-makers and administrators, whether they flow from state or federal sources. This allows the decision makers ready access to information on efforts to offset the differential costs of special education as they expand programs and services to meet mandates.

PL 94-142 EXPENDITURE PRIORITIES

The Education for All Handicapped Children Act of 1975 established priorities for the expenditure of funds under Part B. The first priority was to provide free appropriate public education to handicapped children who were not receiving any education. The second priority was to fully provide for children with the most severe handicaps, who heretofore were receiving an inadequate education. The final priority was to meet all other requirements of the act. A comment is made following section 121a.320 of the regulations:

> Comment. After September 1, 1978, there should be no second priority children, since States must insure, as a condition of receiving Part B funds for fiscal year 1979, that all handicapped children will have available a free appropriate public education by that date.

> New "First priority children" will continue to be found by the State after September 1, 1978 through on-going efforts to identify, locate, and evaluate all handicapped children. (*Federal Register*, August 23, 1977, p. 42489)

Many of the handicapped children yet to be served may be "high cost" children, such as the emotionally disturbed, severely handicapped, and multiply handicapped as opposed to mildly handicapped children, such as educable retarded or speech therapy cases that are approaching the full-service level. These high cost areas of special education typically have lower pupil-teacher ratios and require more related services, thus elevating costs. The necessity of teacher aides, materials, and equipment may also increase costs for some unserved children. LEA administrators must be aware of this possibility.

DOES LEAST RESTRICTIVE ENVIRONMENT (LRE) COST LESS?

Another note of caution to LEA administrators is that placement of handicapped children in the least restrictive environment should not be pursued strictly on the basis of lower costs. Most state guidelines and regulations do allow a resource or itinerant special education teacher to serve a larger number of children than the teacher of the self-contained class. Thus, on the face of it, it would appear less costly to utilize the resource or itinerant model. However, the following factors must be considered:

1. Service to be provided should be based on the needs of the individual child, not on a preexisting model of 30 minutes per day (or similar arbitrary time allocation) for the program model utilized. Thus the special education teacher may not be able to serve the maximum number of children allowed.
2. The cost of special education in a resource or itinerant model is a total add-on charge to the basic program, when a child is enrolled in the regular class.
3. The special education teacher's instructional time may be lost as the teacher travels or consults with the regular classroom teachers.

If any financial gains are realized through placement in the least restrictive environment, it may be at the expense of an appropriate program. Certainly the least restrictive environment is the preferred setting for children in special education programs, but only when it is so determined based on their educational needs. The service model adopted, whether it be resource or itinerant, should not have limits established for such things as individual or small-group instruction, amount of time per day or week, or other logistical details. These decisions can only be made after the needs of the handicapped learners are known.

Caution in this area is crucial, given the fact that an appeal could be based on the fact that the preset program did not take into account the needs of the child. It could be difficult to convince an impartial hearing officer that an established program and procedures were appropriate for a specific child or group of children, when individual needs underlie the philosophy of PL 94–142.

EXPENDITURE OF PART B FUNDS

Before other expenditures are made, Part B funds should go to eligible children who are not receiving any education. This is in keeping with the priorities established by law.

Excess Costs

Expenditures of Part B funds are to be made only for the excess costs of providing special education and related services to handicapped children. In reality, this requirement means the LEA must spend an amount for a handi-capped child that is at least equal to the amount expended for a nonhand-icapped child before Part B funds are utilized.

Relevant sections of the regulations dealing with excess costs are:

Sec. 121a.182 The excess cost requirement.
A local education agency may only use funds under Part B of the Act for the excess costs of providing special education and related services for handicapped children.

Sec. 121a.183 Meeting the excess cost requirement.
(a) A local educational agency meets the excess cost requirement if it has on the average spent at least the amount determined under Sec. 121a.184 for the education of each of its handicapped children. This amount may not include capital outlay or debt service.
(b) Each local educational agency must keep records adequate to show that it has met the excess cost requirement.

Sec. 121a.184 Excess costs—computation of minimum amount.
The minimum average amount a local educational agency must spend under Sec. 121a.183 for the education of each of its handicapped children is computed as follows:
(a) Add all expenditures of the local educational agency in the preceding school year, except capital outlay and debt service:
   (1) For elementary school students, if the handicapped child is an elementary school student, or
   (2) For secondary school students, if the handicapped child is a secondary school student.
(b) From this amount, subtract the total of the following amounts spent for ele-mentary school students or for secondary school students, as the case may be:
   (1) Amounts the agency spent in the preceding school year from funds awarded under Part B of the Act and Title I and VII of the Elementary and Secondary Education Act of 1965, and
   (2) Amounts from State and local funds which the agency spent in the preceding school year for:
      (i) Programs for handicapped children,
      (ii) Programs to meet the special educational needs of educationally de-prived children, and
      (iii) Programs of bilingual education for children with limited English-speaking ability.
(c) Divide the result under paragraph (b) of this section by the average number of students enrolled in the agency in the preceding school year:
   (1) In its elementary schools, if the handicapped child is an elementary school student, or
   (2) In its secondary schools, if the handicapped child is a secondary school stu-dent. (*Federal Register,* August 23, 1977)

It is clear the local education agency should have (or should develop) an accounting procedure through which such costs as those enumerated above can be isolated and utilized in the computation. Certainly this procedure is one more reason for keeping special education sections of a budget clearly visible within the total budget. The potential for fiscal audit of Part B expenditures exists, and the process contained in the regulations would seem to be an automatic portion of such an audit.

Appropriate Use of Part B Funds

What types of expenditures of Part B funds appear to be most appropriate? Even though a financial study of the per capita cost of special education can probably demonstrate a cost above that of regular education, the using of Part B funds for salaries of special education teachers may not be a wise procedure. Since forty-eight states had mandatory special education acts prior to the passage of PL 94–142, school districts would have been required by state law to support special education teaching positions even if PL 94–142 did not exist. Therefore, Part B funds, which could be used for some extra services, would be used up on a service that must be provided anyway.

The question then becomes, What is a true excess cost? If the program or service is provided to the nonhandicapped child, then it is probably not an excess cost. Generally a teacher, desk, chair, pencils, books, etc. are provided for a nonhandicapped child when he or she enters school. Expenditures beyond such basic requirements could be considered excess costs. Excess costs, then, could be defined as those personnel, equipment, and service costs not provided to nonhandicapped children. A teacher-aide could be considered an excess cost if teacher-aides are not provided in other programs of the school. Or, something like psychiatric consultation in evaluation or programing, which is not a usual expenditure for the nonhandicapped child, could also fall into this category. Other such personnel items could include occupational and/or physical therapists; aides on buses for severely handicapped children; speech therapists or school psychologists to serve *only* specified handicapped children (assuming these services presently exist in the overall educational program); teachers of adapted physical education, if the handicapped child is unable to participate in regular physical education; or other such special personnel costs.

Creative Use of Part B Funds

It would appear wise to deploy Part B funds where state and/or local funds are not typically utilized. This could be for personnel costs such as those suggested above.

Or it could occur in the specialized equipment area. The purchase of equipment not normally used in programs for nonhandicapped children would be logical and legitimate Part B expenditures. Some of the more costly equipment needed in programs for the hearing- or visually-impaired, or orthopedically handicapped, constitute areas where it might be difficult to obtain funds through the usual budgetary process, particularly if no specific state assistance is provided for major equipment costs.

The best rule of thumb might be to maximize the use of Part B funds by planning expenditures in areas not subject to state reimbursement and other allocations difficult to obtain through the local budget.

The Test of the Audit

The school district that employs special education teachers with Part B funds will probably face a great deal of difficulty in meeting the minimum expenditure figure, while the district that focuses expenditures on necessary related service personnel and specialized equipment should have little problem in meeting such a test. Personnel salaries constitute a major portion (75–85 percent) of the instructional budget. Lower pupil-teacher ratios in special education are often used to justify the use of Part B funds to employ special education teachers. However, such ratios are usually about half of that found in the regular program and the salaries (75–85 percent) quickly overtake any excess cost resulting from the special education lower pupil-teacher ratio.

NO COST TO PARENTS

Regulations implementing PL 94–142 contain highly significant sections regarding the nature of free education and costs.

Sec. 121a.301 Free appropriate public education—methods and payments.
(a) Each State may use whatever State, local, Federal, and private sources of support are available in the State to meet the requirements of this part. For example, when it is necessary to place a handicapped child in a residential facility, a State could use joint agreements between the agencies involved for sharing the cost of that placement.
(b) Nothing in this part relieves an insurer or similar third party from an otherwise valid obligation to provide or to pay for services provided to a handicapped child.

Sec. 121a.302 Residential placement.
If placement in a public or private residential program is necessary to provide special education and related services to a handicapped child, the program, including nonmedical care and room and board, must be at no cost to the parents of the child. (*Federal Register,* August 23, 1977, p. 42488)

Third-Party Payments

The provision of special education and related services can be quite costly to the LEA, and LEA administrators may be overlooking assistance in providing adequately for handicapped children. It may be that the LEA is paying total costs when an insurance carrier, governmental agency, private agency, or service club could assist in payment of needed services. The ultimate responsibility for providing all necessary education and related services—at no cost to parents—rests with the LEA. However, the LEA may be able to receive funds from other sources, thus insuring the needed programs at the lowest possible cost to the LEA.

For example, health insurance carried by the parents may cover the cost of physical or occupational therapy, or the local Easter Seal clinic, as well as others, may be involved in such services. The local or county health department may provide necessary medical exams. And often service clubs donate funds to programs for handicapped children to purchase needed equipment, materials, or educational experiences.

The bottom line is that the LEA must provide for the free appropriate public education required by any given handicapped child. But the LEA should also make a thorough investigation of possible alternative sources of assistance or provision of services within the community. The LEA must seek out such resources, not wait for outsiders to volunteer help. Interagency cooperation can facilitate financial assistance to LEAs in meeting the requirements of the Education for All Handicapped Children Act.

OTHER SOURCES OF FUNDS FOR SPECIAL EDUCATION

Do other sources of funds exist which may be utilized in provision of special education and related services? Yes! Most other sources are discretionary (competitive) in nature and a project proposal must be developed and submitted to the appropriate state or federal agency. Federal programs, federal programs operated through state education agencies (SEAs), and SEA programs are sources of such competitive project funds.

Vocational Education Funds

Ten percent of federal vocational education funds are "set aside" for providing vocational education programs for handicapped learners. While only 10 percent of the federal funds are mandated for use in serving handicapped children, some states have followed the original Congressional intent of 1967 and matched this amount with state funds. Expenditures may be for personnel or equipment.

Vocational Rehabilitation Funds

Many states provide vocational rehabilitation funds to assist in providing prevocational and vocational programs for special education students. Depending on the state policies, vocational rehabilitation may provide funds to employ prevocational or vocational counselors or the rehabilitation agency may employ personnel directly and assign them to the school district. Vocational rehabilitation funds may also be available for equipment purchases, safety equipment, corrective and/or cosmetic surgery, payments to employers to provide work-study stations, and other program-related expenditures.

The local vocational rehabilitation counselor can help determine which funded programs may be available to your schools. Typically the local counselor is all-powerful in his or her district or region. A rehabilitation plan (not unlike an IEP) is developed for each client (student) and, when signed by all concerned, the needed funds are committed. In general, it is wise not to have the local counselor call the state office to determine whether a certain type of expenditure is needed or legitimate. The answer could be, "No!" Rather, all concerned should work together cooperatively to convince the counselor of the need to have the expenditure placed in the individual rehabilitation plan.

Title IV-C, ESEA

Title IV-C, Elementary and Secondary Education Act (ESEA) funds allocated through the SEA may be sought for innovative and/or demonstration programs for the handicapped, including regional or innovative programs to serve secondary age or severely handicapped children. Check with the state Title IV-C coordinators for requirements and application procedures.

Crippled Children's Service Agency

Title V of the Social Security Act provides for a state service program for crippled children. Each state assigns this program to one of its state agencies, usually either the health or welfare agency. Wisconsin is unique in that its program for crippled children is assigned to the SEA.

Services for eligible children include diagnosis and evaluation, surgical procedures, special equipment (wheelchairs, hearing aids, etc.), therapy, and consultation. If the appropriate state agency for these services is unknown, the state branch of the federal Social Security Administration can provide this information.

Medicaid Funds

Title XIX and Title XX of the Social Security Act *may* be a resource for services for certain eligible children. The individual state plan or the state administrator can help determine if this is a source of funds for handicapped children. Typically Title XIX and XX eligibility requirements are less flexible than other programs. Their personnel are usually found in the state health, welfare, or social service agency, and their paper requirements are such that their utilization is not cost efficient in small districts.

Personnel Preparation Funds

Various states may make available preservice or in-service education funds for regular educators or special educators through state appropriations. The state special education office can provide information on grants to LEAs and traineeships, fellowships, or loans to individuals.

Each SEA also participates in personnel preparation programs under Part D, Education of the Handicapped Act (EHA). State plans typically concentrate on in-service education activities of the short course, workshop, or institute format. Costs of attendance are generally covered by the funds from Part D. Fellowships and traineeships to prepare personnel to teach targeted groups of handicapped children are often available under Part D, when training is not available in that state. The funds allow residents of the state to obtain the necessary training in out-of-state institutions of higher education. Again, the special education unit in the SEA can provide information on the state Part D plan.

Part B State Funds and Preschool Incentive Grants

The SEA retains up to 25 percent of the Part B funds generated under the PL 94–142 child count. After allowable SEA administrative charges are deducted, the balance is generally available for competitive projects in targeted areas of need. If the needs of a district are consistent with those established by the SEA, a proposal should be developed to initiate or expand the particular program. The SEA will provide necessary information and forms.

The preschool incentive grant funds, generated under authority of PL 94–142, are also for discretionary use by the SEA. Statewide projects of technical assistance for preschool programs have been initiated in some states. Other states allocate the incentive funds to LEA or regional programs and services for handicapped preschoolers on a competitive project basis.

Direct Federal Funding

Other federal programs operate in whole or in part directly from the federal funding agency. Funds are available to support research and demonstration, personnel preparation, model program development, and other such activities. Since the passage of PL 94–142, many of these federal sources are allocating resources to improve the implementation of the law.

The funds are allocated on a competitive proposal basis and are announced in such publications as the *Federal Register, Commerce Business Daily,* commercially available newsletters, and other sources. The announcements state the purpose of the program, requirements for eligibility, deadline dates, and how to obtain information and applications.

Information regarding availability of federal discretionary funds is available from a variety of sources. The Department of Education publishes an annual listing of discretionary programs administered by the agency. Title, purpose, intent, eligibility, projected deadlines, and names of persons to contact for information are included in the listing. Copies of the listing are available upon request from the Department.

The *Catalog of Federal Domestic Assistance* (CFDA) gives brief, basic information about every federally funded program, including education. Given the fact that it is all-inclusive, it is more difficult for a novice to utilize. It is, however, a tremendous resource. The catalog is usually available in larger libraries, the SEA, or from the Government Printing Office.

A 1979 publication entitled *Getting the buck to stop here: A Guide to Federal Resources for Special Needs* is available from The Council for Exceptional Children (CEC). The first section of the publication summarizes each federal program under a series of descriptors of categories and specific needs. After scanning the chart to locate possible appropriate funding sources, the user may obtain detailed information in the second section. Organization of the guide relies heavily on CFDA numbers. The guide will soon be outdated, but it appears to be the type of document CEC will revise periodically so it does not lose its usefulness. The guide is less cumbersome than the CFDA and contains programs of interest only to persons involved with handicapped and gifted children.

A WORD ABOUT DISCRETIONARY PROGRAMS

In general, it is much easier to obtain grants through state-level sources, whether the funds are actual state appropriations or federal programs administered by the state. In most cases, project proposals to the state are shorter and less complicated. State personnel are more accessible for assistance. However, federal sources should not be overlooked because they are more difficult to obtain. It should be remembered, that some proposals are successful, so the proposal writer should not give up if his or her first project proposal is not funded. A 25–30 percent average on approval of projects is considered excellent.

Program objectives should never be compromised just to be eligible for funds, and all available project funds should not be spent just because there is a deadline. A budget is a plan, not a contract! It is true that unused funds must be returned unless extensions are granted for remaining funds to be expended on the project purposes.

Funds should not be spent prior to receipt of a grant, for such expenditures are not generally allowed as charges against the grant. Delays in receipt of project approval are to be expected. The review process is usually quite time consuming.

OVERALL FUNDING OF SPECIAL EDUCATION

This chapter has reviewed the basic local, state, and federal funds available to provide programs for handicapped children on a continuing basis. In addition to these basic sources, the cost-conscious LEA should not overlook interagency agreements, third-party sources, or discretionary funding sources.

It is true that most basic funding sources are derived from tax revenues. The local taxpayer is most concerned about the local tax bill and, to a lesser extent, the state and federal tax burden. The creative administrator may be able to keep local taxes down by aggressively seeking out funds from state, federal, and other sources.

REFERENCES

Bernstein, C. D., Kirst, M. W., Hartman, W. T., and Marshall, R. S. *Financing Educational Services for the Handicapped.* Reston, Va.: Council for Exceptional Children, 1976.

Federal Register, Part II, Education of Handicapped Children. Implementation of Part B of the Education of the Handicapped Act, August 23, 1977, pp. 42474–42518.

Jones, P. R., and Wilkerson, W. R. "Factors To Consider in Planning Special Education Financing." In K. F. Jordan and K. Alexander, eds., *Futures in School Finance: Working toward a Common Goal.* Bloomington, IN: Phi Delta Kappa, 1975.

Rossmiller, R. A., Hale, J. A., and Frohreich, L. E. *Educational Programs for Exceptional Children: Resource Configurations and Costs.* Madison: The University of Wisconsin, 1970.

Snell, D. "Special Education Program Cost Analysis for Three Selected School Corporations in Indiana." Unpublished Ed.D. dissertation, Indiana University, 1973.

Sorensen, F. W. *A Cost Analysis of Selected Public School Special Education Systems in Illinois.* Springfield, IL: Office of Superintendent of Public Instruction, 1973.

Thomas, M. A. "Finance: Without Which There Is No Special Education." *Exceptional Children, 39*(1973):475–480.

Wilkerson, W. R. "Indiana School Finance Study: A Summary Report." Bloomington, IN: Indiana University, 1978.

CHAPTER 5 QUESTIONS

Q: Must a handicapped child receive special education and related services in the building serving his or her normal attendance area?

A: While it may be possible to serve many mildly handicapped children in their normal attendance area, it is doubtful this can always be accomplished for more severely handicapped children or those in low incidence categories. Inter-school and inter-district cooperative efforts are necessary to meet the least restrictive environment requirements.

Q: Must every handicapped child participate in the regular program?

A: No, all decisions must be made on an individual basis considering nature, intensity, and duration of the handicapping condition, as well as current needs.

Q: Are special day schools, residential schools, or other separate facilities in violation of the law?

A: Absolutely not, if such facilities can be justified as the appropriate facility at that point in the handicapped child's life.

Q: Should a child always continue in his or her initial placement for the remainder of the school year?

A: If the needs or conditions change, movement to a less restrictive placement should be completed as soon as possible, after all relevant parties are informed and parental approval is received.

Q: If a child has been served by the LD resource teacher for two periods per day, and is in a regular fifth grade the rest of the day, must the parents be consulted if the school feels that reducing service to one hour per day is more appropriate?

A: Yes! Due process rights must be assured.

Least Restrictive Environment

The Education for All Handicapped Children Act of 1975 has been called the "mainstreaming" law, even though this term does not actually appear anywhere in the law! (See Appendix A, which is a reprint of PL 94–142, and try to find the word "mainstreaming.")

Unfortunately, the word "mainstreaming" has come to denote the concept of least restrictive environment. Mainstreaming appears to be a utility word used to justify many current programs for handicapped children.

ALL HANDICAPPED CHILDREN IN REGULAR CLASSES?

In one school district which has long been recognized as a prototype for educating handicapped children, every self-contained special education class was closed. Children who had previously been served in special classes—many of them for several years—were all returned to regular classes serving children of comparable ages. Many special education teaching positions were eliminated from the budget entirely, and the remaining special education staff provided very limited itinerant support services to the handicapped children now in regular classrooms. This arrangement caused dissension among everyone involved.

Regular class teachers were upset and rejected the inclusion, and intrusion, of handicapped children into their classes. Their complaints centered around their lack of training to work with the handicapped, and the need to spend disproportionate amounts of time with handicapped children, thus taking instructional time away from nonhandicapped children.

Many special educators also rejected the movement of handicapped children from specialized to regular programs. Their concerns focused on the fact that regular class teachers would not be able to spend as much time with handicapped children, since their class sizes were two and three times as great as those of the special classes. The lack of time, coupled with the regular teachers' perceived lack of special training, resulted in a fear that the handicapped children would actually regress from their present achievement levels.

Parents of the handicapped objected to the relocation of their children to nonspecially designed facilities and equipment, which was unlike what they had become accustomed to in special classes. They also expressed concern that their children might be exploited by some nonhandicapped students and might possibly engage in immoral and/or illegal behaviors or practices.

On the other hand, parents of nonhandicapped children feared that their children would suffer educationally as a result of being enrolled with handicapped students. They felt that teachers might lower the level of instruction and spend too much time with handicapped children.

Some of the handicapped students were able to cope with the transfer to regular classes and continue their learning. Others, however, were unable to learn in the new situation. They became frustrated and developed a dislike for school.

The above conditions have been described as mainstreaming, both by regular as well as special educators.

In another school district, school buses picked up handicapped as well as nonhandicapped children each morning. The buses made stops at all the schools in town to discharge the nonhandicapped students; they then continued on to a school located in the rural area surrounding the town to discharge the handicapped students.

This type of situation is also called mainstreaming. In the first example, all handicapped children attend school and receive instruction with nonhandicapped students; thus they are mainstreamed. In the second situation, mainstreaming consists only of handicapped and nonhandicapped children riding together on the same bus—but to different facilities.

It would be difficult for most professional educators to defend either of the two situations described. Both are somewhat extreme examples of mainstreaming, and therefore it is not surprising that the term has acquired negative connotations in the minds of many parents and professionals. A precise definition of the term is difficult to formulate.

One Element of Least Restrictive Environment (LRE)

Reynolds and Birch (1977) suggest that mainstreaming should be considered in the multiple contexts of academic, social, and physical arenas. Physical placement in regular classes may still result in social and academic isolation; and social isolation may well occur even though a handicapped child in the regular program has little or no difficulty with the academic material.

In 1976, the governing bodies of The Council for Exceptional Children (CEC) published an official definition of mainstreaming. It is relatively comprehensive and reads as follows:

> Mainstreaming is a belief which involves an educational placement procedure and process for exceptional children, based on the conviction that each such child should be educated in the least restrictive environment in which his educational and related needs can be satisfactorily provided. This concept recognizes that exceptional children have a wide range of special educational needs, varying greatly in intensity and duration; that there is a recognized continuum of educational settings which may, at a given time, be appropriate for an individual child's needs; that to the maximum extent appropriate, exceptional children should be educated with nonexceptional children; and that special classes, separate schooling, or other removal of an exceptional child from education with nonexceptional children should occur only when the intensity of the child's special education and related needs is such that they cannot be satisfied in an environment including nonexceptional children, even with the provision of supplementary aids and services. (CEC, "Official Actions . . .," 1976, p. 43)

Several features of the above definition deserve mention:

1. Mainstreaming is described as a "belief"; it is not a descriptive term.
2. The definition refers to education in the "least restrictive environment," which begins to add meaning.
3. Widely varying "needs," "intensity," and "duration" are acknowledged for each child.
4. A "continuum of educational settings" is required.
5. The definition calls for education to be provided to the "maximum extent appropriate" with nonexceptional children, but yet allows for more restrictive settings when the "intensity" of the exceptional child's needs cannot be accommodated in a setting with nonexceptional students.

Unfortunately, the vast majority of individuals who use the term "mainstreaming" do not consider all of the elements of the definition presented, but focus only on the physical proximity aspect. As a result, the term mainstreaming has developed negative connotations for many individuals and groups. For this reason, this writer suggests that the term mainstreaming be deleted from the professional literature and from common usage, and be replaced by the more proper term "least restrictive environment (LRE)."

LRE IS NOT NEW

The concept of least restrictive environment is not new. It was included in many of the state special education statutes that were passed well before the enactment of PL 94–142. The Education Amendments of 1974 (PL 93-380), enacted some fifteen months prior to PL 94–142, referred to the need for educational programs for handicapped children to be provided in the least restrictive environment.

Continuum of Services

Thirteen years before the passage of PL 94–142, Reynolds (1962) described a "hierarchy of special education programs." While the term "least restrictive environment" had not yet been applied to the education of handicapped children, Reynolds gave an excellent overview of the concept. He described a continuum of services necessary to provide educational and related service programs for all handicapped children. The model is by no means static: A child can move in either direction as needs change. Reynolds' hierarchy is summarized in Figure 5.1.

The successive levels of administrative arrangements or service options described by Reynolds are as appropriate today as they were in 1962. The severity or intensity of the educational or related needs at a given time for an individual child determine which level of the model will be needed to offer an appropriate program. The less severe the condition, the closer placement can be to the baseline of regular classrooms.

It would not be at all unusual for a seriously emotionally disturbed child to be placed in the most restrictive setting of a hospital or treatment center.

Figure 5.1
SPECIAL EDUCATION PROGRAMS

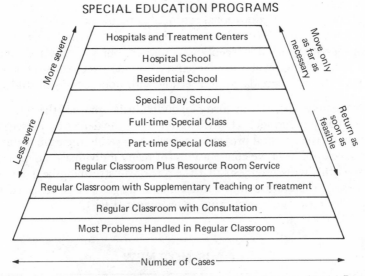

Source: Reynolds, M.C. "A Framework for Considering Some Issues in Special Education." *Exceptional Children, 28* (March 1962): 367–370. Copyright 1962 by The Council for Exceptional Children. Reprinted with permission.

However, as the child's needs for intensive psychiatric treatment diminish, he or she can be returned to the school environment, perhaps initially in a full-time special class. As further academic and social needs can be met at less restrictive levels, the child may move in successive steps toward the regular class, or possibly to a resource room, before full placement in a regular class is achieved. Fewer and fewer handicapped children should be served at the higher levels of the model.

With the possible exception of speech therapy, which is usually provided on an itinerant basis to children enrolled in the regular class, most public school special education programs have developed in the form of full-time special classes or special day schools. Through the mid- to late 1960s, the only options available in many schools were the regular classroom or the full-time special class or special day school. In such cases, handicapped children were required to fit the program, rather than vice-versa.

The essence of PL 94–142 and most state statutes today is that programs must be individualized, based on the child's needs at a given point in time. Thus, the continuum of service approach described by Reynolds (1962) and restructured by Willenberg (1967), and Deno's (1970) Cascade System, may serve as suitable models for implementing the Education for All Handicapped Children Act.

Regulatory Factors

The regulations for implementing PL 94–142 (*Federal Register*, August 23, 1977) closely parallel the statutory language of the law when references are made to the least restrictive environment. The regulations state:

Section 121a.550 General
(b) Each public agency shall insure:
   (1) That to the maximum extent appropriate, handicapped children; including children in public or private institutions or other care facilities, are educated with children who are not handicapped, and
   (2) That special classes, separate schooling or other removal of handicapped children from the regular educational environment occurs only when the nature or severity of the handicap is such that education in regular classes with the use of supplementary aids and services cannot be achieved satisfactorily.

Section 121a.551 Continuum of alternative placements.
(a) Each public agency shall insure that a continuum of alternative placements is available to meet the needs of handicapped children for special education and related services.
(b) The continuum required under paragraph (a) of this section must:
   (1) Include the alternative placements listed in the definition of special education under Section 121a.13 of Subpart A (instruction in regular classes, special classes, special schools, home instruction, and instruction in hospitals and institutions), and

(2) Make provision for supplementary services (such as resource room or itinerant instruction) to be provided in conjunction with regular class placement.

Section 121a.552 Placements.
Each public agency shall insure that:
(a) Each handicapped child's educational placement:
    (1) Is determined at least annually,
    (2) Is based on his or her individualized education program, and
    (3) Is as close as possible to the child's home;
(b) The various alternative placements included under Section 121a.551 are available to the extent necessary to implement the individualized education program for each handicapped child;
(c) Unless a handicapped child's individualized education program requires some other arrangement, the child is educated in the school which he or she would attend if not handicapped; and
(d) In selecting the least restrictive environment, consideration is given to any potential harmful effect on the child or on the quality of services which he or she needs. (p. 42497)

DECISIONS TO BE MADE FOR EACH CHILD

The regulations stress throughout that all decisions must be made on an individual basis. Of particular interest to those individuals who are fearful that *all* handicapped children might be placed in the regular classroom, is the fact that any potential harmful effect on the child is carefully considered. This cautionary measure tends to eliminate most severely handicapped children from regular class placement. Additional sections of the regulations call for participation of handicapped students to the maximum extent appropriate in nonacademic and extracurricular activities, such as meals and recess.

LRE FOR CHILDREN IN INSTITUTIONS

In cases where children are residents of a public or private institution, the application of least restrictive environment requires that there be access to education with nonhandicapped children. This can be accomplished by attendance on a full- or part-time basis in the local public schools.

State statutes vary as to financial responsibility for children in institutions who attend full- or part-time programs in the local schools. In some states, the state government may have responsibility while in others the district of legal residence may be responsible. Local school districts should clarify this issue by careful study of state statutes, but the local district cannot deny access to local programs.

LEAST RESTRICTIVE/MOST PRODUCTIVE ENVIRONMENT

The concept of least restrictive environment, when properly considered on an individual basis for each child, goes well beyond placement. With due consideration for academic, social, physical, psychological, and medically related needs for each handicapped child, the least restrictive environment becomes the most productive environment for the child.

In considering the appropriate educational program for a handicapped child, two basic questions must be asked:

1. Is the proposed program in the least restrictive environment possible?
2. Is the proposed program in the most productive environment possible?

In making a final decision, it seems that the answer to the second question should receive more attention than the first.

For example, if an educable mentally retarded child is being considered for placement in the regular program, with resource service, both questions may be answered in the affirmative. But if an institutionalized, severely handicapped child is being considered for return to the home, the first answer would appear to be "yes," but the second answer could well be "no" if the child required 24-hour medical supervision.

Lowenbraun and Affleck (1978) proposed some thirty-five criteria to be utilized in determining adequacy of a given placement. Their first criterion states that a self-contained institutional education program may be considered the least restrictive environment "if and only if" legal and/or medical opinions suggest the child or society would be harmed by the child's departure from such a protective environment. The Lowenbraun and Affleck criteria deal with the self-contained facility; the local education agency; mildly handicapped; hearing impaired; and severely behavior disordered; and include such areas as ancillary special education services for handicapped children in the regular classroom; in-service training for staff; and physical accommodations for children with orthopedic, visual, or hearing impairments.

PARENTAL CONCERNS

Parents of handicapped children may frequently resist placement in a less restrictive environment. Often such resistance is only an initial reaction, but some parents continue to resist even after a proposed program and the philosophy of least restrictive environment is fully explained to them. Educators may find such resistance surprising, particularly when so much effort was expended in developing a full continuum of service delivery within the schools.

However, it must be kept in mind that parents of handicapped children with observable physical disabilities have probably seen rejection of, and discrimination against, their children by many segments of society. Thus their protective attitude is understandable and may cause them to seek a more sheltered situation for their child.

As mentioned earlier, exploitation of handicapped children is also a concern, especially in areas such as sexual abuse, drugs, alcohol, theft, and vandalism. The media coverage of such activities in today's schools certainly has not lessened concerns of parents of handicapped or nonhandicapped children.

While special educators do not like to acknowledge it, the instruction in special classes has not always been geared to individual needs. The lower pupil–teacher ratio of special classes was initially established to allow for more individualization. However, this has not always been the result, and parents who have recognized the lack of quality in more restrictive settings seriously question the possibility of improving quality by moving their child to a less restrictive setting with a greater pupil-teacher ratio.

Educators must be cognizant of the concerns of parents and the reasons such concerns exist. In addition to those already mentioned, many parents have unwarranted guilt feelings about having produced a handicapped child. These feelings may not always be readily observable, but may produce some parental reactions such as overprotection.

GETTING PARENTS INVOLVED

The Education for All Handicapped Children Act calls for parental involvement at several stages of the referral, evaluation, IEP development, and placement process. Honest attempts at actively involving the parents—as opposed to only seeking a signed permission statement—can provide positive opportunities to help reduce fears or concerns that might otherwise be expressed by parents. Such opportunities could be likened to in-service education efforts with staff.

Ballard (1978) suggested some possible methods of involving parents in the development of their child's IEP. The methods he suggested could apply equally well to the other stages of the process. Ballard's list proposes the following:

1. Each local educational agency shall take steps to insure that one or both of the parents of the handicapped child are present at each meeting or are afforded the opportunity to participate, including scheduling the meeting at a mutually agreed upon time and place.
2. If neither parent can attend, the local education agency shall use other methods to insure parent participation, including individual or conference telephone calls.
3. A meeting may be conducted without a parent in attendance if the local education agency is unable to convince the parents that they should

attend. In this case the local education agency must have a record of its attempts to arrange a mutually agreed upon time and place, such as:

    a. Detailed records of telephone calls made or attempted and the results of those calls

    b. Copies of correspondence sent to the parents and any responses received

    c. Detailed records of visits made to the parents' home or place of employment and the results of those visits.

4. The local education agency shall take whatever action is necessary to insure that the parent understands the proceedings at a meeting, including arranging for an interpreter for parents who are deaf or whose native language is other than English.

Some parental concerns may be real and some may be imagined. Whichever the case, school personnel must work with the parents cooperatively to develop an appropriate program for the child.

Many parents have not had active positive involvement with the schools. All too often, parental involvement was sought only when disciplinary actions were necessary for a child. As contacts with parents are initiated, school personnel must realize the history of negative contacts many parents have had with school personnel.

The federal statute is oriented toward the individual child. It is not oriented toward the school or the parents. The desired outcome is the appropriate education of handicapped children. Schools and parents must work together effectively to achieve this end, and hopefully a feeling of mutual trust and understanding will result from this partnership.

IN-SERVICE EDUCATION: MAKING LRE A VIABLE CONCEPT

Is the education of handicapped children in the least restrictive environment a viable concept? Is a continuum of services possible in the schools today?

Chapter 8 of this book will focus specifically on the area of personnel development, but it is appropriate at this time to mention briefly the need for in-service education. Successful implementation of the least restrictive environment will require an on-going in-service education program for a district's total professional and ancillary staff. Teachers of handicapped and nonhandicapped students, building administrators, counselors, diagnostic personnel, central office staff, bus drivers, food service personnel, and custodial staff will all need to understand various aspects of the concept.

Teachers of regular classes have been heard to complain that in-service all too often is very general, and focuses mainly on descriptions and characteristics of various types of handicapped children. The real concern of the regular class teacher, however, is specifically what to do when a given handicapped child is assigned to the class; how to deal with and handle the child.

Regular classroom teachers should be assured that many of the methods and techniques they have used in the past also work for the handicapped child, although some modifications of the curriculum or classroom management may be necessary for some handicapped children.

WHAT REGULAR TEACHERS CAN EXPECT

At the very minimum, regular classroom teachers should have access to the child's individualized education program (IEP). In addition, they should receive a brief statement as to what the child can accomplish on his or her own. This is particularly true for a physically disabled, blind, or hearing-impaired child. Without such information, the regular class teacher does not know whether the child can physically get about the building to restrooms, cafeteria, etc. Teachers should know whether an aide or interpreter will accompany the hearing-impaired child to class. Special education support staff should be available to the regular class teacher to respond to questions or suggest techniques of dealing with specific problems.

Special education support staff must continuously monitor the progress of the child in the regular program to determine whether additional services are needed. Perhaps it may be necessary for a resource or itinerant teacher to provide some supplementary tutoring to maintain the child in the program. In such a case, the monitoring responsibility might be assumed by that individual.

The regular classroom teacher also needs to know the child's schedule for receiving supportive or related services. In some cases, the child may have regularly scheduled periods of time with the resource teacher; in other cases, the child may have access to the resource teacher only when an unscheduled crisis or need occurs.

Laying the proper foundation for the least restrictive environment can solve many potential and time-consuming problems.

THE NEIGHBORHOOD SCHOOL CONCEPT

It is unrealistic to assume that every handicapped child is going to be able to attend the neighborhood school serving the given residential area. Few schools are of sufficient size to provide the full range of services, from regular classes to full-time special classes. Many small school districts will have difficulty in providing comprehensive special education and related service programs if they attempt to do so on their own. Cooperative efforts both within and between districts are required to implement a comprehensive special education program for all types of handicapped children, with a full continuum of services.

COOPERATIVE AND REGIONAL PROGRAMING

State statutes and regulations in special education vary greatly with regard to cooperative programing. Some states have formally created intermediate districts, other states allow formal and informal cooperative or joint programing. Only the largest urban area school districts can probably operate a truly comprehensive program by themselves.

Comprehensive special education programing and implementation of a full continuum of services for the higher prevalence areas of special education will typically require a pupil population base of 10,000 to 15,000 students. More than 25,000 students may well be necessary for full implementation of state and federal mandates for the low prevalence special education areas. Even with the 25,000 and over pupil population base, regional and/or statewide cooperation may be required to effectively serve all handicapped children.

Creative planning and programing are necessary prerequisites in sparsely populated and geographically isolated areas. Artificial boundries imposed by state lines may require school districts in two or more states to work together jointly. Cost efficiency will also require inter- and intra-district cooperation. The continuum of services necessary to implement the least restrictive environment for all handicapped children in the schools will not be achieved without effort.

DO PARENTS KNOW THE REQUIREMENTS?

Parents of handicapped children are becoming more knowledgeable of their rights to a free, appropriate public education for their handicapped children. Advocacy groups are continually providing information to their members. The media—popular magazines in particular—are making parents more aware of their rights.

One issue of *Better Homes and Gardens* (September 1979) contains a thorough article on PL 94–142. Topics addressed include: Who is covered; Identification; Least restrictive environment; Individual planning; Due process rights; What happens to nonhandicapped kids; and Key problems.

The article concludes with a section entitled, "If Your Child Is Handicapped." Six steps outlined in this section are:

First, face your own feelings head on. "You shouldn't be ashamed of your mixed feelings about your child's problems," says Martha Ziegler, whose daughter is handicapped. "They're normal reactions to an often difficult situation. It helps to talk with parents of children with similar problems."

Second, become informed about your rights and the proper procedures under PL 94–142 and your state's laws. Organizations for the parents of handicapped children can tell you a lot and even provide training sessions on how to utilize your rights effectively. Many of these groups will also send an experienced member with you to the IEP session and to hearings, if you wish.

Third, insist on proper testing for your child. Get an outside evaluation, if necessary.

Fourth, be firm but cooperative in developing your child's IEP. Offer your views about the child as well as your observations about specific behavior. Make certain the program relates to your child's special needs. Don't accept a program that is too general ("Johnny will read better by the year's end"). See that the IEP outlines related services in addition to educational programs.

Fifth, keep on top of how the child is progressing through the year and request a revision of the IEP if you think it's necessary.

Sixth, if you fail to get a remedy through the school or district, report the matter to the state department of education and to the Bureau of Education for the Handicapped in Washington. But don't lose sight of the fact that PL 94–142 is meant to be worked out on the local scene. (Daly, 1979, pp. 45, 49)

The article cited above is merely one example of much factual information currently available to parents of handicapped children. It takes a positive approach to cooperation with the schools, but also emphasizes that parents should remain firm in their position.

Parents are learning more about state and federal statutes for the handicapped on a continuing basis. Hopefully, the same is true for members of the professional and educational community.

IMPLEMENTING LRE IN THE SCHOOLS

Whether the least restrictive placement setting is an institution, a total school district, a single building, single classroom, or a uniquely individual setting for one handicapped child, several key points must be considered.

Consider the Individual

First and foremost, decisions should be made based on each individual child's needs at the time. Each child has different needs at different times. It is wrong to assume that *all* educable mentally retarded or learning disabled children should be placed in regular classes two periods per day. Nor can it be assumed that all blind children should be served at the state residential school for the blind. Before the LRE concept, which dictates that programs be developed for each handicapped child, came into use, the predominant trend was that handicapped children were fitted into existing programs. However, under the LRE concept, if no existing program is appropriate, a new or modified program must be developed.

Inform All Relevant Parties

All staff, parents, and the child or children involved should be made fully aware of the type of placement and the reason for it. The information presented to a child may necessarily be less comprehensive than that shared with regular and special teachers, principals, other staff, and parents. The age of the child and the severity of the handicap are critical factors to be considered with respect to the type of information shared with a child. Depending on the extent to which LRE has been implemented, it may be necessary to inform a regular class that a new child who is blind will be enrolling. Hopefully, information sensitizing nonhandicapped children to the accomplishments as well as the problems of handicapped individuals has been presented previously.

Appropriate in-service education for staff should precede implementation. If a choice must be made as to who should receive in-service training, the building administrator is a likely candidate, since he or she is a key person in influencing the building staff and, without his or her acceptance of LRE placements, the program may be doomed.

Groups of parents, such as the local Association for Retarded Citizens (ARC) unit or other formal and informal groups, should be prepared before the LRE concept is implemented. Individual parents may become more knowledgeable about the concept if they have attended a group meeting about it. Concerns expressed by individual, or groups of, parents need to be worked out. If the child has been served in a more restrictive placement, some parental resistance may be encountered; therefore, the reasons for moving the child to less restrictive levels of service should be documented.

Relevant support service personnel in the local education agency (LEA) or institution must be made aware of the LRE concept and the rationale for its implementation for individual children. It is important that clerical, custodial, food service, transportation, nursing, and aide personnel who may be directly or indirectly involved with children not be overlooked.

LRE placement may be easier to accomplish in departmentalized buildings where handicapped children changing classes will be involved in a normal flow with other children. Elementary buildings are less likely to be departmentalized and may require additional preparation.

Some regular teachers will be less able to accept a handicapped child in the classroom. While we would like to believe that all teachers are accepting and understanding, this is probably not the case. Some selective assignments may be necessary, but teachers should not be overloaded just because they are cooperative or have attended workshops or taken additional coursework.

Separate facilities are still appropriate when severity of handicap or special needs of the individual cannot be met otherwise.

Children should be moved from placement to placement as needs change— not necessarily at a semester, quarter, or grading period break, unless this is absolutely necessary to assure relevant material is not missed by changing placement in the middle of a grading period.

USE OF A DECISION-MAKING MODEL

Professional people frequently use a formal or informal decision-making model. A variety of such models may be found in the literature in any field. Common elements include considering all possible alternatives and selecting the best one. Planning for all possible "system breaks" in implementing the LRE concept is crucial. All possible reactions—both positive and negative—to measures taken should be thought through and capitalized on or remediated. Implementation should then be easy and operate smoothly.

REFERENCES

Ballard, J. *Public Law 94–142 and Section 504—Understanding What They Are and Are Not* (rev. ed.). Reston, Va.: The Council for Exceptional Children, 1978, p. 5.

Daly, M. "Handicapped Children in the Classroom—What Mainstreaming Is All About." *Better Homes and Gardens, 57* (1979): 38, 40, 42, 45, 49.

Deno, E. "Special Education as Developmental Capital." *Exceptional Children, 37* (1970): 229–237.

Federal Register, Part II. "Education of Handicapped Children; Implementation of Part B of the Education of the Handicapped Act," (August 23, 1977): pp. 42474–42518.

Lowenbraun, S., and Affleck, J. *Developing Criteria for the Evaluation of the Least Restrictive Environment Provision.* USOE, BEH, Division of Innovation and Development, State Program Studies Branch (1978).

Reynolds, M. C. "A Framework for Considering Some Issues in Special Education." *Exceptional Children, 28* (1962): 367–370.

———, and Birch, J. W. *Teaching Exceptional Children in All America's Schools: A First Course for Teachers and Principals.* Reston, Va.: The Council for Exceptional Children, 1977.

CHAPTER 6 QUESTIONS

Q: Must the building principal attend IEP meetings?

A: No, but in most cases the building principal will be the other representative of the school district who is "legally qualified to provide or supervise the provision of special education." In districts where several personnel are qualified as special education supervisors, these individuals certainly meet the criteria as the other representative and can serve in that capacity. Designees of the principal may serve if they meet the criteria. For example, an assistant principal would qualify but a guidance counselor would not, unless the guidance counselor held certification as a building administrator or a special educator.

Q: Does PL 94–142 require that the identification, IEP, and placement process be completed within a minimum length of time?

A: PL 94–142 does not establish a fixed number of days, weeks, or months for such activities. Again, this is a case where state standards apply. Various state laws and regulations differ in the number of days stipulated (calendar and/or administrative) for completing the above process. Only IEP development has a fixed number of days requirement in federal law and regulations. There is no reason for long delays (3 months or more), unless additional diagnosis is required and then all parties, including parents, should be fully informed.

Q: If a physical therapist is not employed in the school district, but medical reports indicate that a child should be receiving physical therapy, must physical therapy be included in the IEP and be provided by the schools?

A: If physical therapy is indicated by appropriate documentation, it should be included in the IEP as a related service. The schools must either provide the therapy or arrange for another agency, such as the city or county health department, to provide it. If other options are not available, the part-time service of a physical therapist at the local hospital may be utilized.

Individualized Education Programs

One major new requirement in The Education for All Handicapped Children Act of 1975 is that an individualized education program (IEP) be developed for each handicapped child. This requirement is outlined in Section 4(a)(4)(19) of PL 94–142. The reader is encouraged to read this section of the statute in the Appendix of this text.

PROPOSED RULES

What appears to be a relatively straightforward section in the statute has created confusion among teachers, administrators, and parents throughout the country, possibly stemming from the "proposed rules" for PL 94–142 (*Federal Register,* 1976).

The "proposed rules" on IEP development and content were much more specific and detailed than the final regulation published on August 23, 1977 (*Federal Register,* 1977). Appendix A of the final regulations contains an analysis which, when referring to IEP contents, states:

> Comment: Hundreds of commenters responded to this section. Some commenters requested that additional services or other items be added. Other commenters recommended that the section be sharply cut back, because they felt that this went unnecessarily beyond the items listed in the statute. Many of the commenters wanted the specific service areas they represent added to the list of services to be provided in the IEP. Others felt that this went unnecessarily beyond the items listed in the statute.

> Response: The Office of Education has elected to amend this section by adopting

substantially verbatim the language from section 602(19) of the statute. The regulation retains one clarification from the proposed rules, that the individualized education program must include related services to be provided to the child, as well as special education and the extent to which the child can participate in regular education programs. However, given the controversy over this section and whether it is appropriate to add items not specifically covered in the statute, the Office of Education has decided that some experience operating under the statute would be useful before considering whether further regulations on this point would be appropriate. (*Federal Register*, 1977, p.42508)

FINAL REGULATIONS

Differences in the proposed rules and the final regulations are illustrated by the following excerpts from the *Federal Register* of December 30, 1976 (proposed) and August 23, 1977 (final).

Proposed

Final

121a.223 Participants in meetings.

121a.344 Participants in meetings.

(a) A representative of the local educational agency, other than the child's teachers, who is qualified to provide, or supervise the provision of, special education.

(1) A representative of the public agency, other than the child's teacher, who is qualified to provide, or supervise the provision of, special education.

(b) The child's teacher or teachers, special or regular, or both, who have a direct responsibility for implementing the child's individualized education program.

(2) The child's teacher.

(c) One or both of the child's parents, . . .

(3) One or both of the child's parents, . . .

(d) Where appropriate, the child.

(4) The child where appropriate.

(e) Other individuals, at the discretion of the parent or agency.

(5) Other individuals, at the discretion of the parent or agency.

(b) Evaluation personnel. For a handicapped child who has been evaluated for the first time, the public agency shall insure:

(1) That a member of the evaluation team participates in the meeting; or

(2) That the representative of the public agency, the child's teacher, or some other person is present at the meeting, who is knowledgeable about the evaluation procedures used with the child and is familiar with the results of the evaluation.

121a.225 Content of individualized education program.

...

(a) A statement of the child's present levels of educational performance, including academic achievement, social adaptation, prevocational and vocational skills, psychomotor skills, and self-help skills.

(b) A statement of annual goals which describes the educational performance to be achieved by the end of the school year under the child's individualized education program;

(c) A statement of short-term instructional objectives, which must be measurable intermediate steps between the present level of educational performance and the annual goals;

(d) A statement of specific educational services needed by the child (determined without regard to the availability of those services) including a description of:

(1) All special education and related services which are needed to meet the unique needs of the child, including the type of physical education program in which the child will participate, and

(2) Any special instructional media and materials which are needed;

(e) The date when those services will begin and length of time the services will be given;

(f) A description of the extent to which the child will participate in regular education programs;

(g) A justification for the type of educational placement which the child will have;

(h) A list of the individuals who are responsible for implementation of the individualized education program; and

(i) Objective criteria, evaluation procedures, and schedules for determining, on at least an annual basis, whether the short-term instructional objectives are being achieved.

121a.346 Content of individualized education program.

...

(a) A statement of the child's present levels of educational performance;

(b) A statement of annual goals, including short-term instructional objectives;

(c) A statement of the specific special education and related services to be provided to the child, and the extent to which the child will be able to participate in regular educational programs;

(d) The projected dates for initiation of services and the anticipated duration of the services; and

(e) Appropriate objective criteria and evaluation procedures and schedules for determining, on at least an annual basis, whether the short-term instructional objectives are being achieved.

The issuance of the final regulations, while hailed by many as a reversal of the over-regulation of the proposed rules, did revert to the basic statutory language of PL 94–142. Very little direction beyond the statute is provided by the final regulations. This in part is felt to create much of the confusion surrounding the IEP process. Many of the items deleted from the proposed rules did give interpretive direction and in several cases may be viewed as sound educational practice.

PROVIDE ONLY AVAILABLE SERVICES?

A specific area that created confusion between the proposed rules and the final regulations concerned provision of available services. The deletion of the parenthetical phrase "determined without regard to availability of those services," which appeared in the proposed rules, but not in the final regulations, is an example. In response to what appeared to be the commonly emerging practice of writing into the IEP only those services available within the schools or agency, Edwin W. Martin, then Deputy Commissioner of the Bureau of Education for the Handicapped (BEH), issued an "Informal Letter to Chief State School Officers," on November 17, 1977. The subject of Martin's letter was a clarification of the Bureau's position on IEP content.

Martin's letter stated in part that:

> ... As a result of this change, some parties have interpreted the final regulations to mean that a public agency must provide to a handicapped child only those services which are available in the agency. This interpretation is not correct.
>
> Although the wording on IEP content was changed in the final regulations, our position on the critical issues of need and required services for individual handicapped children has not been altered. We do not wish to change this basic position and, under the statute and extensive legislative history on IEPs, we have no authority to do so. (Martin, 1977)

Reasons for the wording of the final regulation, as explained by Martin's (1977) letter, included the fact that the BEH decided that additional details could have had a "negative effect on the implementation of the IEP requirement." Martin further pointed out that reverting to the statutory language did not mean that a handicapped child would receive any lesser level services than those required by law.

According to Martin (1977), the fact that the parents participate in IEP planning allows them to accept or reject the proposed services. Parental dissatisfaction could be the basis of a formal request for an impartial due-process hearing to resolve an issue.

Further elaboration on the IEP as the basis of the required free appropriate public education (FAPE) under both PL 94–142 and Section 504 of the

Rehabilitation Act of 1973 (PL 93–112) is provided in the Martin letter as follows:

> The regulations under Section 504 (45CFR Part 84) state that an appropriate education "... is the provision of regular or special education and related aids and services that (i) are designed to meet the individual educational needs of handicapped persons as adequately as the needs of nonhandicapped persons are met and (ii) are based upon adherence to procedures that satisfy the requirements of section 84.34 (Educational setting), 84.35 (Evaluation and placement), and 84.36 (Procedural safeguards)."
>
> The Section 504 regulations also require recipients to achieve full compliance with the FAPE requirements of section 84.33 as expeditiously as possible, but in no event later than September 1, 1978.
>
> Under Part B, "FAPE" means special education and related services ... which are provided in conformity with an IEP. The timelines for FAPE are the same for both Part B and Section 504.
>
> Read together, these two statutes and their implementing regulations require that by September 1, 1978, each handicapped child must be provided all services necessary to meet his/her special education and related needs. (Martin, 1977)

CONGRESSIONAL OVERSIGHT HEARINGS

Efforts like those of Martin did not totally resolve the problems and confusion surrounding the IEP development process. Congress held oversight hearings on the implementation of PL 94–142 during July of 1979. Both parents and teachers who testified included comments on the IEP. Parents expressed: (a) a need for in-service training relating to their role in the IEP process, and (b) full information on due-process rights provided by the local schools. Teachers who testified included remarks indicating that: (a) IEPs have increased paperwork requirements for teachers; and (b) they needed in-service training and additional time allowed in their schedules for development and implementation of IEPs. Teachers did acknowledge that many of their problems with the IEP process might subside as they gained additional experience with it (NASDSE, 1979).

BEH REGIONAL MEETINGS

Similar concerns were expressed in five regional meetings held by the Bureau of Education for the Handicapped (BEH) during July 1979. The meetings were planned to determine issues and to clarify the process of implementing PL 94–142. In these regional meetings, the IEP surfaced as a major area of concern. The problems expressed were not relevant to the statutory requirement for an IEP but to state and local interpretation thereof (Education of the

Handicapped, 1979). The regional meetings also raised concerns about such issues as the following: (a) an IEP constituting a contract; (b) schools providing only those programs and services available, rather than all needed services; (c) computer-generated IEPs; (d) persons mandated to participate in the IEP development meeting; and (e) individuals permitted to issue official policy.

NO FEDERALLY REQUIRED FORMAT

The Education for All Handicapped Children Act does not specify an official format for the IEP; it merely delineates content. Some state education agencies (SEAs) have developed a uniform IEP format for use in the state while other states have provided one or more sample formats to school districts. In still other states, the local district is left to develop its own format, as long as the required elements of the IEP are included.

ADDED PAPERWORK—IS IT REALLY NECESSARY?

Teachers have complained about added paperwork. In some instances, state and local forms require information above and beyond that required by PL 94–142. IEPs can be used by state and local education agencies in lieu of the previously required annual progress reports. Typically, the IEP has been viewed as one additional paperwork task for teachers rather than as a replacement for other teacher-prepared reports. With additional columns for checks or dates, the IEP could become a very effective progress report or report card to be shared with parents. The teachers could enter check marks or dates to indicate achievement of certain goals and/or objectives.

IEP RESOURCE MATERIAL

A useful resource in IEP development and implementation is available from the Foundation for Exceptional Children in Reston, Virginia. The IEP package contains three sound filmstrips as well as "A Primer on Individualized Education Programs for Handicapped Children." The primer is also available at low cost without the kit. Utilization of these materials is valuable for in-service education of school staff or parents.

A MANAGEMENT TOOL

A variety of terms, including "management tool" and "contract," have been used to describe the IEP. The intent of Congress appears to have been for the

IEP to serve as a possible accountability device, to assure individual planning for each handicapped child.

Such accountability, however, does not extend to the schools or the teacher. In the December 30, 1976, *Federal Register,* the initial discussion of the organization of the proposed rules cited this statement made in the *Congressional Record* by Congressman Albert Quie:

> It is important to point out that [the individualized educational program] is an educational program developed jointly, but it is not intended as a binding contract by the schools, children and parents. (p. 56970)

Further elaboration indicates that the educational agency is responsible for providing the services contained in the IEP, but is not responsible if the projected goals and objectives are not achieved by the child.

The final regulations include the following section, which was added to clarify whether or not the IEP is a contract:

> 121a.349 Individualized Education Program—Accountability
> Each public agency must provide special education and related services to a handicapped child in accordance with an individualized education program. However, Part B of the Act does not require that any agency, teacher, or other person be held accountable if a child does not achieve goals and objectives. (*Federal Register,* 1977, p. 42491)

Parents have a valid complaint if the agency does not provide all elements of the education program and related services called for in the child's IEP. A complaint is not valid, however, if all elements of the program and services were provided but the child did not achieve the goals or objectives specified. Failure to meet the goals and objectives could be a result of a variety of factors, including overestimating the child's potential to achieve.

AN EDUCATIONAL BUDGET

The IEP may be most accurately described as an educational budget for the child. A budget is a plan or schedule, usually of a fiscal nature, for a set period of time. The IEP has many of the same characteristics (plan, schedule) from the educational point of view. But a budget is not a contract, and neither is an IEP.

KEY POINTS TO REMEMBER

What key points should be kept in mind regarding the IEP?

  1. The IEP must be developed before the child is placed in a special education program. This fact has been questioned by LEA teachers and admin-

istrators who maintain that only the special education teacher who receives the child can designate the required goals and objectives. It is difficult to assume the validity of this point when one considers that the evaluation prior to the IEP development will ascertain present levels of educational performance. Annual goals and short-term instructional objectives are developed from such present levels of performance. Without knowledge of goals and objectives, it is extremely difficult to place the child in the appropriate program. The child's teacher or teachers utilize the goals and objectives in developing lesson plans which further delineate the daily instructional and related service plan for the child.

2. The participants in the IEP development meeting are clearly specified both by statute and regulation. The representative of the agency must be someone other than the child's teacher, who is qualified to provide or supervise the provision of special education. Persons qualified to *provide* special education services include those certified, licensed, or endorsed by the state education agency in an appropriate area of special education. A special education teacher other than the child's teacher would meet the requirement. Those qualified to *supervise* could include building principal, assistant principal, special education director or special education supervisor. Whenever possible, a person qualified to supervise is preferable to someone qualified to provide services, for the presence of an administrator or supervisor demonstrates to the parents the school's intent to serve the child appropriately.

3. While it may be desirable to have all teachers and service personnel who have worked, or will work, with the child present for the IEP meeting, caution should be exercised so as to avoid overwhelming the parents. Parents may be hesitant to offer input if they are greatly outnumbered. The goal should be to sincerely and actively solicit parent input and understanding.

4. It is doubtful that school personnel will come to the IEP meeting without some preplanning. However, it should not be merely a token meeting just to meet a legal requirement, when in fact all decisions have already been made. Parents can legitimately criticize the process if they feel their attendance is useless or perfunctory.

5. Involving the handicapped child, particularly older children, can result in a high level of motivation to learn. The writer visited one secondary-level class for the educable mentally retarded (EMR) where the students had participated in IEP development. The students had access to their IEPs and checked off the objectives as they were met. This appeared to be a strong motivating factor for the EMR students.

6. Educational jargon should be avoided at the IEP conference. Rather, language that is readily understood by parents should be used, particularly for developing annual goal statements, short-term instructional objectives, and evaluation criteria.

7. It is not necessary to wait for the beginning of the school year to develop IEPs for all handicapped children. The statute and regulations require at least an annual review and updating of the IEP. Thus IEP development may be more intensive in the fall, but can be accomplished in the spring or at any time so long as twelve months have not elapsed since the previous IEP was developed.

A COMPREHENSIVE APPROACH

Larsen and Poplin (1980) offer a fairly comprehensive approach to IEP development. They suggest that broad areas such as self-help and basic living skills; academic skills; vocational and career skills; and sociobehavioral skills be considered as IEP goals and objectives are developed. Emphasis from one area to another may shift depending upon severity of handicap or age of child. The work of Larsen and Poplin may prove useful to personnel involved in writing IEPs. If IEP manuals have not been developed locally, regionally, or statewide, personnel involved in writing IEPs may wish to refer to this source and other similar works on the market.

DEFINITION OF "APPROPRIATE"

The Education for All Handicapped Children Act of 1975 guarantees the provision of a free appropriate public education for all handicapped children aged 3 through 21. What does "appropriate" education mean? Ballard (1978) indicates:

> "Appropriate" is not defined as such, but rather receives its definition for each child through the mechanism of the individualized written education program (IEP) as required by PL 94–142. Therefore, what is agreed to by all parties becomes in fact the "appropriate" educational program for each particular child. (p. 4)

The IEP process is critical to the implementation of PL 94–142. It should not be taken lightly or circumvented in any way. The IEP constitutes a primary issue in procedural due-process hearings and any subsequent litigation.

The concept of individualizing instruction is not unique. The individualized education program for handicapped children is a formalized step in implementing an old concept.

IEPs FOR ALL CHILDREN?

The two major teacher organizations in the United States (American Federation of Teachers and National Education Association) have both called for federal financial aid to elementary and secondary education. It is conceivable that such aid will be forthcoming in the 1980s, and when it does come, it will not be surprising if an IEP or similar mechanism will be required for every child.

SAMPLE IEP FORMS

As noted in this chapter, PL 94–142 does not require a specific form for the IEP. The statute does specify what information must be included. Two sample formats that meet the federal requirements are included in the Appendix. They are both very simple, and are included to illustrate the simplicity which may be used *if* no further SEA or LEA requirements have been imposed. Both formats allow for multiyear usage by allowing for annual review/revision information to be recorded on the initial IEP.

The reader is cautioned not to adopt either format without first checking with the SEA special education unit and LEA authorities to determine if additional requirements exist (see Appendix for current SEA addresses and telephone numbers).

FURTHER FEDERAL CLARIFICATION ON IEPs

Following Congressional oversight hearings and regional meetings which generated concerns about the IEP, the Office of Special Education (Department of Education) issued a policy paper on IEPs on May 23, 1980. The policy paper was disseminated to state directors of special education, state Part B coordinators, and state PL 89–313 coordinators. LEA personnel may or may not have received this information from their SEA.

Included in the policy paper are clarifications on many issues mentioned in this chapter. The document contains the most current federal interpretation available of the entire IEP process. For this reason, the entire paper has been reproduced in the Appendix. The interested reader should study the paper for additional information and clarification of the IEP.

The introduction to the paper concludes with a key paragraph which reads:

> In effect, the paper is an extension of the final regulations under PL 94–142. Thus the interpretations included in the paper will be followed by the Office of Special Education in enforcing compliance with the law.

This paragraph alone should demonstrate a need for reading the policy paper included in the Appendix.

REFERENCES

Ballard, J. *Public Law 94–142 and Section 504—Understanding What They Are and Are Not* (rev. ed.). Reston, VA.: The Council for Exceptional Children, 1978.

Education of the Handicapped. "IEPs Biggest Concern at PL 94–142 Meetings." Washington, D.C.: Capitol Publications, 1979, p. 2.

Federal Register, December 30, 1976, Part IV, Education of Handicapped Children and Incentive Grants Program. Assistance to States, pp. 56966-56998.

Federal Register, August 23, 1977, Part II, Education of Handicapped Children. Implementation of Part B of the Education of the Handicapped Act, pp. 42474-42518.

Larsen, S. C., and Poplin, M. S. *Methods for Educating the Handicapped: An Individualized Education Program Approach.* Boston: Allyn & Bacon, 1980.

Martin, E. W. "Informal Letter to Chief State School Officers." Division of Assistance to States *Bulletin, 5* (November 17, 1977).

National Association of State Directors of Special Education, Inc., *Liaison Bulletin,* August 3, 1979, pp. 1 and 2.

Office of Special Education, "Individualized Education Programs (IEPs)—OSE Policy Paper." Department of Education, May 23, 1980.

CHAPTER 7 QUESTIONS

Q: The parents of a child suspected of having a handicap gave written consent for the school to evaluate him. If the child is found eligible for special education and related services, can the school initiate placement without additional parental consent?

A: No. Consent must be obtained prior to evaluation and a second consent must be obtained prior to placement. If consent for placement is denied the school may initiate the due-process hearing procedure to obtain a decision on placement.

Q: The school has acted properly in all respects. The parents have none-the-less initiated a due-process hearing. Can the school request that the hearing be open to the public to prove they have acted properly?

A: No. While most of the rights in the hearing are the same for either party, the parents have the exclusive right to request an open hearing.

Q: A family recently moved to our district from a rural area out of the state. Their child is enrolled in a private school for handicapped children. They have asked that we pay the tuition for their child. Are we obligated to do so?

A: If the parents have not formally requested a special education program for their child from your district, you are probably not obligated. Your district should be allowed to evaluate the child to determine if he can receive a free appropriate program in your district. If he cannot, then you are obligated to see that the program is provided at no cost to the parents.

Due-Process
Procedures

7

The procedural safeguards afforded to handicapped children and their parents under The Education for All Handicapped Children Act of 1975 have been criticized by local and state education agency personnel. The critics claim the due-process procedures are time-consuming, require additional paperwork, and result in added costs—particularly when a due-process hearing is involved. The statute and regulations are very specific and include timelines to be met for hearings. While the procedures are of great significance, in reality they merely call for fair play and parental involvement in decisions regarding a handicapped child. Active and open communication with parents can resolve many disputes and reduce the number of potential due-process hearings.

The due-process hearing procedure contained in PL 94–142 was not intended to result in adversarial proceedings. But in reality, when the formal hearing procedure stage is reached, it is doubtful that adversarial relationships have not already developed between the parents and the schools.

A PROTECTION FOR LOCAL EDUCATION AGENCIES (LEAs)

While it is true that the rights of parents and their handicapped children have resulted in the concern for procedural safeguards, this section of the statute and regulations actually affords protection to the LEA. Prior to passage of the Act in 1975, many states and LEAs had not developed clear procedures for dealing with complaints or concerns of parents. LEAs were essentially in a position of playing a game where the rules were unknown. The Act made it clear that an LEA could initiate a due-process hearing when a parent refused to give consent for evaluation or initiation of service. Prior to this time, some state legislation had provided the appeal route only for parents and not for schools.

The US Office of Education (August 1979) reported that since September 1977, forty-one states had changed their laws and regulations to meet the requirements of PL 94–142 in due-process areas. Four additional states were in the process of reviewing their laws, while five states had comparable provisions in law and/or regulations and did not require changes (USOE, August 1979, p. 30).

INFORMED CONSENT

The procedural safeguards section, and more specifically the discussion on due-process hearings, border on quasilegal proceedings. School personnel must be cautious not to use practices that may intimidate parents when informing them of their rights. For explaining procedures and obtaining consent, a personalized approach is far superior to formal written notice. While written notice must be provided, it is more appropriate to present it during a conference with the parents rather than mail this information to them. Either approach should certainly allow adequate opportunity for the parent to ask questions concerning all processes and procedures.

Also, there is a difference between obtaining consent—a signature from parents giving approval to evaluate their child—and what is known as informed consent, as defined in the regulations of PL 94–142. According to Section 121a.500 of the regulations implementing PL 94–142, consent is defined as follows:

(a) The parent has been fully informed of all information relevant to the activity for which consent is sought, in his or her native language, or other mode of communication;
(b) The parent understands and agrees in writing to the carrying out of the activity for which his or her consent is sought, and the consent describes that activity and lists the records (if any) which will be released and to whom; and
(c) The parent understands that the granting of consent is voluntary on the part of the parent and may be revoked at any time. (*Federal Register*, August 23, 1977, p. 42494)

Provision of notice in the native language of the home has presented problems for some LEAs. The US Office of Education (USOE, August 1979) reported that Delaware used migrant workers to act as interpreters for Hispanic individuals. Members of the American Association of University Women in Delaware offered assistance in translating notices into fifty languages (p. 57). State universities may, and often do, assist in this area.

To comply with regulations and assure full understanding on the part of parents, a conference with the parents to present and review written procedures is the most logical approach. Parental involvement should continue throughout the process of identification and provision of special education and related services. As was pointed out in Chapter 6, which focused on IEPs, school personnel should be aware that parents must never be made to feel outnumbered or overwhelmed in any meeting or conference.

AN INFORMATION GUIDE FOR PARENTS

A locally developed guide for parents can be a good communication device. As an alternative to locally developed materials, some state education agencies (SEAs) have developed information guides for parents and furnish them to the LEA either free or at low cost. Organizations such as the National School Public Relations Association (NSPRA) have also produced guides for parents. The local or state publications have the advantage of incorporating the unique local or state features, while publications such as those of the NSPRA must out of necessity focus on federal requirements only. NSPRA provides a low-cost imprinting service to list the school name or other particular information on their guides. Various local businesses may assist in providing funds to produce or purchase information guides as a public service.

THE BEST DEFENSE IS FULL DISCLOSURE

School districts which make the extra effort to inform parents of their rights may reduce the potential number of appeals. Parents of a handicapped child may feel that such a district at least has a real commitment to educating their child, and thus may be willing to negotiate before calling for a due-process hearing.

In an article entitled "Exceptional Law or Law with Exceptions," Pechter (1979) cites school practices which attempt to circumvent the procedural safeguards. He states:

> Under these pressures to serve more children more effectively, administrators' approach to parents has been directed at paper compliance. Signatures on necessary documents to show proof of notice, informed consent, and compliance with time deadlines take precedence over guaranteeing the parents' genuine understanding and approval. (p. 72)

Pechter, as an advocate, has frequently observed such actions. In concluding his article, Pechter indicates:

The school's unwillingness sincerely to promote active parent involvement reflects skepticism that parents can and will provide useful assistance. It is not surprising, given these institutional obstacles and a history of powerlessness in the face of them, that the fears, anger, and cynicism of parents as they enter into this process are rarely diminished once they have been "involved" in it. (p. 73)

ADVOCACY IS HERE TO STAY

Many organizations and agencies are providing advocacy assistance to parents of handicapped children, and attempts by schools to compromise the goal of free appropriate public education to meet the unique needs of each handicapped child do not go unnoticed. Advocates observing such behaviors can assist parents in pursuing due-process hearing procedures that can be very time-consuming and frustrating, not only to parents but also to schools. (See Appendix for a partial listing of advocacy groups.) Other costs to the system beyond staff time involved in a hearing include hiring hearing officers, making transcripts, and providing multiple copies of materials. Ultimately, the cost incurred by the hearing process could have been used to provide direct service and instruction not only to handicapped children but to all children in the schools.

NEGOTIATION—A GOOD PRACTICE

Schools have the responsibility of proposing an appropriate program for the handicapped child. When a parent objects to the child's proposed program, it seems logical to find out what exactly the parents object to and what they would consider appropriate. The parents can often provide valuable information about their child, and perhaps only minor modifications of the program will be necessary. Negotiations should take place in good faith.

By avoiding the hearing process whenever possible, a saving of human and fiscal resources for all parties concerned will result. Although the time consumed in assuring parents' rights can be extensive, a sincere willingness to propose and negotiate an appropriate program for each specific child will probably still incur less time and energy than a hearing. And more importantly, the schools will gain the confidence of the parents, which should result in a more effective program for the child. Cooperation, communication, and fair play are keys to avoiding formal due-process hearings.

On the other hand, if the school has acted properly and can substantiate the fact that the program offered is appropriate, the school should not just give in to parents' demands. In such cases, the hearing may provide a valid forum for the school.

PREPARATION FOR THE HEARING

Preparation for a hearing is more important than the hearing itself. This is true for everyone involved.

At least five days prior to the hearing, all preparation should be completed. This will allow both parties to share the documents that will be presented as evidence, as well as the names of witnesses who will present testimony. If both parties are adequately prepared, all necessary and relevant information can be presented in an organized and sequential fashion. Such a procedure will allow the hearing officer to make a well-informed decision based on the evidence presented.

Exhibits for the Hearing

The initial step in preparing for the hearing should be a review of the child's school file. All relevant records should be utilized as evidence at the hearing. Placement of such records in chronological order is advantageous and greatly assists the hearing officer in obtaining an educational history of the child. A face sheet should be numbered and labeled for each document, such as School Exhibit 1, etc. This practice allows easy access to specific documents during the hearing. Generally, relevant documents would include: (a) a school history (annual progress reports, etc.); (b) diagnostic and evaluation reports that identify the child's handicapping condition and need for special education and related services; and (c) a full description of the proposed program and services (the individualized education program should suffice if it is properly completed). It may also be necessary to have documented evidence of proper notice, parent involvement (or lack of it), and signed consent forms if these issues will be considered in the hearing.

Witnesses

Once all relevant documents are selected as evidence, it is necessary to determine who will serve as witnesses at the hearing. It is usually necessary for witnesses to review the contents of documents, describe procedures, or testify about other relevant facts. Witnesses selected to testify should have a thorough knowledge of the child. For ease in conducting the hearing, witnesses can refer to specific documents by their exhibit number.

Disclosure of Evidence—No Surprises

Either party to the hearing may prohibit introduction of evidence which was not disclosed at least five days prior to the hearing.

HEARING OFFICER IS IN CONTROL

Once the hearing begins, the hearing officer has full control of the proceedings. The hearing officer can determine whether or not certain evidence is relevant. An opportunity must be provided for opposing parties to cross-examine any of the witnesses regarding their testimony. While this is an administrative hearing as opposed to a judicial hearing, many of the same procedures (such as cross-examination of witnesses) do apply. The major difference is that the administrative hearing may be much more informal.

RIGHTS OF PARTIES SIMILAR

Both parties to the hearing have the same rights with only minor exceptions. If deemed necessary, the school can request that the child be a witness at a hearing, but it cannot compel the child to attend without the parent's consent. Only the parents have the right to determine whether or not the child will attend. In general, the open discussion of the child's handicap, disability, and problems could have a very negative effect on the child. Parents also have the exclusive right to determine whether the hearing will be open to the public.

LEGAL ASSISTANCE

Legal counsel is not required at due-process hearings, but it is permitted. An attorney representing the school or other public agency is usually in attendance, either to present the school or agency position or to advise whomever else is presenting the school position. Parents are often hesitant to file a request for a due-process hearing without legal representation. The school or agency is required to provide parents with information regarding free or low cost legal representation.

AN UNFAIR ADVANTAGE FOR THE SCHOOLS?

Parents and advocacy groups have complained that the school or agency has an unfair advantage in the hearing process. The area of legal counsel is one such area upon which complaints are based. Simply stated, the parents feel their tax dollars are actually supporting competent counsel for the other party (the schools) while they must provide their own counsel. This allegation is basically true and the schools must recognize this advantage. The school or agency also has full-time staff to prepare for a hearing while the parent does not. And finally, the institutional party has more ready access to experts to support testimony. Thus an overall advantage does appear to rest with the school or agency in local due-process hearings.

HEARING OFFICERS

The local due-process hearing itself is subject to the competence of the hearing officer selected. The differences in state procedures for developing hearing processes and selecting a pool of potential hearing officers are significant. Some states specifically indentify who or what class of individuals may be used as hearing officers. Other states are not so specific and merely state that all potential hearing officers must complete a prescribed training component. A wide variety of individuals serve as hearing officers; examples include: professors of school law or special education; lawyers; administrators of special education in other LEAs; ministers; public service commission hearing examiners; retired school administrators; and others.

Training of Hearing Officers Is Critical

Given the diverse backgrounds of persons employed as hearing officers, it appears that a prescribed training program for hearing officers is necessary. While professors may know a great deal about school law or special education, they may know little about conducting a due-process hearing. The reverse can be true for an attorney. Each class of individuals serving as hearing officers may lack certain knowledge or skills. Therefore, a training program conducted by the state to assure a firm base of knowledge or skills for all potential hearing officers makes the process more effective. Refresher courses may also be advisable on a periodic basis.

APPEAL OF HEARING OFFICER'S DECISION

An administrative appeal of the hearing officer's decision in a local hearing is available to either party. Such an appeal should be made to the state education agency. Until an appeal is filed, the local hearing officer's decision is final and binding.

If an appeal is made, the state education agency is charged with conducting an impartial review of the hearing. While primarily concerned with the procedural conduct of a hearing, the state can seek additional evidence if necessary: An additional hearing can be convened. Following the review, a decision by the state is rendered, and considered final, unless either party wishes to pursue civil action through the court system. If civil action is sought by either party the process at that point moves from an administrative to a judicial procedure.

TIMELINES FOR HEARING MUST BE MET

The timeline established for the due-process hearing procedure is forty-five days (from the receipt of the request for a hearing until a decision is made and mailed to each party). The hearing officer may specify an extended time period upon request by either party. Mediation by the hearing officer can be utilized to resolve any issues raised for the hearing at any time in the process. When either party requests state-level involvement, a decision must be made within thirty days following the receipt of the request. The state official conducting the review may also extend the thirty-day time period at the request of either party. State regulations may be more specific on these timelines and may inject intermediate steps, such as appointment of a hearing officer or setting the date of hearing.

Throughout the hearing process, the handicapped child must remain in the educational placement held prior to the initiation of the process. Changes in placement are allowed only under mutual consent of both parties. If the child is not currently in school, the child must be placed in the public schools with the consent of the parents.

TUITION PAYMENT TO NONPUBLIC PROGRAMS—A MAJOR ISSUE

To date, the most frequent issue leading to hearings has been the payment of tuition to nonpublic programs. In many instances such requests have been made for handicapped children who had never been enrolled in public educational programs first. While parents of handicapped children have the right to enroll their child in any nonpublic school they choose, the LEA does not have to pay for the child's education unless all administrative procedures have been followed. The correct procedure for placement in a nonpublic facility involves the full diagnostic and evaluation activities required for placement in public programs, but parents must request service for their handicapped child through the public school first. Then, if the LEA cannot or is unable to provide an appropriate program locally or through other public agencies, they are obliged to pay for the nonpublic program.

THE PROCESS CAN WORK BOTH WAYS!

The schools should make every attempt to provide an appropriate program for each handicapped child, which includes all necessary special education and related services, not only those readily available. Open communication with parents from the point of initial referral until the initiation of services for the child appears to be the best way to avoid complaints leading to the administrative and judicial procedures open to the parent. However, when it is apparent that a handicapped child is in need of special education and related services and the parents of the child refuse the necessary consent, the LEA should not hesitate to initiate due-process hearing procedures. The process was designed to work both ways!

REFERENCES

Federal Register, August 23, 1977, Part II, Education of Handicapped Children. "Implementation of Part B of the Education of the Handicapped Act," pp. 42474-42518.
Pechter, S. E. "Exceptional Law or Law with Exceptions." *Amicus, 4* (March/April 1979): 68–73.
U.S. Office of Education. *Progress toward a Free Appropriate Public Education.* (Semiannual update on the implementation of PL 94–142). Washington, D.C. (August 1979), 61 pp.

CHAPTER 8 QUESTIONS

Q: Where can I obtain speakers for in-service education in my rural district?

A: Never overlook your own staff! Other sources are state education agency (SEA) and state college and university personnel. Advocacy groups at the state or local level are also potential resources, particularly on due-process procedures. National information sources (see partial list in Appendix) can often supply films, slide–tape programs, cassettes, and even speakers for in-service sessions.

Q: Our budget is tight. How much will in-service cost?

A: In-service may not cost anything if SEA and other public representatives are utilized. Federal and state funds may also be available to assist. Contact your SEA.

Q: Who should receive in-service?

A: *All* school personnel and the school board are potential and logical targets for in-service.

Q: A parent of a handicapped child asked if she could attend an in-service meeting. Can parents attend?

A: They certainly can attend. As a matter of fact, a positive approach would be to invite parents to in-service meetings. Specially designed in-service for parents may be an investment that will pay dividends as programs and services are implemented.

Personnel Development

"Why do I have a blind child in my third-grade class? That is what special education is for in our schools."

"The opening of school is just a week away and we can't find a teacher of the severely handicapped for the new class we opened."

"The special class teachers we shifted to resource teaching positions last fall seem to have more problems than the new resource teacher we hired."

THE NEED FOR QUALIFIED PERSONNEL

Comments and questions such as those expressed above have been heard many times since the passage of the Education for All Handicapped Children Act. They relate to the overall qualifications required of regular and special educators. The preparation of personnel in special education, both in terms of quality and quantity, has been a concern of state education agencies (SEAs), institutions of higher education, professional organizations, and the US Office of Education for many years. The passage of PL 94–142 gave renewed emphasis to personnel development not only for special educators but also for regular educators.

COMPREHENSIVE SYSTEM OF PERSONNEL DEVELOPMENT (CSPD)

Under the provisions of PL 94–142, each state annually describes its programs and procedures for developing and implementing a comprehensive system of personnel development (CSPD). The process of developing the CSPD requires an assessment of personnel needs at both preservice and in-service levels to assure that all personnel working with handicapped children are appropriately trained.

IN-SERVICE EDUCATION

As was noted in Chapter 5, successfully educating handicapped children in the least restrictive environment requires an on-going in-service education program for a total district staff. Such in-service training should be provided to teachers of handicapped and nonhandicapped students, as well as to administrators, counselors, diagnostic personnel, school nurses, therapists, aides, central office staff, and support service staff (including bus drivers, food service, and custodial personnel).

PRESERVICE EDUCATION

Many states have adopted a certification requirement stipulating that all new teachers entering the schools must complete one or more courses, experiences, or practica in special education. Institutions of higher education have met this requirement by giving survey courses on exceptionalities or possibly by giving a course or set of experiences on providing for the handicapped child in the regular classroom. As recent graduates of schools and colleges of education accept positions in local education agencies (LEAs), employers will notice that such experiences have been completed. Even if the LEA relied only on recent graduates to fill vacant positions, it would take many years to develop a teaching staff with complete knowledge of educating handicapped children.

FUNDING FOR IN-SERVICE

A major shift in allocation of federal funds under Part D of the Education of the Handicapped Act has occurred since the passage of PL 94–142. While the majority of funds allocated under Part D have gone toward preservice training of special educators, the Division of Personnel Preparation (DPP), Bureau of Education for the Handicapped (BEH), US Office of Education (USOE), projected the expenditure of almost 27 million dollars for in-service activities for the 1980–1981 school year. This amount is nearly half of the total appropriation of slightly over 55 million dollars. Over 19 million dollars were targeted for preservice and in-service special education training for regular education teachers (USOE, July 1979, p. 19).

Further evidence of the shift of efforts toward in-service training programs may be noted in the USOE's semiannual update on the implementation of PL 94–142, which reported:

In-service training programs for regular educators have increased in number and in the precision of training delivered. For example, projects funded by the BEH Division of Personnel Preparation (DPP) will provide in-service training to approximately 20,000 more regular education teachers next year than this (approximately 47,000 will be provided training next year compared to 26,700 this year). (USOE, August 1979, p. 39)

WHO MAY APPLY FOR PART D FUNDS?

Grants under Part D of the Education of the Handicapped Act are made to state and local education agencies, institutions of higher education, private and other nonprofit agencies. Funds granted to state education agencies are utilized to a great extent in providing in-service education programs for local education agency personnel.

STATE EDUCATION AGENCY IN-SERVICE FUNDS

In addition to federal funds being made available, some states have allocated additional funds to local education agencies to support in-service education programs for staff members. LEA personnel should contact the state education agency regarding the availability of such funds. State education agencies have also utilized federal and state funds to sponsor statewide or regional in-service education programs for LEA personnel. To facilitate inquiries, a list of SEA special education units is reproduced in the Appendix. Call or write the SEA in your state.

CURRENT ISSUES IN PERSONNEL PREPARATION

In the following statement the Office of Education (August 1979) summarized several remaining issues in comprehensive personnel development:

States have demonstrated significant advances in personnel training at both the preservice and in-service levels, but problems remain in providing a sufficient number of appropriately and adequately trained personnel to meet the full intent of the law.

- Annual program plans from the states indicate that a lack of in-service training, particularly for teachers of children with low-incidence handicapping conditions, continues to limit the ability of state and local agencies to offer a full continuum of alternatives to all handicapped children, especially in rural areas.
- Data from the Wisconsin Annual Program Plan (APP) and a study conducted by the Idaho state education agency indicate an attrition rate among special education personnel in rural areas well in excess of an expected 6% rate. It

has yet to be determined whether changes in administrative assignments and procedures could prevent this rapid turnover or whether new recruitment initiatives will be needed to attract new teachers for the handicapped.
• Certification for special education personnel continues to be a pressing need. Data from the National Center for Education Statistics' Survey of Recent College Graduates in 1975 show that approximately one-third of the teachers employed yearly by local school districts to teach the handicapped have not been trained as special educators.

BEH, in attempting to meet the needs of state and local agencies for qualified personnel, has increased the number of teachers receiving in-service training by approximately 75%. However, the need for in-service training for special education personnel as well as for regular education teachers continues to be critical. (USOE, August 1979, pp. 40–41)

LOCAL EDUCATION AGENCY EFFORTS REQUIRED

In compliance with one of several mandates required by PL 94–142 for participation in funding, local education agencies must describe their personnel development plan in applications to the state education agency. Several key areas must be considered by the LEA when planning in-service training on the education of handicapped children. Needless to say a once-a-year in-service session for teachers is hardly a comprehensive plan for personnel development. It may be seen as a starting point for in-service, if it is followed up with several meetings at the building, grade, or department level.

PLANNING AND DELIVERING IN-SERVICE

LEA personnel responsible for planning the necessary in-service must consider the following issues: timing; presenters; frequency of sessions; method of delivery; clientele; incentives to staff; and topics to be covered.

Timing—A Contract Issue

Timing of in-service sessions may be a critical factor for success or failure. The teacher who has taught all day is not always receptive to an in-service session scheduled for an hour or two at the end of the school day or in the evening. From the teacher's viewpoint, released time from other duties is generally preferred, and may be arranged through early dismissal of school or scheduled teacher work days. Negotiated teacher contracts may specify when in-service sessions are to be conducted thus making the decision for the administrator. Should it be deemed that contract language is inhibiting the scheduling or success of in-service efforts, the administration should attempt to modify the language in future negotiations. Whenever possible, in-service should not be scheduled on the day preceding a holiday. This writer recalls presenting an in-service session the morning before Thanksgiving. The effectiveness of the session was greatly diminished due to the fact that the LEA staff were anticipating their vacation.

Who Are the Presenters?

In-service sessions may be conducted by existing LEA staff, SEA staff, university faculty members, professional organization staff, or private consultants. The specific topic to be covered may determine who conducts the training. Obviously, the availability of funds to support the in-service program may also be a deciding factor. Teachers generally prefer sessions to be conducted at the building level. Utilizing a combination of LEA staff familiar with the district, as well as personnel external to the LEA to offer a fresh approach, may be advantageous. Teachers frequently seek answers to specific questions (such as how to provide for a particular child in their class) as opposed to the general philosophy and overview type of session. The latter, however, is often useful in a year-long planned sequence which progresses from the general to the specific. When the in-service sessions deal with particular classroom methods and techniques, other teachers, whether internal or external to the LEA, may have more credibility with the teaching staff.

In-Service Frequency

Frequency of in-service sessions may be another area that is spelled out in existing negotiated contracts. If possible, it may be more relevant to have five sessions given over five weeks than to spread five sessions over five months or the entire school year. Conducting the training sessions every week also provides for more continuity than having sessions spread over an extended period of time.

Approach

The method of delivery of in-service sessions can also make or break the activity. A varied approach, with the active involvement of the participants is superior to the lecture approach. Utilization of audiovisual aids may also make a session more interesting.

Clientele

Knowing the clientele designated to receive the training is extremely critical in planning successful in-service education. If the ultimate targets of the in-service courses are teachers, it is best to concentrate it first on building-level administrators, who in turn will be supportive of the activity with teachers. If, for example, in-service education on serving handicapped children in the least restrictive environment is to be presented for classroom teachers, it is essential for the building-level administrator to be knowledgeable about the philosophy and information regarding implementation of that concept, because he or she is the person most likely to receive teacher questions and concerns. The initial responses of the building administrator to teacher questions may greatly influence the success not only of the in-service course, but also its ultimate implementation in the school.

Support Staff Depending on the topics to be covered in in-service education, there may be a need to incorporate training for support service staff. For instance, uninformed food service personnel in the school cafeteria might make negative comments toward handicapped children being served in the least restrictive environment. Attempts should be made to overcome this possibility. Obviously, in-service programs for service staff should differ from those provided for professional staff in terms of topics covered and type of presentation.

In general, all school employees should have some basic knowledge of programs provided in the schools, whether such programs are designed for handicapped or nonhandicapped children. All school employees are potential recipients of questions from patrons of the school and should at least be able to refer them to the proper individuals or offices for the information sought.

The School Board A group that should not be overlooked is the school board. As the policy-makers for the schools they must certainly be knowledgeable about all school programs.

Incentives

Another consideration in planning in-service education should be possible incentives for the staff. Will participants receive professional growth or continuing education credit as a result of such training? Many schools require such credit for advancement on salary schedules or recommendation for recertification. If a school district contracts with an institution of higher education for delivery of in-service programs, it is possible to arrange for academic credit or formal continuing education units to be awarded to participants. In some school districts staff incentives may not be required to gain the necessary participation, while in other districts staff incentives may be a very important motivator.

Topics

In-service topics to be covered will vary greatly from district to district, depending on the existing level of programing and prior in-service activities.

Instruction for professional staff may be necessary on topics such as individualized education programs, nondiscriminatory testing, least restrictive environment, procedural safeguards, and surrogate parents. Interagency cooperation might be an appropriate topic for administrative and business office staff. It may be necessary to assess the district's needs so as to determine the current and projected in-service topics for the staff. The topics mentioned here as possible areas of focus for in-service education are far from an exhaustive list.

Evaluation Leads to Better In-Service

Evaluation of in-service education is a necessity. Not only will evaluation efforts provide valuable information about the usefulness of the activity completed, it may also assist greatly in planning for future in-service. Evaluation of the activity should be done both by the individual or individuals presenting the in-service and by the persons receiving the training. The method of evaluation may take the form of a listing of objectives with a scale (numerical or descriptive) indicating to what extent the objective was met. Other features of the evaluation could relate to the method of presentation, location, or timing. Future topics for in-service can often be proposed by participants or presenters.

KNOWLEDGE PRECEDES ACCEPTANCE AND FULL IMPLEMENTATION

Personnel development is a critical area if schools are to provide quality education for all children. Institutions of higher education have developed many new or modified programs to prepare preservice personnel for emerging roles in the schools. The need for in-service education of existing staff in the schools, however, presents the greater challenge to provide free appropriate public education for all handicapped children. Without the necessary in-service education, personnel in the schools will experience great difficulty in meeting the challenge of their changing roles.

REFERENCES

US Office of Education, "Application for Grants under Handicapped Personnel Preparation Program," July 1979.
US Office of Education, "Progress toward a Free Appropriate Public Education; Semiannual Update on the Implementation of Public Law 94–142," August 1979.

CHAPTER 9 QUESTIONS

Q: Our district is reviewing the administrative organization chart and changing several position titles. What title should be assigned to the person in charge of special education?

A: This question cannot be answered without knowing such things as size of district, job descriptions and position titles of other middle-management staff, and what positions are included in the superintendent's cabinet. Cabinet-level status is wise because the individual's role in special education cuts across all areas of the district operation. The individual should be titled and empowered according to the size and organization of the district. (At times, the person in charge of special education will be given titles that cannot be printed in any book!)

Q: Our district has 3,200 students enrolled. We are employing for the first time a person to be in charge of special education on a full-time basis. Should we employ an administrator or a supervisor?

A: Congratulations on recognizing the difference between administrative and instructional improvement roles. Given the complexities of special education law and regulation as programs are implemented, the best bet would probably be an administrator. If it is possible, through joint cooperation with other small districts in your area, more than one person might be employed—one to provide administrative and one to provide instructional improvement functions—not only for your district but also for the neighboring ones.

Q: Is a good special education teacher the best choice for a leadership position in special education?

A: Answering a question with a question is not always a good approach, but does a good third-grade teacher make a good elementary principal? While the teaching experience may be excellent, additional training and personality factors are critical for such leadership personnel. This answer would be true for all types of educational leadership personnel.

Organizing
To Get
the Job Done

The local education agency (LEA) is faced with a major challenge in implementing mandated special education and related service programs. The statutory and regulatory detail at the federal and state level may appear ominous to LEA administrators and boards of education. How does an LEA, whether large or small, urban or rural, approach the task of assuring the provision of a free appropriate education to all children?

This chapter expresses the need for qualified administrative and supervisory staff in special education. It also includes an overall leadership plan, the development of which should include factors such as: (a) number of children to be served; (b) facilities; (c) transportation; (d) legal and fiscal issues; and (e) other related concerns. The need for cooperative programs in rural areas or decentralization in urban districts also influences the leadership plan. Preferred qualifications of special education leadership staff are outlined.

PERSONNEL DEVELOPMENT FOR LEADERSHIP STAFF

The previous chapter examined issues in personnel development in both special education and regular education, primarily from the standpoint of direct teaching staff. Certainly, personnel development for the direct instructional staff is critical to getting the job done, but what about leadership staff? Principals have become key personnel in special education programing, mainly by serving as representatives of their schools in the IEP team conference. They may or may not feel comfortable in this role, and may or may not have received the proper training to perform adequately in it. Can a principal be expected to be totally knowledgeable about state and federal requirements in special education? It is doubtful that a principal would have the detailed knowledge of procedures beyond those necessary for building-level administration. Neither can superintendents and other central office staff be expected to become totally familiar with all the necessary requirements and regulations of special education.

A NEED FOR LEADERSHIP STAFF IN SPECIAL EDUCATION

Now, more than ever, a need exists for highly trained individuals to administer special education and related service programs at the LEA level. Personnel holding such leadership roles in special education may carry titles such as assistant superintendent, administrator, director, coordinator, or supervisor. Areas of responsibility commensurate with the title may encompass special education, special education and related services, specialized instructional services, supportive instructional services, special services, exceptional children's programs, or exceptional child education. Such a list is not exhaustive, and may or may not fully describe the range of responsibilities for the position.

Changing Roles

Typically, the decision regarding the title for a given position within the administrative structure is made in accordance with the other position titles within the school district. In cases where positions for leadership personnel in special education were created several years ago, the title may no longer be appropriate for the functional position today. The current complexity of leadership positions in special education may have forced an individual to move from a supervisory role to an administrative one.

For example, an individual employed several years ago as a supervisor of special education may have served primarily as a curriculum supervisor for existing programs for the mentally retarded. Such a staff member may have been highly competent in the original role that focused on instructional improvement, but is unable to cope effectively with the administrative role which evolved. Where administrators originally spent most of their time working with teachers in the classroom, they now spend virtually no time with teachers. Tasks such as completion of forms, monitoring timelines, preparing budgets, and interpreting the program to school personnel and the public now require the majority of their time. Individuals in such situations often feel uncomfortable in the administrative posture and actually prefer the previous instructional improvement activities.

Administrative and Supervisory Needs

Both administrative and instructional improvement roles are needed to provide high quality programs for handicapped children. Small school districts may allow a single individual to function in both capacities. However, the qualitative dimension of programs can sometimes be enhanced if such small districts cooperate with other, neighboring districts and jointly employ both administrative as well as supervisory or instructional improvement personnel. Some states have established intermediate districts or regional service areas which formally define units for this type of cooperation. Other states without such formal units make provision for interdistrict cooperation through joint agreement, cooperative, or consortium arrangements. Larger school districts can and should support the employment of administrative and supervisory personnel in order to assure efficient and effective programing.

DEVELOPING A SPECIAL EDUCATION LEADERSHIP PLAN

In developing the leadership plan for special education and related services in a local school district, several factors should be kept in mind: age range of children served; diagnostic and programing functions; numbers of the various categories of handicapped children to be served; facilities required; transportation needs; legal and fiscal issues; negotiated agreements; and titling of positions.

Age Ranges Served

The kindergarten through twelfth-grade curriculum of school districts is often headed by a single administrator. Operationally within school districts, however, sharp demarcations are often found between elementary and secondary levels. Central office curriculum staff are frequently two separate positions for elementary and secondary instruction. In some cases where a K–12 curriculum director is employed, an assistant is also hired to provide service at the elementary or secondary level, depending on the expertise of the director. Special education and related service programs, possibly more than any other programs in the schools, actually span the K–12 age range. In fact, depending on various state statutes, special education programs span preschool through ages 21 and over.

The placement of the special education and related services unit within the district's organizational structure should reflect this broad range of responsibility. It should not be subservient to the elementary or secondary supervisor. Since special education leadership personnel must function at all levels within the LEA, relationships need to be clearly established and followed with building-level administrative personnel, so as to avoid conflict in overlapping areas. Lack of such clearly designated relationships can result in many petty disputes which only impede efficient and effective program development and operation. Unclear relationships may exist relative to evaluation of special education personnel, placement of children in the least restrictive environment, discipline of handicapped children, provision of supplies and materials for programs, budgeting, curriculum, and other areas of building operation.

Diagnostic and Programing Functions

It is critical that the referral, diagnostic, and programing processes involved in providing appropriate education to handicapped children be followed in order to comply with federal and state statutes. Internal and external problems within the process can, and have, result in backlogs and waiting lists, which in turn become the subject of allegations of noncompliance and litigation. For example, in 1979 a federal district court judge ruled that within a sixty-day period the New York City Schools must evaluate and place 8000 handicapped children waiting for services. In reacting to the decision, special education officials indicated " . . . the order would apply to some 2000 children waiting for diagnosis and another 6000 handicapped students awaiting placement in special education programs" (Education of the Handicapped, 1980, p.5).

Backlogs and waiting lists in most school districts do not rival the magnitude of the problem in the largest city in the United States. However, many school districts throughout the nation have problems that proportionately are not that much different, when the ratio of district size is compared to the size of the waiting list.

The administrative separation of diagnostic and programing functions allows greater opportunity for backlogs and waiting lists to develop in a school district. States have established timelines for various phases of the referral, diagnostic, and placement processes. In cases where school districts exceed the established timelines, they become vulnerable to allegations of noncompliance through administrative or judicial proceedings.

It is strongly recommended that the administrative plan for a school district centralize these functions under the jurisdiction of the special education chief. Thus the possibility of backlogs and waiting lists developing is reduced. Also, if a problem does arise, the blame cannot be shifted to another person, which is often what happens when functions are administratively separated.

Number To Be Served

The potential number of handicapped children in a school district ranges up to 12 percent of the enrollment. The unique characteristics of a given local district can result in a number slightly above or below the estimated prevalence figures. Thus a reasonably substantial segment of the school population may require special education and related services. Decisions as to the need for regional or cooperative programing can be considered, based on the efficiency and effectiveness of small districts attempting to provide comprehensive programs. However, handicapped students must be served without regard to size of school district. Regionalization or cooperative programs may be the only available alternative for small districts to obtain necessary leadership personnel.

The number of children served in special education programs can help determine the number and type of leadership staff required. Comparisons of numbers of handicapped children to numbers of nonhandicapped children in an elementary or secondary building may be appropriate. Often the total enrollment of a building determines the need for one or more assistant building administrators. This comparison is not totally accurate, given that the special education and related services program is spread throughout the district rather than centralized in one building.

Facilities

Facilities required for special education and related services programs often must be specialized. While typical classroom space may be appropriate for full- or part-time special classes, adequate clinic space for various therapy services and diagnostic work is also required. If the regular program is not housed in barrier-free facilities, removal of those architectural barriers will be necessary both for those handicapped children requiring special education and other handicapped children who have no need for special education. Adaptations to regular classrooms are required for education of visually-impaired and hearing-impaired students. Instructional space is needed for the resource or itinerant program model, although a full-size classroom may not be required.

Observation rooms for parents of preschool handicapped children, behavior disordered children, and others, while not mandated, may prove extremely valuable in parent education activities. The presence of the parent directly in the classroom can, in some instances, be distracting to both the child and the teacher or therapist. Observation rooms with one-way glass mirrors overcome such distractions. Also the school may be able to enlist the parent's assistance in follow-up and reinforcement activities in the home after live or videotaped teaching and management demonstrations by the instructor are observed by the parent.

Transportation

Transportation of handicapped children can be a major problem in many communities. Under state statutes it is not uncommon to find provision of transportation for nonhandicapped children listed as permissive. On the other hand, special transportation for handicapped children when required for participation in an appropriate program is indeed mandated as a related service. Specially equipped buses or vans, minibuses, taxis, and shuttlebuses may be required. Depending on the severity of a handicap or the age of child, door-to-door transportation is often necessary. Creative planning and scheduling is vital to make certain the education of handicapped students is not slighted by a shorter school day where transportation equipment is utilized first for nonhandicapped children. While length of instructional day is an issue, the spiraling costs and shortages of fuel present other incentives to creative scheduling and planning.

Special transportation costs for handicapped students are generally subject to state categorical aid. Providing appropriate programs for handicapped children in the least restrictive environment and as close as possible to their homes may pay dividends when transportation is considered.

Legal and Fiscal Issues

Legal and fiscal issues in educating handicapped children also call for highly trained leadership staff. Federal and state legal requirements for the operation of programs have been expanded under mandated programing. As acknowledged in Chapter 4, programs for exceptional children are costly. Fiscal resources should be coordinated from all available sources to provide high quality programs. Leadership staff in special education must be continually aware of legal requirements and availability of resources. Without adequate leadership staff, many legal requirements or sources of funds can be overlooked.

Negotiated Agreements

Negotiated agreements or contracts with professional organizations can have tremendous impact on required programing. Length of school day for teachers must be considered in terms of meetings required in the diagnostic and IEP development process. Weighted pupil counts for handicapped children served in regular classes have implications for class size. Disruptive pupil clauses may impact on identification of handicapped children. If not actively involved in the negotiations process, special education leadership staff at least need to monitor the development of contract language carefully. Such involvement or monitoring may result in a reduction of costs for released time or overtime payments in areas that on the surface appear to have little or no fiscal impact.

Titling of Positions

Special education and related services programs of today bear heavily on total school district operation. The reverse is also true. The top level adminstrative position in special education should be included in the superintendent's "cabinet" at the local district level, with a highly trained and experienced person serving in this role. The implications of mandated special education programs require full participation of the top level administrator in the district-wide decision-making body. Without such direct input into the decision-making structure, the local district can easily fall into noncompliance with state and federal statutes.

The actual title of the top level administrator of special education in a local district can and should vary with the district size and administrative organizational structure. The position should be entitled and empowered appropriately.

What position titles function at the cabinet level in the district? In small districts the title of supervisor may be appropriate. In medium-sized districts the title of director or coordinator may be appropriate. In larger school districts, where assistant superintendents constitute the decision-making body, the title of assistant superintendent is appropriate.

Where special education leadership staff from a cooperative arrangement serve a number of smaller districts, the top level administrator should still have cabinet level status within the various member districts, even though he or she may be unable to attend all meetings in each district.

LARGE SCHOOL DISTRICT ORGANIZATION

Decentralization of school district operation has taken place in larger school districts. In these cases, area or regional superintendent positions have been developed. The regional or area offices often have positions that tend to mirror central office organization. In special education, regionalized services may be valuable for high prevalence areas, but may prove difficult in low prevalence areas, strictly from a numerical basis.

PREPARATION OF SPECIAL EDUCATION ADMINISTRATORS

What training and experience should be sought in selecting a top level administrator of special education? Obviously state certification standards may influence these decisions. State standards, however, range from no particular requirements to very specific ones.

Given the range of responsibilities of the position, it is suggested that the administrator of special education have the following qualifications:

Certification in one or more areas of special education.
Coursework in a minimum of three areas of special education.
Three or more years of successful experience as a professional worker in special education. (Additional certification and professional experience in regular education programs would be desirable.)
Masters degree in special education or related field.
Completion of graduate and advanced graduate level training in the areas of:
   Administration and supervision of public education,
   Administration and supervision of special education,
   School law,
   Special education law,
   School finance,
   Special education finance,
   Research and program evaluation, and
   Tests and measurements.
Completion of practica and internship in adminstration of special education.

It would be advisable for the administrator of special education to have additional training in the areas of counseling, budgeting, school–community relations, personnel management, facilities planning, and other such related areas.

In general, many candidates holding the above qualifications will have the sixth-year graduate certificate or doctoral degree. They may also be certified or nearly certified as principals and/or superintendents.

Even with the qualifications listed above, the administrator of special education will need to make conscious efforts at self-improvement through formal and informal study activities. The nature of the field today requires highly competent professional leadership staff.

PREPARATION OF SPECIAL EDUCATION SUPERVISORS

Supervisory or instructional improvement staff on the special education leadership team will also need a high level of training and experience. Depending on the number of such personnel within a district, the training and experience should focus more on learning theory, curriculum development, and in-service education. Advanced training in a specialty area of supervision—i.e., mental retardation, learning disabilities, hearing impairment, etc.—would be very helpful. Based on the size of the program, the instructional improvement staff may supervise one or more areas of special education. Where adequate instructional support can be provided by two persons, the titles may be split as follows: supervisor of programs in learning and behavioral disabilities; and supervisor of programs of physical disabilities may be appropriate. Diagnostic and therapy personnel could be assigned directly to the administrator or the most relevant supervisor.

The overall quality of special education and related services programs for handicapped children is dependent on qualified leadership staff, whether secured at the single district or multiple district level. The factors considered in this chapter should assist in developing the leadership plan for special education in local school districts.

REFERENCES

"Judge Orders Evaluation, Placement for 8000 NYC Handicapped Children." *Education of the Handicapped* (January 2, 1980): 5.

Other Issues and Concerns

10

A wide range of issues and concerns has surfaced since the passage of PL 94–142. Many of them are not new and had existed previously under permissive state legislation. The federal statute appears to have focused attention on these issues and concerns as less restrictive placements were developing and more individuals were encountering handicapped children.

The first five years of implementation of PL 94–142 focused primarily on quantitative issues. As programs mature, the attention will shift to the qualitative aspects of programs and services.

Parents and advocates who initially sought service will likewise shift their attention to the quality of service provided, and the appropriateness of the program for the individual child as will educational administrators who originally were forced to employ teachers who met only minimum certification requirements.

As appropriations move above one billion dollars, Congressional leaders, who have conducted initial rounds of oversight hearings, are also becoming more concerned about quality of programs. Their concerns focus primarily on accountability for expenditure of tax revenues.

Interest in any one or all of these issues will vary with groups composed of parents, administrators, and teachers. This chapter will be devoted to brief discussion of many such issues and suggested approaches for resolution. The issues are presented under the broad headings of evaluation, service, and personnel.

EVALUATION

During the decade prior to the passage of PL 94–142, the attention of researchers and the courts had been focused on issues of diagnosis and evaluation, particularly for the group of handicapped children labeled educable mentally retarded. Findings of both the courts and researchers documented the fact that, in all too many cases, minority group children who scored below a certain level on a single intelligence test were placed in programs for educable retarded children. Disproportionate numbers of minority group children were found in special education classes. Thus the question of the potential discriminatory aspects of intelligence tests was raised. PL 94–142 addressed this as well as other evaluation issues.

Nondiscriminatory Testing and Evaluation

Prior to PL 94–142's nondiscriminatory testing and evaluation regulations, a single test score was often utilized in determining eligibility and subsequent placement in special education. This highly questionable practice was not only discriminatory toward racial and cultural minorities, but also toward nonverbal children, or those with mild disabilities. Regulations for implementing PL 94–142 not only eliminated the single test approach, but also tightened procedures for diagnosing specific learning disabilities.

Presumably, initial diagnostic procedures using the new standards reduce the number of children who are diagnosed as handicapped learners. However, children who may have been misdiagnosed prior to the new standards, and who are already in programs, would not be identified until the required reevaluation within three years, unless the child is referred for some special reason.

A review of Table 3.1 shows that five states (Louisiana, Mississippi, New Jersey, Tennessee, and Texas) showed significant reductions in the number of handicapped children served on December 1, 1978 and December 1, 1979. Since those five states have concentrations of culturally diverse children enrolled in the schools, such drops may be the result of reevaluations using the new criteria established for nondiscriminatory testing and evaluation. While precise data are unknown, it would appear that the new standards may be accomplishing their intended purpose.

Grading the Handicapped Child

Unfortunately, letter grades are still the primary form of reporting and recording student progress. The question then arises, should handicapped children receive grades? The practices in the district should probably be applied to the handicapped as well, with possible exceptions for severe and profoundly handicapped children.

Special class teachers should not "give" undeserved passing grades, but should assign grades based on what is earned. If children who are capable of making progress do not apply themselves, they should receive lower or failing grades just as nonhandicapped children would. On the other hand, consistent hard work should be rewarded with passing grades. The same grading practices should be followed by regular class teachers who have handicapped children enrolled in their classes. If handicapped children earn an A, they should receive the A; if they earn an F, they should receive an F.

Some regular and special class teachers follow a contract procedure for grading. This practice can provide an incentive to learn for all children.

Ideally, parent conferences are a better system of reporting progress for all children. Conferences for parents of handicapped children should still be held, even though letter grades are utilized.

Monitoring

State and local education agencies are subject to evaluation of their implementation of special education.

Under PL 94–142, the Department of Education (formerly US Office of Education), monitors state-level implementation. Monitoring visits to SEAs also include visits to a few LEAs, public, and private residential programs; and meetings with state agencies and advocacy groups. But the primary monitoring of LEAs is the function of the SEA. In the decade prior to passage of PL 94–142, SEAs functioned more in a consultative and technical assistance manner. Local districts have not been accustomed to such SEA monitoring and much fear of it has surfaced.

If an LEA has complied with all of the assurances agreed to in the local application for Part B funds, they should have no fear of a visit. The LEA administrators should make sure all current records are complete and on file in the appropriate locations.

SEA monitoring visits to date have focused on quantitative dimensions. The Office of Special Education Policy Paper on IEPs (see Appendix) suggests more attention be placed on the quality of IEPs as opposed to their mere existence. Such qualitative concern will eventually filter into all aspects of the monitoring process.

Districts attempting to meet only the letter of the law will be more likely to raise the concern of the monitoring teams than will those trying to go beyond the legal requirements to implement best practices.

LEA personnel are not the only ones who have shown concern for this change of the SEA role. SEA employees were quite comfortable in their role as friendly helpers, and sometimes they are not sure they want to accept their new role!

SERVICES

The Education for All Handicapped Children Act requires a free appropriate public education. The definition of "appropriate" hinges upon what is contained in the individualized education program for any given child. Disagreement has often centered on issues relating to services parents deem necessary but which the schools have not traditionally provided or are uncertain about their ability to provide. A series of such issues is described in this section.

Year-Round School for Handicapped Children

In 1978, the Education Law Center initiated litigation in the US District Courts of Pennsylvania. The suit, Armstrong v. Kline, claimed the 180-day school year policy of the state violated provision of appropriate education for three severely handicapped children. The basis of the complaint centered on the fact that interruption of the education program by the traditional summer vacation resulted in a loss of skills for severely handicapped children. The 1979 decision concluded that such interruption could preclude the students from achieving self-sufficiency and avoiding institutionalization. Pennsylvania filed an appeal but proceeded to provide summer programs in 1980. On July 16, 1980, the Third US Circuit Court of Appeals upheld the district court decision and said the 180-day rule violated PL 94–142 by precluding the proper determination of the content of the required free appropriate public education (Education of the Handicapped, July 30, 1980).

Similar litigation is pending in other states. The decisions in this type of case will have far-reaching implications in future years.

Currently, the Pennsylvania decision applies only to severely handicapped children, not to all handicapped children. The major factor in determining which handicapped children will be afforded the year-round program is the definitive proof as to whether or not a significant loss of learned content or behaviors results from an interruption of program. The Pennsylvania decision was based on PL 94–142.

It appears that such cases are more relevant to the language of Section 504, PL 93–112. (However, it is doubtful that federal funds would be utilized in many summer school programs.) The real issue could be summarized by concluding that if any summer school programs were offered in whole or in part with public support, it would be discriminatory not to also make available programs for handicapped children. States and LEAs vary in their support of summer programs.

Summer programs do appear to be useful and appropriate for certain groups of handicapped children. The intensity of the disabling condition and the age of the child are important factors to consider in determining who can benefit from year-round schooling.

Length of School Day

Many school districts provide morning transportation for handicapped children after the vehicles have completed routes for nonhandicapped learners.

Afternoon routes pick these children up first. The resultant late start and early dismissal is subject to challenge by many parents and advocacy groups, who view this as a qualitative issue. Is it appropriate for handicapped children to have a reduced instructional day to facilitate transportation?

School districts should attempt to overcome this problem before the challenges begin. Those handicapped children who can utilize regular transportation routes should do so, and then the necessary equipment for special education routes should be obtained to insure that the transportation requirements can be met without loss of instructional time. When possible, provision of appropriate services at the neighborhood school of the handicapped child will alleviate this problem. Obviously, this type of arrangement would also be less restrictive than transporting a child to services delivered across town.

Location of Services in Building

Assignment of space for special education programs and services should not have a low priority. Again, challenges of appropriateness may be well taken in administrative hearings or judicial proceedings. A given school should not be overloaded with programs and services due to declining enrollment or acceptance of programs by building staff. Such a practice has implications for least restrictive placements and transportation.

Medical and Health Services

The provision of medical and health services in today's schools varies from state to state and from district to district within a given state. Relevant medical information is to be reviewed as a part of the diagnostic process. Some states, such as Virginia, require a physical examination routinely as part of the diagnostic procedure. The latter requirement is open to question unless available data suggest the examination or the disability is medically based.

Whether provided directly by the schools or a local health department, school nurses are invaluable in collecting the relevant data, assisting with interpretation, and acting as liaisons with the medical community.

Medication

In cases where medication is utilized and is to be administered at school, a release form should be developed by competant legal sources. This release should include such information as type and dosage of medication, prescribing physician, and person(s) authorized to administer the medication. Again, a nurse is extremely valuable in such areas. Medication should be kept in a locked location to avoid misuse.

Educators should not refer a child to a physician for medication, but rather for general or specific evaluations, such as neurological examinations. Willingness to work cooperatively and share relevant information can result in mutually beneficial relationships with the medical community.

A child should never be referred to a specific physician or dentist. In cases involving vision, the term "eye" doctor should be used to avoid a specific reference to an optometrist or ophthalmologist—unless state policy allows you that option. Violation of such referral practices almost always results in the wrath of the medical community being brought to bear on the schools.

Safety

The potential for accident or injury may well be greater for handicapped students, and thus extra caution is advised. All personnel and students should receive instruction in safety and accident prevention.

In the early 1960s courts decreed that school districts could be held liable for damages in the case of injury to a student. Adequate liability insurance protection has become a must for all districts. The best rule of thumb to avoid charges of negligence is the same for handicapped as it would be for nonhandicapped students. Whenever a given activity increases the risk factor over that incurred in a classroom, the ratio of supervision should be increased. Such activities include lunchrooms, playgrounds, and field trips. If one teacher has responsibility for ten students in the classroom, then two or three adults should supervise the group of ten students on a field trip.

Transporting any schoolchild creates a variety of problems, not the least of which is safety. Additional liability may be incurred in transporting certain handicapped children. It is recommended that two-way radios be available in all vehicles used for transporting schoolchildren and specifically for handicapped children. Aides may also be necessary to assist with medical or behavioral needs the driver is unable to take care of while driving the vehicle. While accidents are to be avoided at all costs, they do happen. Radios and aides can become critical in such situations, as well as those instances involving failure of equipment.

PERSONNEL

Education is a labor-intensive endeavor. Consequently a variety of issues involving employment and dismissal, salary, and working conditions are faced by every school district. While it is true that some states do not allow collective bargaining, the trend has been toward approval of collective bargaining for school employees. Regardless of the situation in your state, the following issues and suggestions relating to personnel should be of assistance in operating special education programs.

The Role of Principals

Prior to PL 94–142, many building administrators had very little contact with special education programs in their building. Now concern is being expressed by building administrators on a variety of issues they face in implementing programs. Since their roles have changed, principals who may have had no formal preparation or experience in working with special education programs now find these programs housed in their buildings, and additional demands are being made on their time in the referral, diagnostic, and IEP development process. It is possible most of the concerns expressed by principals are due to their changing roles as opposed to a reluctance to work with handicapped children and their parents.

Hopefully, the additional time required of principals involving special education tasks will be acknowledged through allocation of additional professional and/or clerical support.

Referrals and IEP Meetings An informed principal will discuss potential referrals of children with regular classroom teachers in advance of a formal request for screening or evaluation. In addition, the principal should observe the child in question after the referral is received, if this has not been done previously. It is possible that building-level resources exist which would eliminate the need for a special education referral. The teacher may or may not be aware of such resources.

The practice of merely signing a referral and forwarding it to the appropriate office should be a thing of the past. Principals may be assigned responsibility for obtaining the informed consent of parents prior to proceeding with the evaluation.

Conferences with parents to develop the IEP also require an "other representative of the school" to be present. This representative is usually the principal.

Discipline of Special Education Students Principals are often confused about which disciplinary procedures may be utilized for handicapped children attending self-contained or resource programs. The best rule of thumb is that building procedures should be utilized for *all* students in the building, assuming of course that handicapped children know and understand the building rules and procedures. Modifications may be necessary for certain severely handicapped or physically handicapped children.

Can handicapped children be suspended or expelled from school? The answer is *yes*, if the rules and penalties do not discriminate against the handicapped child. In *many* states, formal expulsion does not relieve the schools of their responsibility to provide an educational program for *nonhandicapped* children of compulsory age. The location and timing of the alternative program may be away from the school or at different hours from the traditional school day.

In *all* states, expulsion of *handicapped* children within the mandated age range of the state does not relieve the LEA of its responsibility to provide a free appropriate public education for them. A more restrictive setting may be required due to the behaviors of the child. Such education might be provided through home instruction or in combination with evening adult education programs (as could also be done with nonhandicapped children). If the expulsion is for extreme behavioral reasons, the required education may be provided in alternate public or private day or residential facilities so long as it is at no cost to the child's parent or guardian.

State and local policies should be reviewed carefully to determine whether specific mention is made concerning handicapped children and disciplinary procedures. This is particularly true in cases where suspension and expulsion are to be considered.

Teacher and Staff Evaluation   Building administrators have expressed concerns regarding who should evaluate special education teachers and related service personnel. Some principals do not feel qualified to evaluate special education staff who are based in their building. Other principals want to insure they have an opportunity to evaluate all staff who are assigned to their building in any capacity.

The resolution of these concerns may be found in district policies and procedures. The best practice, however, is for special education teachers and all other personnel to be evaluated by the building principal *and* the special education leadership staff. A highly competent special education teacher, speech therapist, or psychologist should not receive a strong positive evaluation if they are always late in arrival or cause other problems that can only be observed at the building level.

In general, specialist supervisors or directors should deal with evaluation as it relates to technical expertise, while principals' evaluations should focus on overall performance in the building. Feedback to the specialist leadership staff should be sought from each building in which itinerant staff are assigned. The best evaluation procedure also involves self-evaluation by the staff member, with a follow-up conference involving the staff member and the evaluators.

Substitute Teachers for Special Education

Classes are often dismissed when the special education teacher is away for medical, personal, or professional leave. This practice is discriminatory since this is not the procedure followed for regular class teachers.

Substitute teaching is not easy in regular education and, in some instances, may be even more difficult in special education, where true individualized instruction is taking place. Ideally, a pool of certified special education teachers should be developed to serve as substitutes in classes for handicapped children. However, since this is not usually possible, due to the lack of special education teachers available, the second best approach is to develop a cadre of substitutes who are certified in general education, but have demonstrated the interest in and ability to work with handicapped learners.

Certainly the principal should be available as a resource for any substitute teacher. When at all possible, special education leadership staff should be available, or at least on call, as a resource for special education substitute teachers.

Teacher Shortages and Attrition

Qualified professionals and nonprofessionals prepared to work with handicapped children are still in short supply. This is not only the case with certain special education teaching personnel, but with therapists (occupational, physical, language, music, recreation), and qualified adapted physical educators as well. The same is true for psychologists, social workers, qualified aides, and other related personnel.

Teacher "burn out" is also more prevalent in some special education areas than in other teaching fields. This fact, coupled with usual attrition factors, compounds the lack of qualified personnel.

Recruitment is vital. In some cases, it may be necessary to support attendance of existing staff at summer school to obtain required certification. As mentioned in Chapter 8, the SEA may have state or federal funds available to assist in payment of stipends or tuition.

Negotiated Contracts

In states where collective bargaining for teachers exists, the bargaining unit is sure to identify many potentially negotiable issues contained in PL 94–142. Additional compensation or released time for teachers involved in IEP development is one of the first areas to surface. The fact that IEP meetings are usually held after the negotiated work day or even on weekends to be at a "mutually convenient time and place," lends support to such requests. Additional compensation or released time is also requested for participation in required in-service programs.

Another issue often brought to the bargaining table relates to reduction of class size when an identified handicapped child is placed in a regular classroom. Typically, a form of weighted counting of the handicapped child is requested to be utilized in determining the pupil-teacher ratio of the teacher involved. Care should be taken in negotiating the weighted count, since it could be found to be a negative incentive in implementing least restrictive alternative placements.

In lieu of reducing class size under weighted counting of handicapped children, the Charlottesville, Virginia City Schools are allowing regular classroom teachers to document the situation through the counts and make specific requests for assistance. While the program is in its early stages, it is anticipated that teachers may request such things as teacher aides, tuition or fees to obtain additional training, special equipment, or support to attend professional meetings. It is assumed the teacher could also request a reduction in class size. Teacher requests are reviewed by a committee of regular and special education teachers and administrators to determine whether the request is valid and should be granted. Such an approach requires action on the part of the teacher to identify the problem and, more importantly, to help decide how it may be resolved.

Where teacher-parent conferences are required and it is necessary for the teacher to travel to the child's home, requests for mileage or transportation costs are heard. Parent conferences can be valuable and consideration of requiring them must be balanced with consideration of potential costs.

Length of teacher day may often be an issue, particularly when significant funds for teacher salary increases are not readily available. Reduction of the length of the day may present a serious problem in obtaining required teacher input at case conference, eligibility, or IEP meetings. Thus, what may have appeared to have little or no fiscal implication, actually results in the need to pay overtime or employ substitutes to allow teachers to attend.

It would be wise for special education administrative staff to be either directly or indirectly involved in negotiating sessions. This could avoid the acceptance of a proposal with tremendous implications for special education programs.

A list of issues and concerns cannot be all inclusive. This chapter has attempted to deal with those most frequently mentioned. New issues and concerns will continue to arise. In some cases, common sense may provide the best answer; in other instances, technical expertise will be required.

REFERENCES

"Appeals Court Affirms Year-Round Programs for Handicapped." *Education of the Handicapped* (July 30, 1980): 1.

Future Implementation Challenges

11

Over five years have elapsed since the enactment of The Education for All Handicapped Children Act of 1975 (PL 94–142). The initial five years of implementation resulted in many challenges to local, state, and national policy-makers and administrators. Parents and advocacy groups have tested the law through administrative and legal proceedings. To date only one case brought under PL 94–142 or Section 504 of PL 93–112, involving elementary and secondary-age handicapped learners, has reached the US Appelate Courts (Armstrong v. Kline, No. 79–2158, 3rd USCCA, 1980). One other case under Section 504 was heard by the Supreme Court, but it involved postsecondary issues (Southeastern Community College v. Davis, No. 78–711, USSC, 1979).

LEGAL CHALLENGES

Challenges will continue to be heard, primarily in LEA and SEA administrative due-process hearings. It is highly probable that a case involving elementary- and secondary-age handicapped children will reach the Supreme Court. Precisely which issue will be the first to receive interpretation by the highest court of the land is unknown. The Pennsylvania case (Armstrong v. Kline), regarding the provision of summer programs for handicapped children, may be appealed to the Supreme Court. That case is closest to such review if the Commonwealth files an appeal.

Other cases pending in lower courts may reach the high court before Armstrong. The issues involved are difficult to predict, but financing special educa-

125

tion and related services will be involved either directly or indirectly. Certainly this is an issue in extended year programs.

Only time will tell if the Supreme Court is ever asked to rule on whether or not all handicapped children have a constitutional right to an education.

ADDITIONAL FUNDS NEEDED

Appropriations for education of handicapped children at the local, state, and national levels have increased dramatically in the last five years. Authorized funding levels contained in PL 94–142 have not been met for the third and fourth years of the program. Over three times the amount appropriated for fiscal year 1981 will be required if appropriations are to meet authorizations for fiscal year 1982. The fiscal year 1982 authorization for PL 94–142 exceeds 3.16 billion dollars.

The recovery from the 1980 recession will play a large part in determining the future federal funding levels. The pattern of federal mandates and funding mirrors the history of state mandates and funding seen in the past two decades.

Current economic conditions also have had an effect on local and state appropriations. Budget priorities must shift to become consistent with local, state, and national policy if adequate funding levels are to be achieved at the state and national level. The local taxpayer may be forced to assume a greater burden for total implementation.

THE BACKLASH

When will parents of nonhandicapped children start demanding IEPs? Will parents of slow learners insist on the development of remedial reading and math classes? What additional programs are needed for gifted children? Are the citizens of this country willing to support quality educational programs for *all* children?

Curtailment of school budgets will ultimately result in reduction of programs. All mandated programs, including programs for handicapped children, must survive. Nonmandated programs and activities, which are often popular, are targets for legal reductions. Although school budgets were declining before the push to implement special education, special education may be viewed as the cause for program retrenchment.

Parents should rally support for all educational programs before cuts are made, and they should not put the blame for cutbacks on educational programs designed for handicapped learners.

All educators and policy-makers should attempt to avoid head-on confrontations between parents of nonhandicapped and handicapped children. Many other issues in education should consume our energy.

THE FATE OF PERMANENT LEGISLATION

PL 94–142 was enacted with permanent authorization. This is somewhat unique compared to other funded educational and social programs, which require reauthorization every four years or at other predetermined intervals. It is doubtful that any politician would feel comfortable in singling out PL 94–142 for revocation.

Advocacy groups and others interested in the education of handicapped children must be on the alert to make sure the authorizations contained in PL 94–142 are not included in omnibus "sunset" legislation. Sunset laws could require the periodic reauthorization or subsequent demise of many funded programs, including those under PL 94–142.

BEH IDENTIFIED CHALLENGES

In the August 1979 Semiannual Update on the Implementation of PL 94–142, remaining challenges identified by the Bureau of Education for the Handicapped (now Office of Special Education) included:

- The Bureau of Education for the Handicapped will continue its initiative to develop and implement the federal, state, and local interagency agreements necessary to coordinate and maximize the use of federal monies for providing health, education, and social services to the handicapped.
- The Bureau will continue to provide technical assistance and target discretionary monies to increase current efforts to identify, locate, and evaluate all handicapped children.
- The Bureau will continue its parent initiative which is intended to help develop leadership and continuity in local parent organizations so that these organizations can effectively support active parent involvement in the special education pupil planning and programming process.
- The Bureau will continue its technical assistance efforts to identify and disseminate management techniques for designing efficient pupil appraisal systems capable of meeting the demands of our nation's large city school districts where the largest backlogs for evaluation have occurred.
- The Bureau will continue to target and prioritize discretionary training monies in responding to the needs of state and local programs. (pp. xvii–xviii)

FULL IMPLEMENTATION

Progress has been made. More handicapped children than ever before are receiving an education. The quality and appropriateness of programs, however, must continue to improve.

Many more handicapped learners remain to be identified and served before we can attest to full implementation of state and national policy. This goal certainly is humanitarian, realistic and *attainable*.

Just as was the case with state mandates, the first five years under federal legislation were the easy ones. *The real hard work lies ahead!*

REFERENCES

US Office of Education. "Progress toward a Free Appropriate Public Education: Semi-annual Update on the Implementation of Public Law 94–142 (August 1979).

APPENDIX A
PL 94-142

Public Law 94-142
94th Congress, S. 6
November 29, 1975

An Act

To amend the Education of the Handicapped Act to provide educational assistance
to all handicapped children, and for other purposes.

*Be it enacted by the Senate and House of Representatives of the
United States of America in Congress assembled,* That this Act may
be cited as the "Education for All Handicapped Children Act of 1975".

Education for
All Handicapped
Children Act of
1975.
20 USC 1401
note.

EXTENSION OF EXISTING LAW

SEC. 2. (a)(1)(A) Section 611(b)(2) of the Education of the
Handicapped Act (20 U.S.C. 1411(b)(2)) (hereinafter in this Act
referred to as the "Act"), as in effect during the fiscal years 1976 and
1977, is amended by striking out "the Commonwealth of Puerto Rico,".

(B) Section 611(c)(1) of the Act (20 U.S.C. 1411(c)(1)), as in
effect during the fiscal years 1976 and 1977, is amended by striking
out "the Commonwealth of Puerto Rico,".

(2) Section 611(c)(2) of the Act (20 U.S.C. 1411(c)(2)), as in
effect during the fiscal years 1976 and 1977, is amended by striking
out "year ending June 30, 1975" and inserting in lieu thereof the
following: "years ending June 30, 1975, and 1976, and for the fiscal
year ending September 30, 1977", and by striking out "2 per centum"
each place it appears therein and inserting in lieu thereof "1 per
centum".

(3) Section 611(d) of the Act (20 U.S.C. 1411(d)), as in effect during the fiscal years 1976 and 1977, is amended by striking out "year
ending June 30, 1975" and inserting in lieu thereof the following:
"years ending June 30, 1975, and 1976, and for the fiscal year ending
September 30, 1977".

(4) Section 612(a) of the Act (20 U.S.C. 1412(a)), as in effect
during the fiscal years 1976 and 1977, is amended—

(A) by striking out "year ending June 30, 1975" and inserting
in lieu thereof "years ending June 30, 1975, and 1976, for the
period beginning July 1, 1976, and ending September 30, 1976,
and for the fiscal year ending September 30, 1977"; and

(B) by striking out "fiscal year 1974" and inserting in lieu
thereof "preceding fiscal year".

(b)(1) Section 614(a) of the Education Amendments of 1974 (Public Law 93–380; 88 Stat. 580) is amended by striking out "fiscal year
1975" and inserting in lieu thereof the following: "the fiscal years
ending June 30, 1975, and 1976, for the period beginning July 1, 1976,
and ending September 30, 1976, and for the fiscal year ending September 30, 1977,".

20 USC 1411
note.

(2) Section 614(b) of the Education Amendments of 1974 (Public
Law 93–380; 88 Stat. 580) is amended by striking out "fiscal year 1974"
and inserting in lieu thereof the following: "the fiscal years ending
June 30, 1975, and 1976, for the period beginning July 1, 1976, and
ending September 30, 1976, and for the fiscal year ending September 30,
1977,"

20 USC 1411
note.

89 STAT. 773

20 USC 1413
note.
(3) Section 614(c) of the Education Amendments of 1974 (Public Law 93–380; 88 Stat. 580) is amended by striking out "fiscal year 1974" and inserting in lieu thereof the following: "the fiscal years ending June 30, 1975, and 1976, for the period beginning July 1, 1976, and ending September 30, 1976, and for the fiscal year ending September 30, 1977,".

Ante, p. 773.
(c) Section 612(a) of the Act, as in effect during the fiscal years 1976 and 1977, and as amended by subsection (a)(4), is amended by inserting immediately before the period at the end thereof the following: ", or $300,000, whichever is greater".

20 USC 1412.
(d) Section 612 of the Act (20 U.S.C. 1411), as in effect during the fiscal years 1976 and 1977, is amended by adding at the end thereof the following new subsection:

Publication in
Federal Regis-
ter.
"(d) The Commissioner shall, no later than one hundred twenty days after the date of the enactment of the Education for All Handicapped Children Act of 1975, prescribe and publish in the Federal Register such rules as he considers necessary to carry out the provisions of this section and section 611.".

Ante, p. 773.
20 USC 1411
note.
(e) Notwithstanding the provisions of section 611 of the Act, as in effect during the fiscal years 1976 and 1977, there are authorized to be appropriated $100,000.000 for the fiscal year 1976, such sums as may be necessary for the period beginning July 1, 1976, and ending September 30, 1976, and $200,000,000 for the fiscal year 1977, to carry out the provisions of part B of the Act, as in effect during such fiscal years.

STATEMENT OF FINDINGS AND PURPOSE

20 USC 1401
note.
SEC. 3. (a) Section 601 of the Act (20 U.S.C. 1401) is amended by inserting "(a)" immediately before "This title" and by adding at the end thereof the following new subsections:

"(b) The Congress finds that—

"(1) there are more than eight million handicapped children in the United States today;

"(2) the special educational needs of such children are not being fully met;

"(3) more than half of the handicapped children in the United States do not receive appropriate educational services which would enable them to have full equality of opportunity;

"(4) one million of the handicapped children in the United States are excluded entirely from the public school system and will not go through the educational process with their peers;

"(5) there are many handicapped children throughout the United States participating in regular school programs whose handicaps prevent them from having a successful educational experience because their handicaps are undetected;

"(6) because of the lack of adequate services within the public school system, families are often forced to find services outside the public school system, often at great distance from their residence and at their own expense;

"(7) developments in the training of teachers and in diagnostic and instructional procedures and methods have advanced to the point that, given appropriate funding, State and local educational agencies can and will provide effective special education and related services to meet the needs of handicapped children;

"(8) State and local educational agencies have a responsibility to provide education for all handicapped children, but present financial resources are inadequate to meet the special educational needs of handicapped children; and

"(9) it is in the national interest that the Federal Government assist State and local efforts to provide programs to meet the educational needs of handicapped children in order to assure equal protection of the law.

"(c) It is the purpose of this Act to assure that all handicapped children have available to them, within the time periods specified in section 612(2)(B), a free appropriate public education which emphasizes special education and related services designed to meet their unique needs, to assure that the rights of handicapped children and their parents or guardians are protected, to assist States and localities to provide for the education of all handicapped children, and to assess and assure the effectiveness of efforts to educate handicapped children.".

Ante, p. 773.

(b) The heading for section 601 of the Act (20 U.S.C. 1401) is amended to read as follows:

"SHORT TITLE; STATEMENT OF FINDINGS AND PURPOSE".

DEFINITIONS

SEC. 4. (a) Section 602 of the Act (20 U.S.C. 1402) is amended—

(1) in paragraph (1) thereof, by striking out "crippled" and inserting in lieu thereof "orthopedically impaired", and by inserting immediately after "impaired children" the following: ", or children with specific learning disabilities,";

(2) in paragraph (5) thereof, by inserting immediately after "instructional materials," the following: "telecommunications, sensory, and other technological aids and devices,";

(3) in the last sentence of paragraph (15) thereof, by inserting immediately after "environmental" the following: ", cultural, or economic"; and

(4) by adding at the end thereof the following new paragraphs:

"(16) The term 'special education' means specially designed instruction, at no cost to parents or guardians, to meet the unique needs of a handicapped child, including classroom instruction, instruction in physical education, home instruction, and instruction in hospitals and institutions.

"(17) The term 'related services' means transportation, and such developmental, corrective, and other supportive services (including speech pathology and audiology, psychological services, physical and occupational therapy, recreation, and medical and counseling services, except that such medical services shall be for diagnostic and evaluation purposes only) as may be required to assist a handicapped child to benefit from special education, and includes the early identification and assessment of handicapping conditions in children.

"(18) The term 'free appropriate public education' means special education and related services which (A) have been provided at public expense, under public supervision and direction, and without charge, (B) meet the standards of the State educational agency, (C) include an appropriate preschool, elementary, or secondary school education in the State involved, and (D) are provided in conformity with the individualized education program required under section 614(a)(5).

20 USC 1401.

"(19) The term 'individualized education program' means a written statement for each handicapped child developed in any meeting by a representative of the local educational agency or an intermediate educational unit who shall be qualified to provide, or supervise the provision of, specially designed instruction to meet the unique needs of handicapped children, the teacher, the parents or guardian of such child, and, whenever appropriate, such child, which statement shall include (A) a statement of the present levels of educational performance of such child, (B) a statement of annual goals, including short-term instructional objectives, (C) a statement of the specific educational services to be provided to such child, and the extent to which such child will be able to participate in regular educational programs, (D) the projected date for initiation and anticipated duration of such services, and (E) appropriate objective criteria and evaluation procedures and schedules for determining, on at least an annual basis, whether instructional objectives are being achieved.

"(20) The term 'excess costs' means those costs which are in excess of the average annual per student expenditure in a local educational agency during the preceding school year for an elementary or secondary school student, as may be appropriate, and which shall be computed after deducting (A) amounts received under this part or under title I or title VII of the Elementary and Secondary Education Act of 1965, and (B) any State or local funds expended for programs which would qualify for assistance under this part or under such titles.

20 USC 241a note, 881.

"(21) The term 'native language' has the meaning given that term by section 703(a)(2) of the Bilingual Education Act (20 U.S.C. 880b-1(a)(2)).

"(22) The term 'intermediate educational unit' means any public authority, other than a local educational agency, which is under the general supervision of a State educational agency, which is established by State law for the purpose of providing free public education on a regional basis, and which provides special education and related services to handicapped children within that State.".

(b) The heading for section 602 of the Act (20 U.S.C. 1402) is amended to read as follows:

"DEFINITIONS".

ASSISTANCE FOR EDUCATION OF ALL HANDICAPPED CHILDREN

SEC. 5. (a) Part B of the Act (20 U.S.C. 1411 et seq.) is amended to read as follows:

"PART B—ASSISTANCE FOR EDUCATION OF ALL HANDICAPPED CHILDREN

"ENTITLEMENTS AND ALLOCATIONS

20 USC 1411.
Post, p. 793.

"SEC. 611. (a)(1) Except as provided in paragraph (3) and in section 619, the maximum amount of the grant to which a State is entitled under this part for any fiscal year shall be equal to—
    "(A) the number of handicapped children aged three to twenty-one, inclusive, in such State who are receiving special education and related services;
multiplied by—
    "(B)(i) 5 per centum, for the fiscal year ending September 30, 1978, of the average per pupil expenditure in public elementary and secondary schools in the United States;

"(ii) 10 per centum, for the fiscal year ending September 30, 1979, of the average per pupil expenditure in public elementary and secondary schools in the United States;

"(iii) 20 per centum, for the fiscal year ending September 30, 1980, of the average per pupil expenditure in public elementary and secondary schools in the United States;

"(iv) 30 per centum, for the fiscal year ending September 30, 1981, of the average per pupil expenditure in public elementary and secondary schools in the United States; and

"(v) 40 per centum, for the fiscal year ending September 30, 1982, and for each fiscal year thereafter, of the average per pupil expenditure in public elementary and secondary schools in the United States;

except that no State shall receive an amount which is less than the amount which such State received under this part for the fiscal year ending September 30, 1977.

"(2) For the purpose of this subsection and subsection (b) through subsection (e), the term 'State' does not include Guam, American Samoa, the Virgin Islands, and the Trust Territory of the Pacific Islands.   **"State."**

"(3) The number of handicapped children receiving special education and related services in any fiscal year shall be equal to the average of the number of such children receiving special education and related services on October 1 and February 1 of the fiscal year preceding the fiscal year for which the determination is made.

"(4) For purposes of paragraph (1)(B), the term 'average per pupil expenditure', in the United States, means the aggregate current expenditures, during the second fiscal year preceding the fiscal year for which the computation is made (or, if satisfactory data for such year are not available at the time of computation, then during the most recent preceding fiscal year for which satisfactory data are available) of all local educational agencies in the United States (which, for purposes of this subsection, means the fifty States and the District of Columbia), as the case may be, plus any direct expenditures by the State for operation of such agencies (without regard to the source of funds from which either of such expenditures are made), divided by the aggregate number of children in average daily attendance to whom such agencies provided free public education during such preceding year.   **"Average per pupil expenditure."**

"(5) (A) In determining the allotment of each State under paragraph (1), the Commissioner may not count—

"(i) handicapped children in such State under paragraph (1) (A) to the extent the number of such children is greater than 12 per centum of the number of all children aged five to seventeen, inclusive, in such State;

"(ii) as part of such percentage, children with specific learning disabilities to the extent the number of such children is greater than one-sixth of such percentage; and

"(iii) handicapped children who are counted under section 121 of the Elementary and Secondary Education Act of 1965.   **20 USC 241c-1.**

"(B) For purposes of subparagraph (A), the number of children aged five to seventeen, inclusive, in any State shall be determined by the Commissioner on the basis of the most recent satisfactory data available to him.

"(b)(1) Of the funds received under subsection (a) by any State for the fiscal year ending September 30, 1978—

"(A) 50 per centum of such funds may be used by such State in accordance with the provisions of paragraph (2); and

"(B) 50 per centum of such funds shall be distributed by such State pursuant to subsection (d) to local educational agencies and intermediate educational units in such State, for use in accordance with the priorities established under section 612(3).

"(2) Of the funds which any State may use under paragraph (1) (A)—

"(A) an amount which is equal to the greater of—

"(i) 5 per centum of the to.al amount of funds received under this part by such State; or

"(ii) $200,000;

may be used by such State for administrative costs related to carrying out sections 612 and 613;

"(B) the remainder shall be used by such State to provide support services and direct services, in accordance with the priorities established under section 612(3).

"(c)(1) Of the funds received under subsection (a) by any State for the fiscal year ending September 30, 1979, and for each fiscal year thereafter—

"(A) 25 per centum of such funds may be used by such State in accordance with the provisions of paragraph (2); and

"(B) except as provided in paragraph (3), 75 per centum of such funds shall be distributed by such State pursuant to subsection (d) to local educational agencies and intermediate educational units in such State, for use in accordance with priorities established under section 612(3).

"(2)(A) Subject to the provisions of subparagraph (B), of the funds which any State may use under paragraph (1)(A)—

"(i) an amount which is equal to the greater of—

"(I) 5 per centum of the total amount of funds received under this part by such State; or

"(II) $200,000;

may be used by such State for administrative costs related to carrying out the provisions of sections 612 and 613; and

"(ii) the remainder shall be used by such State to provide support services and direct services, in accordance with the priorities established under section 612(3).

"(B) The amount expended by any State from the funds available to such State under paragraph (1)(A) in any fiscal year for the provision of support services or for the provision of direct services shall be matched on a program basis by such State, from funds other than Federal funds, for the provision of support services or for the provision of direct services for the fiscal year involved.

"(3) The provisions of section 613(a)(9) shall not apply with respect to amounts available for use by any State under paragraph (2).

"(4)(A) No funds shall be distributed by any State under this subsection in any fiscal year to any local educational agency or intermediate educational unit in such State if—

"(i) such local educational agency or intermediate educational unit is entitled, under subsection (d), to less than $7,500 for such fiscal year; or

"(ii) such local educational agency or intermediate educational unit has not submitted an application for such funds which meets the requirements of section 614.

"(B) Whenever the provisions of subparagraph (A) apply, the State involved shall use such funds to assure the provision of a free appropriate education to handicapped children residing in the area served by such local educational agency or such intermediate educational unit. The provisions of paragraph (2)(B) shall not apply to the use of such funds.

"(d) From the total amount of funds available to local educational agencies and intermediate educational units in any State under subsection (b)(1)(B) or subsection (c)(1)(B), as the case may be, each local educational agency or intermediate educational unit shall be entitled to an amount which bears the same ratio to the total amount available under subsection (b)(1)(B) or subsection (c)(1)(B), as the case may be, as the number of handicapped children aged three to twenty-one, inclusive, receiving special education and related services in such local educational agency or intermediate educational unit bears to the aggregate number of handicapped children aged three to twenty-one, inclusive, receiving special education and related services in all local educational agencies and intermediate educational units which apply to the State educational agency involved for funds under this part.

"(e)(1) The jurisdictions to which this subsection applies are Guam, American Samoa, the Virgin Islands, and the Trust Territory of the Pacific Islands.

"(2) Each jurisdiction to which this subsection applies shall be entitled to a grant for the purposes set forth in section 601(c) in an amount equal to an amount determined by the Commissioner in accordance with criteria based on respective needs, except that the aggregate of the amount to which such jurisdictions are so entitled for any fiscal year shall not exceed an amount equal to 1 per centum of the aggregate of the amounts available to all States under this part for that fiscal year. If the aggregate of the amounts, determined by the Commissioner pursuant to the preceding sentence, to be so needed for any fiscal year exceeds an amount equal to such 1 per centum limitation, the entitlement of each such jurisdiction shall be reduced proportionately until such aggregate does not exceed such 1 per centum limitation.

Ante, p. 774.

"(3) The amount expended for administration by each jurisdiction under this subsection shall not exceed 5 per centum of the amount allotted to such jurisdiction for any fiscal year, or $35,000, whichever is greater.

"(f)(1) The Commissioner is authorized to make payments to the Secretary of the Interior according to the need for such assistance for the education of handicapped children on reservations serviced by elementary and secondary schools operated for Indian children by the Department of the Interior. The amount of such payment for any fiscal year shall not exceed 1 per centum of the aggregate amounts available to all States under this part for that fiscal year.

"(2) The Secretary of the Interior may receive an allotment under this subsection only after submitting to the Commissioner an application which meets the applicable requirements of section 614(a) and which is approved by the Commissioner. The provisions of section 616 shall apply to any such application.

89 STAT. 779

"(g)(1) If the sums appropriated for any fiscal year for making payments to States under this part are not sufficient to pay in full the total amounts which all States are entitled to receive under this part for such fiscal year, the maximum amounts which all States are entitled to receive under this part for such fiscal year shall be ratably reduced. In case additional funds become available for making such payments for any fiscal year during which the preceding sentence is applicable, such reduced amounts shall be increased on the same basis as they were reduced.

"(2) In the case of any fiscal year in which the maximum amounts for which States are eligible have been reduced under the first sentence of paragraph (1), and in which additional funds have not been made available to pay in full the total of such maximum amounts under the last sentence of such paragraph, the State educational agency shall fix dates before which each local educational agency or intermediate educational unit shall report to the State educational agency on the amount of funds available to the local educational agency or intermediate educational unit, under the provisions of subsection (d), which it estimates that it will expend in accordance with the provisions of this part. The amounts so available to any local educational agency or intermediate educational unit, or any amount which would be available to any other local educational agency or intermediate educational unit if it were to submit a program meeting the requirements of this part, which the State educational agency determines will not be used for the period of its availability, shall be available for allocation to those local educational agencies or intermediate educational units, in the manner provided by this section, which the State educational agency determines will need and be able to use additional funds to carry out approved programs.

"ELIGIBILITY

20 USC 1412.

"SEC. 612. In order to qualify for assistance under this part in any fiscal year, a State shall demonstrate to the Commissioner that the following conditions are met:

"(1) The State has in effect a policy that assures all handicapped children the right to a free appropriate public education.

"(2) The State has developed a plan pursuant to section 613(b) in effect prior to the date of the enactment of the Education for All Handicapped Children Act of 1975 and submitted not later than August 21, 1975, which will be amended so as to comply with the provisions of this paragraph. Each such amended plan shall set forth in detail the policies and procedures which the State will undertake or has undertaken in order to assure that—

"(A) there is established (i) a goal of providing full educational opportunity to all handicapped children, (ii) a detailed timetable for accomplishing such a goal, and (iii) a description of the kind and number of facilities, personnel, and services necessary throughout the State to meet such a goal;

"(B) a free appropriate public education will be available for all handicapped children between the ages of three and eighteen within the State not later than September 1, 1978, and for all handicapped children between the ages of three and twenty-one within the State not later than September 1, 1980, except that, with respect to handicapped children aged three to five and aged eighteen to twenty-one, inclusive, the requirements of this clause shall not be applied in any State if the application of such requirements would be inconsistent with State law or practice, or the order of any court, respecting public education within such age groups in the State;

"(C) all children residing in the State who are handicapped, regardless of the severity of their handicap. and who are in need of special education and related services are identified, located, and evaluated, and that a practical method is developed and implemented to determine which children are currently receiving needed special education and related services and which children are not currently receiving needed special education and related services;

"(D) policies and procedures are established in accordance with detailed criteria prescribed under section 617(c); and

"(E) the amendment to the plan submitted by the State required by this section shall be available to parents, guardians, and other members of the general public at least thirty days prior to the date of submission of the amendment to the Commissioner.

"(3) The State has established priorities for providing a free appropriate public education to all handicapped children, which priorities shall meet the timetables set forth in clause (B) of paragraph (2) of this section, first with respect to handicapped children who are not receiving an education, and second with respect to handicapped children, within each disability, with the most severe handicaps who are receiving an inadequate education. and has made adequate progress in meeting the timetables set forth in clause (B) of paragraph (2) of this section.

"(4) Each local educational agency in the State will maintain records of the individualized education program for each handicapped child, and such program shall be established, reviewed, and revised as provided in section 614(a)(5).

"(5) The State has established (A) procedural safeguards as required by section 615, (B) procedures to assure that, to the maximum extent appropriate, handicapped children; including children in public or private institutions or other care facilities, are educated with children who are not handicapped, and that special classes, separate schooling, or other removal of handicapped children from the regular educational environment occurs only when the nature or severity of the handicap is such that education in regular classes with the use of supplementary aids and services cannot be achieved satisfactorily, and (C) procedures to assure that testing and evaluation materials and procedures utilized for the purposes of evaluation and placement of handicapped children will be selected and administered so as not to be racially or culturally discriminatory. Such materials or procedures shall be provided and administered in the child's native language or mode of communication, unless it clearly is not feasible to do so, and no single procedure shall be the sole criterion for determining an appropriate educational program for a child.

"(6) The State educational agency shall be responsible for assuring   Administration. that the requirements of this part are carried out and that all educational programs for handicapped children within the State, including all such programs administered by any other State or local agency, will be under the general supervision of the persons responsible for educational programs for handicapped children in the State educational agency and shall meet education standards of the State educational agency.

"(7) The State shall assure that (A) in carrying out the requirements of this section procedures are established for consultation with
individuals involved in or concerned with the education of handicapped
children, including handicapped individuals and parents or guardians
of handicapped children, and (B) there are public hearings, adequate
notice of such hearings, and an opportunity for comment available to
the general public prior to adoption of the policies, programs, and
procedures required pursuant to the provisions of this section and
section 613.

"STATE PLANS

20 USC 1413.

"SEC. 613. (a) Any State meeting the eligibility requirements set
forth in section 612 and desiring to participate in the program under
this part shall submit to the Commissioner, through its State educational agency, a State plan at such time, in such manner, and containing
or accompanied by such information, as he deems necessary. Each such
plan shall—
    "(1) set forth policies and procedures designed to assure that
funds paid to the State under this part will be expended in accordance with the provisions of this part, with particular attention
given to the provisions of sections 611(b), 611(c), 611(d), 612(2),
and 612(3);
    "(2) provide that programs and procedures will be established
to assure that funds received by the State or any of its political
subdivisions under any other Federal program, including section
121 of the Elementary and Secondary Education Act of 1965 (20

20 USC 241c-1.

U.S.C. 241c-2), section 305(b)(8) of such Act (20 U.S.C. 844a
(b)(8)) or its successor authority, and section 122(a)(4)(B) of
the Vocational Education Act of 1963 (20 U.S.C. 1262(a)(4)
(B)), under which there is specific authority for the provision of
assistance for the education of handicapped children, will be
utilized by the State, or any of its political subdivisions, only in a
manner consistent with the goal of providing a free appropriate
public education for all handicapped children, except that nothing
in this clause shall be construed to limit the specific requirements
of the laws governing such Federal programs;
    "(3) set forth, consistent with the purposes of this Act, a
description of programs and procedures for (A) the development and implementation of a comprehensive system of personnel
development which shall include the inservice training of general
and special educational instructional and support personnel,
detailed procedures to assure that all personnel necessary to carry
out the purposes of this Act are appropriately and adequately
prepared and trained, and effective procedures for acquiring and
disseminating to teachers and administrators of programs for
handicapped children significant information derived from educational research, demonstration, and similar projects, and (B)
adopting, where appropriate, promising educational practices
and materials development through such projects;
    "(4) set forth policies and procedures to assure—
        "(A) that, to the extent consistent with the number and
    location of handicapped children in the State who are enrolled
    in private elementary and secondary schools, provision
    is made for the participation of such children in the program
    assisted or carried out under this part by providing for such
    children special education and related services; and

89 STAT. 782

"(B) that (i) handicapped children in private schools and facilities will be provided special education and related services (in conformance with an individualized educational program as required by this part) at no cost to their parents or guardian, if such children are placed in or referred to such schools or facilities by the State or appropriate local educational agency as the means of carrying out the requirements of this part or any other applicable law requiring the provision of special education and related services to all handicapped children within such State, and (ii) in all such instances the State educational agency shall determine whether such schools and facilities meet standards that apply to State and local educational agencies and that children so served have all the rights they would have if served by such agencies;

"(5) set forth policies and procedures which assure that the State shall seek to recover any funds made available under this part for services to any child who is determined to be erroneously classified as eligible to be counted under section 611(a) or section 611(d);

"(6) provide satisfactory assurance that the control of funds provided under this part, and title to property derived therefrom, shall be in a public agency for the uses and purposes provided in this part, and that a public agency will administer such funds and property;

"(7) provide for (A) making such reports in such form and containing such information as the Commissioner may require to carry out his functions under this part, and (B) keeping such records and affording such access thereto as the Commissioner may find necessary to assure the correctness and verification of such reports and proper disbursement of Federal funds under this part;　*Reports and records.*

"(8) provide procedures to assure that final action with respect to any application submitted by a local educational agency or an intermediate educational unit shall not be taken without first affording the local educational agency or intermediate educational unit involved reasonable notice and opportunity for a hearing;　*Notice, hearings.*

"(9) provide satisfactory assurance that Federal funds made available under this part (A) will not be commingled with State funds, and (B) will be so used as to supplement and increase the level of State and local funds expended for the education of handicapped children and in no case to supplant such State and local funds, except that, where the State provides clear and convincing evidence that all handicapped children have available to them a free appropriate public education, the Commissioner may waive in part the requirement of this clause if he concurs with the evidence provided by the State;

"(10) provide, consistent with procedures prescribed pursuant to section 617(a)(2), satisfactory assurance that such fiscal control and fund accounting procedures will be adopted as may be necessary to assure proper disbursement of, and accounting for, Federal funds paid under this part to the State, including any such funds paid by the State to local educational agencies and intermediate educational units;

Evaluation.

"(11) provide for procedures for evaluation at least annually of the effectiveness of programs in meeting the educational needs of handicapped children (including evaluation of individualized education programs), in accordance with such criteria that the Commissioner shall prescribe pursuant to section 617; and

State advisory panel.

"(12) provide that the State has an advisory panel, appointed by the Governor or any other official authorized under State law to make such appointments, composed of individuals involved in or concerned with the education of handicapped children, including handicapped individuals, teachers, parents or guardians of handicapped children, State and local education officials, and administrators of programs for handicapped children, which (A) advises the State educational agency of unmet needs within the State in the education of handicapped children, (B) comments publicly on any rules or regulations proposed for issuance by the State regarding the education of handicapped children and the procedures for distribution of funds under this part, and (C) assists the State in developing and reporting such data and evaluations as may assist the Commissioner in the performance of his responsibilities under section 618.

"(b) Whenever a State educational agency provides free appropriate public education for handicapped children, or provides direct services to such children, such State educational agency shall include, as part of the State plan required by subsection (a) of this section, such additional assurances not specified in such subsection (a) as are contained in section 614(a), except that funds available for the provision of such education or services may be expended without regard to the provisions relating to excess costs in section 614(a).

"(c) The Commissioner shall approve any State plan and any modification thereof which—

"(1) is submitted by a State eligible in accordance with section 612; and

"(2) meets the requirements of subsection (a) and subsection (b).

Notice, hearings.

The Commissioner shall disapprove any State plan which does not meet the requirements of the preceding sentence, but shall not finally disapprove a State plan except after reasonable notice and opportunity for a hearing to the State.

"APPLICATION

20 USC 1414.

"SEC. 614. (a) A local educational agency or an intermediate educational unit which desires to receive payments under section 611(d) for any fiscal year shall submit an application to the appropriate State educational agency. Such application shall—

"(1) provide satisfactory assurance that payments under this part will be used for excess costs directly attributable to programs which—

"(A) provide that all children residing within the jurisdiction of the local educational agency or the intermediate educational unit who are handicapped, regardless of the severity of their handicap, and are in need of special education and related services will be identified, located, and evaluated, and provide for the inclusion of a practical method of determining which children are currently receiving needed special education and related services and which children are not currently receiving such education and services;

"(B) establish policies and procedures in accordance with detailed criteria prescribed under section 617(c);

"(C) establish a goal of providing full educational opportunities to all handicapped children, including—

"(i) procedures for the implementation and use of the comprehensive system of personnel development established by the State educational agency under section 613(a)(3);

"(ii) the provision of, and the establishment of priorities for providing, a free appropriate public education to all handicapped children, first with respect to handicapped children who are not receiving an education, and second with respect to handicapped children, within each disability, with the most severe handicaps who are receiving an inadequate education;

"(iii) the participation and consultation of the parents or guardian of such children; and

"(iv) to the maximum extent practicable and consistent with the provisions of section 612(5)(B), the provision of special services to enable such children to participate in regular educational programs;

"(D) establish a detailed timetable for accomplishing the goal described in subclause (C); and

"(E) provide a description of the kind and number of facilities, personnel, and services necessary to meet the goal described in subclause (C);

"(2) provide satisfactory assurance that (A) the control of funds provided under this part, and title to property derived from such funds, shall be in a public agency for the uses and purposes provided in this part, and that a public agency will administer such funds and property, (B) Federal funds expended by local educational agencies and intermediate educational units for programs under this part (i) shall be used to pay only the excess costs directly attributable to the education of handicapped children, and (ii) shall be used to supplement and, to the extent practicable, increase the level of State and local funds expended for the education of handicapped children, and in no case to supplant such State and local funds, and (C) State and local funds will be used in the jurisdiction of the local educational agency or intermediate educational unit to provide services in program areas which, taken as a whole, are at least comparable to services being provided in areas of such jurisdiction which are not receiving funds under this part;

"(3)(A) provide for furnishing such information (which, in the case of reports relating to performance, is in accordance with specific performance criteria related to program objectives), as may be necessary to enable the State educational agency to perform its duties under this part, including information relating to the educational achievement of handicapped children participating in programs carried out under this part; and

"(B) provide for keeping such records, and provide for affording such access to such records, as the State educational agency may find necessary to assure the correctness and verification of such information furnished under subclause (A); **Recordkeeping.**

"(4) provide for making the application and all pertinent documents related to such application available to parents, guardians, and other members of the general public, and provide that all evaluations and reports required under clause (3) shall be public information; **Public information, availability.**

"(5) provide assurances that the local educational agency or intermediate educational unit will establish, or revise, whichever is appropriate, an individualized education program for each handicapped child at the beginning of each school year and will then review and, if appropriate revise, its provisions periodically, but not less than annually;

"(6) provide satisfactory assurance that policies and programs established and administered by the local educational agency or intermediate educational unit shall be consistent with the provisions of paragraph (1) through paragraph (7) of section 612 and section 613 (a); and

"(7) provide satisfactory assurance that the local educational agency or intermediate educational unit will establish and maintain procedural safeguards in accordance with the provisions of sections 612(5) (B), 612(5) (C), and 615.

Application approval. "(b) (1) A State educational agency shall approve any application submitted by a local educational agency or an intermediate educational unit under subsection (a) if the State educational agency determines that such application meets the requirements of subsection (a), except that no such application may be approved until the State plan submitted by such State educational agency under subsection (a) is approved by the Commissioner under section 613(c). A State educational agency shall disapprove any application submitted by a local educational agency or an intermediate educational unit under subsection (a) if the State educational agency determines that such application does not meet the requirements of subsection (a).

Notice, hearing. "(2) (A) Whenever a State educational agency, after reasonable notice and opportunity for a hearing, finds that a local educational agency or an intermediate educational unit, in the administration of an application approved by the State educational agency under paragraph (1), has failed to comply with any requirement set forth in such application, the State educational agency, after giving appropriate notice to the local educational agency or the intermediate educational unit, shall—

"(i) make no further payments to such local educational agency or intermediate educational unit under section 620 until the State educational agency is satisfied that there is no longer any failure to comply with the requirement involved; or

"(ii) take such finding into account in its review of any application made by such local educational agency or such intermediate educational unit under subsection (a).

"(B) The provisions of the last sentence of section 616(a) shall apply to any local educational agency or any intermediate educational unit receiving any notification from a State educational agency under this paragraph.

"(3) In carrying out its functions under paragraph (1), each State educational agency shall consider any decision made pursuant to a hearing held under section 615 which is adverse to the local educational agency or intermediate educational unit involved in such decision.

"(c) (1) A State educational agency may, for purposes of the consideration and approval of applications under this section, require local educational agencies to submit a consolidated application for payments if such State educational agency determines that any individual application submitted by any such local educational agency will be disapproved because such local educational agency is ineligible to receive payments because of the application of section 611(c)(4)(A)(i) or such local educational agency would be unable to establish and maintain programs of sufficient size and scope to effectively meet the educational needs of handicapped children.

"(2)(A) In any case in which a consolidated application of local educational agencies is approved by a State educational agency under paragraph (1), the payments which such local educational agencies may receive shall be equal to the sum of payments to which each such local educational agency would be entitled under section 611(d) if an individual application of any such local educational agency had been approved.

"(B) The State educational agency shall prescribe rules and regulations with respect to consolidated applications submitted under this subsection which are consistent with the provisions of paragraph (1) through paragraph (7) of section 612 and section 613(a) and which provide participating local educational agencies with joint responsibilities for implementing programs receiving payments under this part. **Rules and regulations.**

"(C) In any case in which an intermediate educational unit is required pursuant to State law to carry out the provisions of this part, the joint responsibilities given to local educational agencies under subparagraph (B) shall not apply to the administration and disbursement of any payments received by such intermediate educational unit. Such responsibilities shall be carried out exclusively by such intermediate educational unit.

"(d) Whenever a State educational agency determines that a local educational agency—

"(1) is unable or unwilling to establish and maintain programs of free appropriate public education which meet the requirements established in subsection (a);

"(2) is unable or unwilling to be consolidated with other local educational agencies in order to establish and maintain such programs; or

"(3) has one or more handicapped children who can best be served by a regional or State center designed to meet the needs of such children;

the State educational agency shall use the payments which would have been available to such local educational agency to provide special education and related services directly to handicapped children residing in the area served by such local educational agency. The State educational agency may provide such education and services in such manner, and at such locations (including regional or State centers), as it considers appropriate, except that the manner in which such education and services are provided shall be consistent with the requirements of this part.

"(e) Whenever a State educational agency determines that a local educational agency is adequately providing a free appropriate public education to all handicapped children residing in the area served by such agency with State and local funds otherwise available to such agency, the State educational agency may reallocate funds (or such portion of those funds as may not be required to provide such education and services) made available to such agency, pursuant to section 611(d), to such other local educational agencies within the State as are not adequately providing special education and related services to all handicapped children residing in the areas served by such other local educational agencies. **Funds, reallocation.**

"(f) Notwithstanding the provisions of subsection (a)(2)(B)(ii), any local educational agency which is required to carry out any program for the education of handicapped children pursuant to a State law shall be entitled to receive payments under section 611(d) for use in carrying out such program, except that such payments may not be used to reduce the level of expenditures for such program made by such local educational agency from State or local funds below the level of such expenditures for the fiscal year prior to the fiscal year for which such local educational agency seeks such payments.

"PROCEDURAL SAFEGUARDS

20 USC 1415.

"SEC. 615. (a) Any State educational agency, any local educational agency, and any intermediate educational unit which receives assistance under this part shall establish and maintain procedures in accordance with subsection (b) through subsection (e) of this section to assure that handicapped children and their parents or guardians are guaranteed procedural safeguards with respect to the provision of free appropriate public education by such agencies and units.

"(b)(1) The procedures required by this section shall include, but shall not be limited to—

"(A) an opportunity for the parents or guardian of a handicapped child to examine all relevant records with respect to the identification, evaluation, and educational placement of the child, and the provision of a free appropriate public education to such child, and to obtain an independent educational evaluation of the child;

"(B) procedures to protect the rights of the child whenever the parents or guardian of the child are not known, unavailable, or the child is a ward of the State, including the assignment of an individual (who shall not be an employee of the State educational agency, local educational agency, or intermediate educational unit involved in the education or care of the child) to act as a surrogate for the parents or guardian;

"(C) written prior notice to the parents or guardian of the child whenever such agency or unit—

"(i) proposes to initiate or change, or

"(ii) refuses to initiate or change,

the identification, evaluation, or educational placement of the child or the provision of a free appropriate public education to the child;

"(D) procedures designed to assure that the notice required by clause (C) fully inform the parents or guardian, in the parents' or guardian's native language, unless it clearly is not feasible to do so, of all procedures available pursuant to this section; and

"(E) an opportunity to present complaints with respect to any matter relating to the identification, evaluation, or educational placement of the child, or the provision of a free appropriate public education to such child.

Hearing.

"(2) Whenever a complaint has been received under paragraph (1) of this subsection, the parents or guardian shall have an opportunity for an impartial due process hearing which shall be conducted by the State educational agency or by the local educational agency or intermediate educational unit, as determined by State law or by the State educational agency. No hearing conducted pursuant to the requirements of this paragraph shall be conducted by an employee of such agency or unit involved in the education or care of the child.

"(c) If the hearing required in paragraph (2) of subsection (b) of this section is conducted by a local educational agency or an intermediate educational unit, any party aggrieved by the findings and decision rendered in such a hearing may appeal to the State educational agency which shall conduct an impartial review of such hearing. The officer conducting such review shall make an independent decision upon completion of such review.

"(d) Any party to any hearing conducted pursuant to subsections (b) and (c) shall be accorded (1) the right to be accompanied and advised by counsel and by individuals with special knowledge or training with respect to the problems of handicapped children, (2) the right to present evidence and confront, cross-examine, and compel the attendance of witnesses, (3) the right to a written or electronic verbatim record of such hearing, and (4) the right to written findings of fact and decisions (which findings and decisions shall also be transmitted to the advisory panel established pursuant to section 613(a)(12)).

"(e)(1) A decision made in a hearing conducted pursuant to paragraph (2) of subsection (b) shall be final, except that any party involved in such hearing may appeal such decision under the provisions of subsection (c) and paragraph (2) of this subsection. A decision made under subsection (c) shall be final, except that any party may bring an action under paragraph (2) of this subsection.

"(2) Any party aggrieved by the findings and decision made under subsection (b) who does not have the right to an appeal under subsection (c), and any party aggrieved by the findings and decision under subsection (c), shall have the right to bring a civil action with respect to the complaint presented pursuant to this section, which action may be brought in any State court of competent jurisdiction or in a district court of the United States without regard to the amount in controversy. In any action brought under this paragraph the court shall receive the records of the administrative proceedings, shall hear additional evidence at the request of a party, and, basing its decision on the preponderance of the evidence, shall grant such relief as the court determines is appropriate. *Civil action.*

"(3) During the pendency of any proceedings conducted pursuant to this section, unless the State or local educational agency and the parents or guardian otherwise agree, the child shall remain in the then current educational placement of such child, or, if applying for initial admission to a public school, shall, with the consent of the parents or guardian, be placed in the public school program until all such proceedings have been completed.

"(4) The district courts of the United States shall have jurisdiction of actions brought under this subsection without regard to the amount in controversy. *District courts jurisdiction.*

"WITHHOLDING AND JUDICIAL REVIEW

"SEC. 616. (a) Whenever the Commissioner, after reasonable notice and opportunity for hearing to the State educational agency involved (and to any local educational agency or intermediate educational unit affected by any failure described in clause (2)), finds— *Notice, hearing. 20 USC 1416.*

"(1) that there has been a failure to comply substantially with any provision of section 612 or section 613, or

"(2) that in the administration of the State plan there is a failure to comply with any provision of this part or with any requirements set forth in the application of a local educational agency or intermediate educational unit approved by the State educational agency pursuant to the State plan,

the Commissioner (A) shall, after notifying the State educational agency, withhold any further payments to the State under this part, and (B) may, after notifying the State educational agency, withhold further payments to the State under the Federal programs specified in section 613(a)(2) within his jurisdiction, to the extent that funds under such programs are available for the provision of assistance for the education of handicapped children. If the Commissioner withholds further payments under clause (A) or clause (B) he may determine that such withholding will be limited to programs or projects under the State plan, or portions thereof, affected by the failure, or that the State educational agency shall not make further payments under this part to specified local educational agencies or intermediate educational units affected by the failure. Until the Commissioner is satisfied that there is no longer any failure to comply with the provisions of this part, as specified in clause (1) or clause (2), no further payments shall be made to the State under this part or under the Federal programs specified in section 613(a)(2) within his jurisdiction to the extent that funds under such programs are available for the provision of assistance for the education of handicapped children, or payments by the State educational agency under this part shall be limited to local educational agencies and intermediate educational units whose actions did not cause or were not involved in the failure, as the case may be. Any State educational agency, local educational agency, or intermediate educational unit in receipt of a notice pursuant to the first sentence of this subsection shall, by means of a public notice, take such measures as may be necessary to bring the pendency of an action pursuant to this subsection to the attention of the public within the jurisdiction of such agency or unit.

Petition for review.

"(b)(1) If any State is dissatisfied with the Commissioner's final action with respect to its State plan submitted under section 613, such State may, within sixty days after notice of such action, file with the United States court of appeals for the circuit in which such State is located a petition for review of that action. A copy of the petition shall be forthwith transmitted by the clerk of the court to the Commissioner. The Commissioner thereupon shall file in the court the record of the proceedings on which he based his action, as provided in section 2112 of title 28, United States Code.

"(2) The findings of fact by the Commissioner, if supported by substantial evidence, shall be conclusive; but the court, for good cause shown, may remand the case to the Commissioner to take further evidence, and the Commissioner may thereupon make new or modified findings of fact and may modify his previous action, and shall file in the court the record of the further proceedings. Such new or modified findings of fact shall likewise be conclusive if supported by substantial evidence.

"(3) Upon the filing of such petition, the court shall have jurisdiction to affirm the action of the Commissioner or to set it aside, in whole or in part. The judgment of the court shall be subject to review by the Supreme Court of the United States upon certiorari or certification as provided in section 1254 of title 28, United States Code.

"ADMINISTRATION

"SEC. 617. (a)(1) In carrying out his duties under this part, the   20 USC 1417.
Commissioner shall—

"(A) cooperate with, and furnish all technical assistance necessary, directly or by grant or contract, to the States in matters
relating to the education of handicapped children and the execu-
tion of the provisions of this part;

"(B) provide such short-term training programs and institutes
as are necessary;

"(C) disseminate information, and otherwise promote the education of all handicapped children within the States; and

"(D) assure that each State shall, within one year after the date
of the enactment of the Education for All Handicapped Children
Act of 1975, provide certification of the actual number of handicapped children receiving special education and related services
in such State.

"(2) As soon as practicable after the date of the enactment of the   Regulations.
Education for All Handicapped Children Act of 1975, the Commissioner shall, by regulation, prescribe a uniform financial report to be
utilized by State educational agencies in submitting State plans under
this part in order to assure equity among the States.

"(b) In carrying out the provisions of this part, the Commissioner
(and the Secretary, in carrying out the provisions of subsection (c))
shall issue, not later than January 1, 1977, amend, and revoke such
rules and regulations as may be necessary. No other less formal method
of implementing such provisions is authorized.

"(c) The Secretary shall take appropriate action, in accordance
with the provisions of section 438 of the General Education Provisions
Act, to assure the protection of the confidentiality of any personally   20 USC 1232g.
identifiable data, information, and records collected or maintained by
the Commissioner and by State and local educational agencies pursuant
to the provisions of this part.

"(d) The Commissioner is authorized to hire qualified personnel
necessary to conduct data collection and evaluation activities required
by subsections (b), (c) and (d) of section 618 and to carry out his
duties under subsection (a)(1) of this subsection without regard to
the provisions of title 5, United States Code, relating to appointments
in the competitive service and without regard to chapter 51 and sub-
chapter III of chapter 53 of such title relating to classification and   5 USC 5101,
general schedule pay rates except that no more than twenty such   5331.
personnel shall be employed at any time.

"EVALUATION

"SEC. 618. (a) The Commissioner shall measure and evaluate the   20 USC 1418.
impact of the program authorized under this part and the effectiveness
of State efforts to assure the free appropriate public education of all
handicapped children.

"(b) The Commissioner shall conduct, directly or by grant or contract, such studies, investigations, and evaluations as are necessary to
assure effective implementation of this part. In carrying out his
responsibilities under this section, the Commissioner shall—

"(1) through the National Center for Education Statistics,
provide to the appropriate committees of each House of the Congress and to the general public at least annually, and shall update
at least annually, programmatic information concerning programs
and projects assisted under this part and other Federal programs

supporting the education of handicapped children, and such information from State and local educational agencies and other appropriate sources necessary for the implementation of this part, including—

"(A) the number of handicapped children in each State, within each disability, who require special education and related services;

"(B) the number of handicapped children in each State, within each disability, receiving a free appropriate public education and the number of handicapped children who need and are not receiving a free appropriate public education in each such State;

"(C) the number of handicapped children in each State, within each disability, who are participating in regular educational programs, consistent with the requirements of section 612(5)(B) and section 614(a)(1)(C)(iv), and the number of handicapped children who have been placed in separate classes or separate school facilities, or who have been otherwise removed from the regular education environment;

"(D) the number of handicapped children who are enrolled in public or private institutions in each State and who are receiving a free appropriate public education, and the number of handicapped children who are in such institutions and who are not receiving a free appropriate public education;

"(E) the amount of Federal, State, and local expenditures in each State specifically available for special education and related services; and

"(F) the number of personnel, by disability category, employed in the education of handicapped children, and the estimated number of additional personnel needed to adequately carry out the policy established by this Act; and

"(2) provide for the evaluation of programs and projects assisted under this part through—

"(A) the development of effective methods and procedures for evaluation;

"(B) the testing and validation of such evaluation methods and procedures; and

"(C) conducting actual evaluation studies designed to test the effectiveness of such programs and projects.

"(c) In developing and furnishing information under subclause (E) of clause (1) of subsection (b), the Commissioner may base such information upon a sampling of data available from State agencies, including the State educational agencies, and local educational agencies.

Report, transmittal to congressional committees.

"(d)(1) Not later than one hundred twenty days after the close of each fiscal year, the Commissioner shall transmit to the appropriate committees of each House of the Congress a report on the progress being made toward the provision of free appropriate public education to all handicapped children, including a detailed description of all evaluation activities conducted under subsection (b).

Contents.

"(2) The Commissioner shall include in each such report—

"(A) an analysis and evaluation of the effectiveness of procedures undertaken by each State educational agency, local educational agency, and intermediate educational unit to assure that handicapped children receive special education and related services in the least restrictive environment commensurate with their needs and to improve programs of instruction for handicapped children in day or residential facilities;

"(B) any recommendations for change in the provisions of this part, or any other Federal law providing support for the education of handicapped children; and

"(C) an evaluation of the effectiveness of the procedures undertaken by each such agency or unit to prevent erroneous classification of children as eligible to be counted under section 611, including actions undertaken by the Commissioner to carry out provisions of this Act relating to such erroneous classification.

In order to carry out such analyses and evaluations, the Commissioner shall conduct a statistically valid survey for assessing the effectiveness of individualized educational programs.

"(e) There are authorized to be appropriated for each fiscal year such sums as may be necessary to carry out the provisions of this section.

Appropriation authorization.

"INCENTIVE GRANTS

"SEC. 619. (a) The Commissioner shall make a grant to any State which—

20 USC 1419.

"(1) has met the eligibility requirements of section 612;

"(2) has a State plan approved under section 613; and

"(3) provides special education and related services to handicapped children aged three to five, inclusive, who are counted for the purposes of section 611(a)(1)(A).

The maximum amount of the grant for each fiscal year which a State may receive under this section shall be $300 for each such child in that State.

"(b) Each State which—

"(1) has met the eligibility requirements of section 612,

"(2) has a State plan approved under section 613, and

"(3) desires to receive a grant under this section,

shall make an application to the Commissioner at such time, in such manner, and containing or accompanied by such information, as the Commissioner may reasonably require.

"(c) The Commissioner shall pay to each State having an application approved under subsection (b) of this section the amount to which the State is entitled under this section, which amount shall be used for the purpose of providing the services specified in clause (3) of subsection (a) of this section.

"(d) If the sums appropriated for any fiscal year for making payments to States under this section are not sufficient to pay in full the maximum amounts which all States may receive under this part for such fiscal year, the maximum amounts which all States may receive under this part for such fiscal year shall be ratably reduced. In case additional funds become available for making such payments for any fiscal year during which the preceding sentence is applicable, such reduced amounts shall be increased on the same basis as they were reduced.

"(e) In addition to the sums necessary to pay the entitlements under section 611, there are authorized to be appropriated for each fiscal year such sums as may be necessary to carry out the provisions of this section.

Appropriation authorization.

"PAYMENTS

"SEC. 620. (a) The Commissioner shall make payments to each State in amounts which the State educational agency of such State is eligible to receive under this part. Any State educational agency receiving payments under this subsection shall distribute payments

20 USC 1420.

to the local educational agencies and intermediate educational units of such State in amounts which such agencies and units are eligible to receive under this part after the State educational agency has approved applications of such agencies or units for payments in accordance with section 614(b).

"(b) Payments under this part may be made in advance or by way of reimbursement and in such installments as the Commissioner may determine necessary.".

Regulations.
20 USC 1411
note.

(b)(1) The Commissioner of Education shall, no later than one year after the effective date of this subsection, prescribe—

(A) regulations which establish specific criteria for determining whether a particular disorder or condition may be considered a specific learning disability for purposes of designating children with specific learning disabilities;

(B) regulations which establish and describe diagnostic procedures which shall be used in determining whether a particular child has a disorder or condition which places such child in the category of children with specific learning disabilities; and

(C) regulations which establish monitoring procedures which will be used to determine if State educational agencies, local educational agencies, and intermediate educational units are complying with the criteria established under clause (A) and clause (B).

Proposed
regulation,
submittal to
congressional
committees.
Publication in
Federal
Register.

(2) The Commissioner shall submit any proposed regulation written under paragraph (1) to the Committee on Education and Labor of the House of Representatives and the Committee on Labor and Public Welfare of the Senate, for review and comment by each such committee, at least fifteen days before such regulation is published in the Federal Register.

20 USC 402.

(3) If the Commissioner determines, as a result of the promulgation of regulations under paragraph (1), that changes are necessary in the definition of the term "children with specific learning disabilities", as such term is defined by section 602(15) of the Act, he shall submit recommendations for legislation with respect to such changes to each House of the Congress.

Definitions.

(4) For purposes of this subsection:

(A) The term "children with specific learning disabilities" means those children who have a disorder in one or more of the basic psychological processes involved in understanding or in using language, spoken or written, which disorder may manifest itself in imperfect ability to listen, think, speak, read, write, spell, or do mathematical calculations. Such disorders include such conditions as perceptual handicaps, brain injury, minimal brain dysfunction, dyslexia, and developmental aphasia. Such term does not include children who have learning problems which are primarily the result of visual, hearing, or motor handicaps, of mental retardation, of emotional disturbance, or environmental, cultural, or economic disadvantage.

(B) The term "Commissioner" means the Commissioner of Education.

20 USC 1411.

(c) Effective on the date upon which final regulations prescribed by the Commissioner of Education under subsection (b) take effect, the amendment made by subsection (a) is amended, in subparagraph (A) of section 611(a)(5) (as such subparagraph would take effect on the effective date of subsection (a)), by adding "and" at the end of clause (i), by striking out clause (ii), and by redesignating clause (iii) as clause (ii).

AMENDMENTS WITH RESPECT TO EMPLOYMENT OF HANDICAPPED INDIVID-
UALS, REMOVAL OF ARCHITECTURAL BARRIERS, AND MEDIA CENTERS

SEC. 6. (a) Part A of the Act is amended by inserting after section 20 USC 1404.
605 thereof the following new sections:

"EMPLOYMENT OF HANDICAPPED INDIVIDUALS

"SEC. 606. The Secretary shall assure that each recipient of assist- 20 USC 1405.
ance under this Act shall make positive efforts to employ and advance
in employment qualified handicapped individuals in programs assisted
under this Act.

"GRANTS FOR THE REMOVAL OF ARCHITECTURAL BARRIERS

"SEC. 607. (a) Upon application by any State or local educational 20 USC 1406.
agency or intermediate educational unit the Commissioner is authorized to make grants to pay part or all of the cost of altering existing
buildings and equipment in the same manner and to the same extent
as authorized by the Act approved August 12, 1968 (Public Law
90-480), relating to architectural barriers.

"(b) For the purpose of carrying out the provisions of this section, Appropriation
there are authorized to be appropriated such sums as may be authorization.
necessary.".

`(b) Section 653 of the Act (20 U.S.C. 1453) is amended to read
as follows:

"CENTERS ON EDUCATIONAL MEDIA AND MATERIALS FOR THE HANDICAPPED

"SEC. 653. (a) The Secretary is authorized to enter into agreements
with institutions of higher education, State and local educational
agencies, or other appropriate nonprofit agencies, for the establishment and operation of centers on educational media and materials
for the handicapped, which together will provide a comprehensive
program of activities to facilitate the use of new educational technology in education programs for handicapped persons, including
designing, developing, and adapting instructional materials, and such
other activities consistent with the purposes of this part as the Secretary may prescribe in such agreements. Any such agreement shall—
　　"(1) provide that Federal funds paid to a center will be used
　solely for such purposes as are set forth in the agreement; and
　　"(2) authorize the center involved, subject to prior approval
　by the Secretary, to contract with public and private agencies and
　organizations for demonstration projects.
"(b) In considering proposals to enter into agreements under this
section, the Secretary shall give preference to institutions and
agencies—
　　"(1) which have demonstrated the capabilities necessary for the
　development and evaluation of educational media for the handi-
　capped; and
　　"(2) which can serve the educational technology needs of the
　Model High School for the Deaf (established under Public Law
　89-694).   80 Stat. 1027.
"(c) The Secretary shall make an annual report on activities carried Report to
out under this section which shall be transmitted to the Congress.".   Congress.

CONGRESSIONAL DISAPPROVAL OF REGULATIONS

SEC. 7. (a)(1) Section 431(d)(1) of the General Education Provisions Act (20 U.S.C. 1232(d)(1)) is amended by inserting "final" immediately before "standard" each place it appears therein.

(2) The third sentence of section 431(d)(2) of such Act (20 U.S.C. 1232(d)(2)) is amended by striking out "proposed" and inserting in lieu thereof "final".

(3) The fourth and last sentences of section 431(d)(2) of such Act (20 U.S.C. 1232(d)(2)) each are amended by inserting "final" immediately before "standard".

(b) Section 431(d)(1) of the General Education Provisions Act (20 U.S.C. 1232(d)(1)) is amended by adding at the end thereof the following new sentence: "Failure of the Congress to adopt such a concurrent resolution with respect to any such final standard, rule, regulation, or requirement prescribed under any such Act, shall not represent, with respect to such final standard, rule, regulation, or requirement, an approval or finding of consistency with the Act from which it derives its authority for any purpose, nor shall such failure to adopt a concurrent resolution be construed as evidence of an approval or finding of consistency necessary to establish a prima facie case, or an inference or presumption, in any judicial proceeding.".

EFFECTIVE DATES

20 USC 1411
note.

SEC. 8. (a) Notwithstanding any other provision of law, the amendments made by sections 2(a), 2(b), and 2(c) shall take effect on July 1, 1975.

(b) The amendments made by sections 2(d), 2(e), 3, 6, and 7 shall take effect on the date of the enactment of this Act.

(c) The amendments made by sections 4 and 5(a) shall take effect on October 1, 1977, except that the provisions of clauses (A), (C), (D), and (E) of paragraph (2) of section 612 of the Act, as amended by this Act, section 617(a)(1)(D) of the Act, as amended by this Act, section 617(b) of the Act, as amended by this Act, and section 618(a) of the Act, as amended by this Act, shall take effect on the date of the enactment of this Act.

(d) The provisions of section 5(b) shall take effect on the date of the enactment of this Act.

Approved November 29, 1975.

LEGISLATIVE HISTORY:

HOUSE REPORTS: No. 94-332 accompanying H.R. 7217 (Comm. on Education and Labor) and 94-664 (Comm. of Conference).
SENATE REPORTS: No. 94-168 (Comm. on Labor and Public Welfare) and No. 94-455 (Comm. of Conference).
CONGRESSIONAL RECORD, Vol. 121 (1975):
        June 18, considered and passed Senate.
        July 21, 29, considered and passed House, amended, in lieu of H.R. 7217.
        Nov. 18, House agreed to conference report.
        Nov. 19, Senate agreed to conference report.
WEEKLY COMPILATION OF PRESIDENTIAL DOCUMENTS, Vol. 11. No. 49:
        Dec. 2, Presidential statement.

APPENDIX B

Sample Format of Basic
Multi-Year Individual
Education Program (IEP)

Student Name: _____

Date of Birth: _____ Date of IEP Conference: _____

Persons Present:

Name	Title
_____	Teacher
_____	Principal
_____	Supervisor (Director) Special Education
_____	Parent
_____	Parent
_____	Student
_____	
_____	
_____	

Special Education Program(s) Required: _____

Annual Reviews:

School Year 19 _____ – 19 _____   Conference Date: _____

Persons Present:

Parent: _____   Teacher: _____

Others: _____   Others: _____

_____   _____

_____   _____

School Year 19 _____ – 19 _____   Conference Date: _____

Persons Present:

Parent: _____   Teacher: _____

Others: _____   Others: _____

_____   _____

_____   _____

School Year 19 _____ – 19 _____   Conference Date: _____

Persons Present:

Parent: _____   Teacher: _____

Others: _____   Others: _____

_____   _____

_____   _____

School Year 19 _____ – 19 _____   Conference Date: _____

Persons Present:

Parent: _____   Teacher: _____

Others: _____   Others: _____

_____   _____

_____   _____

I. Present Levels of Educational Performance:

A. Academic: _____

_____

_____

_____

_____

B. Behavioral: _____

_____

_____

_____

_____

C. Social: _____

_____

_____

_____

_____

D. Emotional: _____

_____

_____

_____

_____

E. Vocational: _____

_____

_____

_____

_____

II. Goals:

    A. ( ) regular education
       ( ) special education _____

      _____

      _____

    B. ( ) regular education
       ( ) special education _____

      _____

      _____

    C. ( ) regular education
       ( ) special education _____

      _____

      _____

    D. ( ) regular education
       ( ) special education _____

      _____

      _____

    E. ( ) regular education
       ( ) special education _____

      _____

      _____

III. Supportive/Related Services Goals:

    A. _____

    B. _____

    C. _____

    Full Time Equivalency Ratio: _____% regular education

                                      _____% special education

IV. Instructional Objectives:

A. _____
_____
_____

Anticipated Duration _____ Level of Mastery _____%

Responsible Personnel _____

Date Completed _____ Objective Attained _____ Yes

_____ No

B. _____
_____
_____

Anticipated Duration _____ Level of Mastery _____%

Responsible Personnel _____

Date Completed _____ Objective Attained _____ Yes

_____ No

C. _____
_____
_____

Anticipated Duration _____ Level of Mastery _____%

Responsible Personnel _____

Date Completed _____ Objective Attained _____ Yes

_____ No

D. _____
_____
_____

Anticipated Duration _____ Level of Mastery _____%

Responsible Personnel _____

Date Completed _____ Objective Attained _____ Yes

_____ No

E. _____

_____

_____

Anticipated Duration _____ Level of Mastery _____%

Responsible Personnel _____

Date Completed _____ Objective Attained _____ Yes

_____ No

V. Other: _____

_____

_____

_____

_____

_____

_____

_____

_____

_____

(Note: Include in Section V such things as school/parent communication record; necessary follow-up consultation, etc.)

APPENDIX B
Sample Format of Multi-Year
Individual Education Program (IEP)

Student Name: _____

Primary Handicap: _____

Original Date of IEP Development _____

Date of Birth: _____

Secondary Handicapping Conditions: _____

Percent of Time in Regular Program: _____

Individuals Present:

Teacher _____

Other School Representative — Title _____

Parent(s) _____

Child _____

Others _____　Title

Others _____　Title

I. Present Levels of Performance:

A. Language Arts _____

B. Mathematics _____

C. Social Studies _____

D. Vocational _____

E. Physical Education _____

F. Social/Emotional _____

II. Goal

Instructional Objective(s)	Evaluation Criteria	Date Initiated	Date Attained
A. 1. 2. 3. 4. Individual(s) Responsible:	1. 2. 3. 4.	1. 2. 3. 4.	1. 2. 3. 4.
B. 1. 2. 3. 4. Individual(s) Responsible:	1. 2. 3. 4.	1. 2. 3. 4.	1. 2. 3. 4.
C. 1. 2. 3. 4. Individual(s) Responsible:	1. 2. 3. 4.	1. 2. 3. 4.	1. 2. 3. 4.
D. 1. 2. 3. 4. Individual(s) Responsible:	1. 2. 3. 4.	1. 2. 3. 4.	1. 2. 3. 4.

III. Review and Revision

A. School Year 19 _____ – 19 _____   Conference Date _____
   Parent _____   Child _____
   Others _____
   Comments _____   Teacher _____

B. School Year 19 _____ – 19 _____   Conference Date _____
   Parent _____   Child _____
   Others _____
   Comments _____   Teacher _____

C. School Year 19 _____ – 19 _____   Conference Date _____
   Parent _____   Child _____
   Others _____
   Comments _____   Teacher _____

D. School Year 19 _____ – 19 _____   Conference Date _____
   Parent _____   Child _____
   Others _____
   Comments _____   Teacher _____

IV. Other Information

APPENDIX C

INDIVIDUALIZED EDUCATION PROGRAMS (IEPs)

Part B,
Education of the Handicapped Act,
As Amended by P. L. 94–142

OSE POLICY PAPER

U.S. Education Department
Assistant Secretary for Special Education
and
Rehabilitation Services
Office of Special Education

CONTENTS

INDIVIDUALIZED EDUCATION PROGRAMS (IEPs)

Restatement & Interpretation of Requirements Under Part B of the EHA, As Amended by P.L. 94–142

I. Introduction

A. *Background.* During the Fall of 1979, the Bureau of Education for the Handicapped (BEH) (Now called the Office of Special Education (OSE)) prepared a draft policy clarification paper on the IEP requirement under P.L. 94–142. The paper was written to respond to policy issues and concerns which had been raised during the first two years of implementing the regulations under P. L. 94–142. Many of the issues were raised during a series of public input meetings on the law conducted during the summer of 1979.

The nearly 500 participants who attended these public input meetings included national representatives and their State and regional counterparts from 60 National associations interested in the education of handicapped children. Four main categories of participants attended these meetings, including (1) parents and advocates, (2) teachers, (3) regular and special education administrators, and (4) related services providers.

During August and September, input papers were submitted by individual members of BEH's Ad Hoc Task Force on IEPs. These papers, together with the comments received during the public input meetings, served as the basis for the draft paper.

The draft paper was disseminated in November, 1979 to State educational agencies and to all of the participants who attended the public input meetings. Nearly one hundred written comments were received on the draft paper, including letters from persons in all of the above categories of participants. All of the letters were reviewed and considered by BEH in preparing this final draft policy paper.

B. *Purpose & Overview of the Paper.* A major purpose of this paper is to clarify what requirements must be met in order for public agencies to be in compliance with the IEP provisions in the Act and regulations.

Experience gained over the past two years in administering P.L. 94–142 indicates that some of the wording in the law and regulations has been interpreted in many different ways by individual agencies at the State and local level. In addition, a number of new implementation questions have been raised regarding the IEP requirements, which were not addressed in the final regulations. Given these new questions, and the fact that the existing IEP provisions are being interpreted differently by individual agencies, the Office of Special

Education feels that it is appropriate at this time to: (1) restate the basic Federal requirements, (2) provide clarification on any specific requirement where experience indicates that a more precise interpretation is needed, and (3) answer some of the major new implementation questions that have been raised.

Part II of this paper sets out the major purposes and functions of the IEP requirement for Federal compliance purposes. Part III is essentially a restatement of the regulations on IEPs (§§121a.340–121a.349), together with additional clarifying information.

C. *Effect of policy paper.* This policy clarification paper provides two basic kinds of information: (1) the essential IEP requirements that must be met in order for public agencies to be in compliance with the Act and regulations, and (2) suggestions and guidelines for use by agencies in implementing some of the key requirements.

In effect, the paper is an extension of the final regulations under P.L. 94–142. Thus, the interpretations included in the paper will be followed by the Office of Special Education in enforcing compliance with the law.

II.   Purpose of the IEP Requirement

The IEP provision in the Act and regulations has two main parts (A) the IEP meeting(s) - at which parents and school personnel jointly make decisions about a handicapped child's "program," and (B) the IEP document itself - which is a written record of the decisions reached at the meeting. The overall IEP requirement, comprised of these two parts, has a number of purposes and functions, as set out below:

1. The IEP meeting serves as a communication vehicle between parents and school personnel, and enables them, as equal participants, to jointly decide upon what the child's needs are, what will be provided, and what the anticipated outcomes may be.

2. The IEP itself serves as the focal point for resolving any differences between the parents and the school; first through the meeting and second, if necessary, through the procedural protections that are available to the parents.

3. The IEP sets forth in writing a commitment of resources necessary to enable a handicapped child to receive needed special education and related services.

4. The IEP is a management tool that is used to insure that each handicapped child is provided special education and related services appropriate to his/her special learning needs.

5. The IEP is a compliance/monitoring document which may be used by monitoring personnel from each governmental level to determine whether a handicapped child is actually receiving the free appropriate public education agreed to by the parents and the school.

6. The IEP serves as an evaluation device for use in determining the extent of the child's progress toward meeting the projected outcomes. (NOTE: The law does not require that teachers or other school personnel be held accountable if a handicapped child does not achieve the goals and objectives set forth in his/her IEP. See § 121a.349.)

III. IEP Requirements

This part (1) lists the basic IEP requirements in Sections 121a.340–121a.349 of the regulations (Boxed material), (2) provides additional clarifications, as necessary, on any section of the regulations (or paragraph and sub-paragraph of a section) where a more precise interpretation is needed, and (3) answers some of the key implementation questions that have been raised regarding the IEP requirements, which were not addressed in the final regulations. The clarifying information and implementation questions are presented in a question and answer format, and are included immediately after the specific section, paragraph, or sub-paragraph that is being addressed. (*Note:* The questions are numbered separately for each section.)

INDIVIDUALIZED   EDUCATION
PROGRAMS
§ 121a.340   Definition.
    As used in this part, the term "individualized   education   program" means   a   written   statement   for   a handicapped child that is developed and   implemented   in   accordance with §§ 121a.341–121a.349. (20 U.S.C. 1401(19).)

---

§   121a.341   State educational agency responsibility.
    (a) *Public agencies.* The State educational   agency   shall   insure   that each public agency develops and implements   an   individualized   education   program   for   each   of   its handicapped   children.

---

1. *Who is responsible for writing IEPs for a handicapped child served by a public agency other than the SEA or LEA?*

The answer will vary from State to State, depending upon State law, policy, or practice. It also depends, in part, upon which agency initiates the placement and which agency is responsible for the education of the child.

In all States, however, the SEA is ultimately responsible for insuring that each public agency in the State is in compliance with the IEP requirement and the other provisions of P.L. 94–142. (See § 121a.600.) (NOTE: Section 121a.2 states that the requirements in the Act and regulations apply to all political subdivisions of the State that are involved in the education of handicapped children, including (1) the SEA, (2) LEAs, (3) other State agencies (such as Departments of Mental Health and Welfare, and State schools for the deaf or blind), and (4) State corrections facilities.)

The SEA must insure that every handicapped child in the State receives a free appropriate public education (FAPE) regardless of which agency, State or local, is responsible for the child. While the SEA has flexibility in deciding the best means to accomplish this (e.g., through interagency agreements, etc.), there can be no failure to provide FAPE due to jurisdictional disputes among agencies.

The following paragraphs define (1) some of the SEA's responsibilities for developing policies or agreements under a variety of interagency situations and (2) what some of the responsibilities are for an LEA when it initiates the placement of a handicapped child in a school or program under another State agency:

a. *SEA POLICIES OR INTERAGENCY AGREEMENTS.* The SEA, through its written policies or agreements, must pinpoint who is responsible for writing and implementing IEPs under each interagency situation that is applicable in the State, including any of the following: (1) when an LEA initiates the placement of a child in a school or program under another State agency, (See "LEA Initiated Placements" on page 6.), (2) when another State agency places a child in a residential facility or other program, (3) parent-initiated placements in public institutions, and (4) placements by the courts in corrections facilities. (NOTE: This is not an exhaustive list. The SEA's policies must include any other interagency situation that is applicable in the State; and the policies must cover placements that are made for both educational and non-educational purposes.)

There is often more than one agency involved in writing or implementing a handicapped child's IEP (e.g., when the LEA remains responsible for the child, even though another public agency provides the special education and related services; or when there are shared cost arrangements). It is important that SEA policies or agreements define the role of each agency that is involved in the above situations, in order to offset any jurisdictional problems which might occur that could result in delaying the provision of a free appropriate public education to a handicapped child.

Therefore, for each interagency situation applicable in the State, the SEA must insure (1) that its policies or agreements define the role of any agency that is involved in writing or implementing a handicapped child's IEP (e.g., the child's LEA, the SEA, another State agency, an institution or school under that agency, and the LEA where the institution is located), and (2) that it is clear which agency is responsible for the child's education and for providing (or paying for) the special education and related services to the child.

NOTE: The SEA also must insure that any agency involved in the education of a handicapped child is in compliance with the least restrictive environment provision in the Act and regulations, and specifically the requirement that each handicapped child's placement (a) is determined at least annually, (b) is based on his or her IEP, and (c) is as close as possible to the child's home. (§ 121a.552(a))

b. *LEA INITIATED PLACEMENTS.* When an LEA is responsible for the education of a handicapped child, the LEA is also responsible for writing the child's IEP. The LEA has this responsibility even if development of the IEP results in a placement in a State-operated school or program. Since the IEP must set out the specific special education and related services to be provided, which includes placement, the IEP would have to be developed before the child is placed. When placement in a State-operated school is appropriate, the affected State agency or agencies would have to be involved by the LEA in the development of the IEP.

After the child enters the State school, any meetings to review or revise the child's IEP could be conducted by either the LEA or the State school, depending upon State law, policy, or practice. However, as a general rule, both agencies would jointly be involved in any decisions made about the child's IEP (either by attending the IEP meetings, or through correspondence or telephone calls). There must be a clear decision made (based on State law) regarding whether responsibility for the child's education had been transferred to the State school or remains with the LEA, since this determines which agency is responsible for reviewing or revising the child's IEP.

2. *Who is responsible for writing IEPs for a handicapped child placed out of State by a public agency?*

The "placing" State is responsible for writing the child's IEP and insuring that it is implemented. The determination of the specific agency in the State that is responsible for the child's IEP would usually be based on State law, policy, or practice. However, as indicated earlier, the SEA must insure (1) that the responsible agency is identified, and (2) that the child receives a free appropriate public education.

Any responsibilities of the "receiving" State and its effected public agencies, in terms of implementing the child's IEP, would be specified in an agreement between the appropriate agencies within the two States.

---

§ 121a.341   *SEA Responsibility*—Continued

(b) *Private schools and facilities.* The State educational agency shall insure that an individualized education program is developed and implemented for each handicapped child who:

(1) Is placed in or referred to a private school or facility by a public agency: or

(2) Is enrolled in a parochial or other private school and receives special education or related services from a public agency.

(20 U.S.C. 1412 (4). (6): 1413(a)(4).)

Comment: This section applies to all public agencies, including other State agencies (e.g. departments of mental health and welfare), which provide special education to a handicapped child either directly, by contract or through other arrangements. Thus, if a State welfare agency contracts with a private school or facility to provide special education to a handicapped child, that agency would be responsible for insuring that an individualized education program is developed for the child.

---

§ 121a.342   When individualized education programs must be in effect.

(a) On October 1, 1977, and at the beginning of each school year thereafter, each public agency shall have in effect an individualized education program for every handicapped child who is receiving special education from that agency.

(b) An individualized education program must:

(1) Be in effect before special education and related services are provided to a child; and

(2) Be implemented as soon as possible following the meetings under § 121a.343.

(20 U.S.C. 1412 (2)(B), (4), (6): 1414 (a)(5); Pub. L. 94–142, Sec. 8(c) (1975).)

Comment. Under paragraph (b) (2). It is expected that a handicapped child's individualized education program (IEP) will be implemented immediately following the meetings under § 121a.343. An exception to this would be (1) when the meetings occur during the summer or a vacation period, *or* (2) where there are circumstances which require a short delay (e.g., working out transportation arrangements). However, there can be no undue delay in providing special education and related services to the child.

1. *In requiring that an IEP must be in effect before special education and related services are provided, what does "be in effect" mean?*

   As used in the regulations, the term "be in effect" means that the IEP (1) has been developed at a meeting(s) involving all of the participants indicated in the Act (parent, teacher, agency representative and, the child, where appropriate), (2) is less than one calendar year old, (3) is regarded by both the parents and school personnel as being appropriate in terms of the child's needs, projected outcomes, and services that are specified, and (4) will be implemented as written.

2. *How much of a delay is permissible between the time a handicapped child's IEP is written and when special education is provided?*

   In general, it is not permissible to have any delay. It is expected that the special education and related services set out in a child's IEP will be provided by the agency immediately after the IEP meeting.

   The comment following Section 121a.342 identifies some exceptions (e.g., (1) when the meetings occur during the summer or a vacation period, or (2) when there are circumstances which require a short delay, such as working out transportation arrangements). However, unless otherwise specified in the IEP, the IEP services must be provided within a few days following the meeting.

3. *For a handicapped child entering special education for the first time, when must an IEP be written—before placement or after placement?*

   The IEP must be finalized before placement. Section 121a.342(b) states that an IEP must "Be in effect *before* special education and related services are provided to the child." (Emphasis added.) The appropriate placement for a given handicapped child cannot be determined until after decisions have been made about what the child's needs are and what will be provided. Since these decisions are made at the IEP meeting, it would not be permissible to first place the child and then develop the IEP.

   The above requirement does not preclude temporarily placing a child in a program as part of the evaluation process—before the IEP is finalized —to aid in determining the appropriate placement. When a "trial placement" is considered to be necessary for an individual child, the placement must be made in accordance with the following:

   a. There must be an "interim" IEP developed for the child, which sets out the specific conditions and timelines for the trial placement. (See "c" following.)

   b. The parents must agree to the placement before it is carried out, and be involved throughout the process of developing, reviewing, and revising the child's IEP.

   c. A specific timeline must be set for completing the evaluation and making judgments about the most appropriate placement for the child. (NOTE: It is expected that these activities will be completed within a 30 day time period.)

   d. At the end of the trial period, a meeting must be conducted to finalize the child's IEP.

NOTE: Once a handicapped child is placed in a special education program, the teacher might develop lesson plans or more detailed objectives *based* on the IEP; however, such plans and objectives are not required and would not be a part of the IEP itself. (Questions and answers about IEP goals and objectives are included later in this paper, under § 121a.346(b).)

4. *If a handicapped child has been receiving special education in one LEA and moves to another community, must the new LEA hold an IEP meeting before the child is placed in a special education program?*

Yes. Before the child begins receiving special education and related services, the new LEA must conduct an IEP meeting. At the meeting, the parents and school personnel would (1) review the child's former placement and school records, and (2) revise the child's IEP, where necessary. (NOTE: If the child's previous IEP is not available, a new IEP would have to be developed.) The meeting should take place within one week after the parents enroll the child in the new LEA; and the child must be placed in a special education program immediately after the IEP is written. (See answer to question No. 2, above.)

If the LEA or the parents feel that additional information is needed before a final placement decision can be made (e.g., the need to receive and review the school records from the former LEA, or the need for a new evaluation), it would be permissible to "temporarily" place the child in a program before the IEP is finalized. (See conditions for such placements in the answer to question No. 3, above.)

---

§ 121a.343   Meetings.

(a) *General.* Each public agency is responsible for initiating and conducting meetings for the purpose of developing, reviewing, and revising a handicapped child's individualized education program.

(b) *Handicapped children currently served.* If the public agency has determined that a handicapped child will receive special education during school year 1977–1978, a meeting must be held early enough to insure that an individualized education program is developed by October 1, 1977.

(c) *Other handicapped children.* For a handicapped child who is not included under paragraph (b) of this action, a meeting must be held within thirty calendar days of a determination that the child needs special education and related services.

---

1. *Does paragraph (c) of Section 121a.343 authorize a public agency to delay the development of a handicapped child's IEP for a period of up to 30 days following placement?*

No. The 30 day timeline in Section 121a.343(c) was written to insure that there would not be a significant delay between the time a child is evaluated and when the child begins to receive special education. Once it is determined—through the the evaluation—that a child is handicapped, the public agency has *up to* 30 days to hold an IEP meeting; and the child must be "placed" immediately after the meeting. (See question No. 2 under § 121a.342.) Thus, as previously stated, the IEP must be finalized before placement.

2. *Must the "multidisciplinary team" hold a separate meeting to determine a child's eligibility for special education and related services, or can this step be combined with the IEP meeting?*

This is a State or local decision. Some agencies hold separate "eligibility staffings" with the multidisciplinary team before the IEP meeting. (NOTE: When separate meetings are conducted, placement decisions would be made at the IEP meeting.) Other agencies combine the two steps into one process. If a combined meeting is conducted, the public agency must insure that the parents are included as participants at the meeting. (See § 121a.345 for requirements on parent participation.) In addition, while not required under the Act, it is recommended that agencies involve parents in the separate eligibility staffings whenever possible.

NOTE: If, at a separate eligibility staffing, a decision is made that a child is *NOT* eligible for special education, the parents must be notified about the decision.

---

§ 121a.343 *Meetings*—Continued

(d) *Review.* Each public agency shall initiate and conduct meetings to periodically review each child's individualized education program and if appropriate revise its provisions. A meeting must be held for this purpose at least once a year. (20 U.S.C. 1412 (2)(B), (4), (6): 1414(a)(5).)

Comment. The dates on which agencies must have individualized education programs (IEPs) in effect are specified in § 121a.342 (October 1, 1977, and the begining of each school year thereafter). However, except for new handicapped children (i.e., those evaluated and determined to need special education after October 1, 1977), the timing of meetings to develop, review, and revise IEPs is left to the discretion of each agency.

In order to have IEPs in effect by the dates in § 121a.342, agencies could hold meetings at the end of the school year or during the summer preceding those dates. In meeting the October 1, 1977 timeline, meetings could be conducted up through the October 1 date. Thereafter, meetings may be held any time throughout the year, as long as IEPs are in effect at the beginning of each school year.

The statute requires agencies to hold a meeting at least once each year in order to review, and if appropriate revise each child's IEP. The timing of those meetings could be on the anniversary date of the last IEP meeting on the child, but this is left to the discretion of the agency.

3. *Must IEPs be reviewed or revised at the beginning of each school year?*

No. The basic requirement in the regulations is that IEPs must *be in effect* at the beginning of each school year. (See question No. 1 under § 121a.342.) Meetings must be conducted at least once each calendar year to review or revise each handicapped child's IEP. However, the meetings may be held anytime throughout the year, including (a) at the end of each school year, (b) during the summer, before the new school year begins, or (c) on the anniversary date of the last IEP meeting on the child.

4. *How frequently must IEP meetings be held?*

The regulations state that each public agency must hold meetings periodically, but not less than annually, to review each child's IEP and, if appropriate, revise its provisions. The legislative history makes it clear that there should be as many meetings a year as any one child may need. (Congressional Record, Senate—November 19, 1975, Mr. Stafford, pp 40428—29.) Moreover, agencies must allow sufficient time at the meetings to insure meaningful parent participation.

5. *Can IEP meetings be initiated at the request of the parents?*

Yes. See (a) question No. 4 under "Parent participation (§ 121a.345), (b) question No. 8 under "Content of IEP" (§ 121a.346), and (c) the comment following Section 121a.349 (IEP—accountability).

6. *Can IEP meetings be initiated at the request of the child's special education teacher?*

Special education teachers are the main implementers of IEPs and are in the best position to determine whether a given handicapped child is or is not progressing in accordance with his/her "program." If a teacher feels that a child's placement or IEP services are not appropriate to the child, it is expected that the teacher would, in accordance with agency procedures, (1) call or meet with the parents and/or (2) request the agency to hold another meeting to review the child's current IEP.

§ 121a.344   Participants in meetings.
(a) *General.* The public agency
shall insure that each meeting includes the following participants:
(1) A representative of the public
agency, other than the child's
teacher, who is qualified to provide,
or supervise the provision of, special
education

1. *Who can serve as the "agency representative" at an IEP meeting?*
The "agency representative" could be any member of the school staff,
other than child's teacher, who is "qualified to provide, or supervise the
provision of, specially designed instruction to meet the unique needs of
handicapped children." (Sec. 602(19) of the Act) Thus, the agency representative could be (1) a qualified special education administrator, supervisor, or teacher (including a speech-language pathologist), or (2) a school
principal or other administrator—if the person is qualified to provide or
supervise special education.
The determination of which specific staff member should serve as
agency representative is left to discretion of the individual state or
agency or school. However, the following points should be considered
in such a determination:
a. A first consideration in selecting the agency representative is the need
   to insure that whatever services are agreed upon at the meeting will
   actually be provided and the IEP will not be "vetoed" at a higher
   administrative level within the agency. Thus, the person selected
   should have the authority to commit agency resources (i.e., to make
   decisions about the specific special education and related services that
   the agency will provide to a particular child).
b. A second consideration might be related to the nature and severity
   of a child's handicap and the amount of services he/she requires. For
   children with less severe handicaps (e.g., a mild learning disability or
   a mild speech impairment), where only a limited amount of special
   education is required, the agency representative could be a special
   education teacher or a speech-language pathologist, other than the
   child's teacher. However, for children with more severe disabilities,
   who require extensive special education and related services, the
   agency representative might be a key administrator in the agency.

NOTE: IEP meetings for continuing placements could be more routine than those for initial placements, and, thus, might not require the participation of a key administrator.

2. *Who is the "agency representative" for a handicapped child who is served by a public agency other than the SEA or LEA?*

The answer depends upon individual State law, policy, or practice. It also might depend upon any one or all of the following: Who is responsible for (a) the child's education, (b) for placing the child and (c) for providing (or paying for) special education and related services to the child.

NOTE: In the following situation, the answer is more specific: If a state agency (1) places a child in an institution, (2) is responsible under State law for the child's education, and (3) has a qualified special education staff at the institution, then a member of that staff would be the agency representative at the IEP meetings. Sometimes there is no special education staff at the institution, and the children are served by special education personnel from the LEA where the institution is located. In this situation, a member of the LEA staff would usually serve as the agency representative.

> § 121a.344   Participants in meetings. (Cont'd)
>
> (a) *General.* The public agency shall insure that each meeting includes the following participants:
>
> (2) The child's teacher.

3. *For a handicapped child being considered for initial placement in special education, what teacher should attend the IEP meeting?*

The "teacher" could be either (1) a teacher qualified to provide special education in the child's area of suspected disability, and/or (2) the child's regular teacher. In any event, there should be at least one member of the school staff at the meeting who is qualified in the child's area of suspected disability.

NOTE: Sometimes more than one meeting is necessary in order to finalize a child's IEP. If in this process, the teacher who will be working with the child is identified, it would be useful to have the teacher participate in the meeting with the parents and other members of the IEP team in finalizing the IEP. When this is not possible, the agency should insure that the teacher (i.e., the "receiving" special education teacher) is given a copy of the child's IEP as soon as possible after the meeting(s) and before the teacher begins working with the child.

4. *If a handicapped child is enrolled in both regular and special education classes, which teacher should attend the IEP meeting?*

The special education teacher. At the option of the agency or the parent, the child's regular teacher also might attend. If the regular teacher does not attend, the agency should insure that he/she either receives a copy of the IEP or is informed about its contents. Moreover, the agency should insure that the special education teacher or other appropriate support person is able, where necessary, to consult with and be a resource to the child's regular teacher.

5. *If a handicapped child in high school attends several regular classes, should all of the child's regular teachers attend the IEP meeting?*

This is a State or local decision. However, the following are some points to be considered in making the decision:

a. Generally, the number of participants at IEP meetings should be small. Holding small meetings has several advantages over large ones. For example, they (1) allow for more open, active parent involvement, (2) are less costly, (3) are easier to arrange and conduct, and (4) are usually more productive. (NOTE: In an informal examination of IEPs from five states, BEH staff found that, on the average, IEP meetings were attended by four persons.)

b. While large meetings are generally inappropriate, there may be specific circumstances where additional participants are essential. The regulations authorize the attendance of other participants at the discretion of the agency or parents. (§ 121a.344(a)(5).) When the participation of the regular teachers is considered by the agency or the parents to be essential to the child's success in school (e.g., in terms of his/her participation in the regular education program), it would be appropriate for them to attend as "other participants." Usually, the need for such attendance is greater for children with severe handicaps.

c. While the child's regular teachers would not routinely attend IEP meetings, they should either (1) be informed about the child's IEP by the special education teacher or agency representative, or (2) receive a copy of the IEP itself. Moreover, as mentioned earlier, the agency should insure that the special education teacher is able, where necessary, to consult with, and be a resource to, the child's regular teachers. (See question No. 6 under § 121a.346(b) regarding goals and objectives in the IEP.)

6. *If a child's primary handicap is a speech impairment, must the child's regular teacher attend the IEP meeting?*

No. A speech-language pathologist would usually serve as the child's "teacher." The regular teacher could attend at the option of the school. However, some member of the "IEP team" must be a qualified speech-language pathologist.

7. *If a child is enrolled in a special education class because of a primary handicap and also receives speech-language pathology services, should both specialists attend the IEP meeting?*

In general the answer is yes. The special education teacher must attend the meeting. The speech-language pathologist could either (1) participate in the meeting itself, or (2) provide a written recommendation concerning the nature, frequency, and amount of services to be provided to the child.

8. *Can representatives of teacher unions attend IEP meetings?*

No. Under the Family Educational Rights and Privacy Act (FERPA), union officials cannot attend IEP meetings if student records are discussed—except with the written consent of the parents. Moreover, even if student records are not involved, P.L. 94–142 does not allow for the participation of union officials at IEP meetings. The legislative history of the Act makes it clear that IEP meetings should be confined to those persons who have an intense interest in a particular child. Thus, since union involvement is intended to protect the interests of the teacher rather than the interests of the child, it would be improper for such officials to attend IEP meetings.

> § 121a.344   Participants in meetings. (Cont'd)
>
> (a) *General.* The public agency shall insure that each meeting includes the following participants:
>
> (3) One or both of the child's parents, subject to § 121a.345.
>
> (4) The child, where appropriate.

9. *When may a handicapped child attend an IEP meeting?*

Generally, a handicapped child should attend his/her IEP meeting whenever the parent decides that it is appropriate. Whenever possible, the agency and parents should discuss the appropriateness of the child's participation before a decision is made, in order to help the parents determine whether or not the child's attendance will be (1) helpful in developing the IEP and/or (2) be directly beneficial to the child. The agency must inform the parents about this provision before each IEP meeting—as part of the "notice of meeting" requirement in Section 121a.345(b).

NOTE: Although not required by the Act or regulations, it is recommended that, through the combined efforts of the parents and agency, older handicapped children (particularly those at the secondary school level) be encouraged to participate in their IEP meetings.

10. *Are the parents precluded from attending IEP meetings when the student reaches the age of majority?*

No. The parents retain the right to participate in IEP meetings after the student reaches the age of majority. (NOTE: The Act is silent concerning the rights of a handicapped student at the age of majority. However, if a student wants to attend his/her IEP meeting, it is expected that the student would be allowed to do so. The only exception would be where a student had been declared legally incompetent. Even in those cases, the student could attend if the parents decide it is appropriate.)

---

§ 121a.344   Participants in meetings. (Cont'd)

(a) *General.* The public agency shall insure that each meeting includes the following participants:

(5) Other individuals at the discretion of the parent or agency.

---

11. *Do related services personnel have a role at IEP meetings?*

Yes, if a handicapped child has an identified need for related services. For example, when the child's evaluation indicates that he/she needs a specific related service in order to benefit from special education (e.g., physical therapy, occupational therapy, or counseling), the agency should insure that a qualified provider of that service either (a) attends the IEP meeting, or (b) provides a written recommendation concerning the nature, frequency, and amount of service to be provided to the child. (NOTE: This could be a part of the evaluation report.)

12. *Are agencies required to use a "case manager" in the development of a handicapped child's IEP?*

No. However, some local schools have found it helpful to have a special educator or some other school staff member (e.g., a social worker, counselor, or psychologist) serve as coordinator or "case manager" of the IEP process for an individual child or for all handicapped children served by the agency. Examples of the kinds of activities which case managers might carry out are: (1) coordinating the multidisciplinary evaluation process, (2) collecting and synthesizing the evaluation reports and other relevant information about a child that might be needed at the IEP meeting, (3) communicating with the parents, and (4) participating in, or conducting, the IEP meeting itself.

§ 121a.344   *Participants in meetings*—Continued

(b) *Evaluation personnel.* For a handicapped child who has been evaluated for the first time, the public agency shall insure:

(1) That a member of the evaluation team participates in the meeting; or

(2) That the representative of the public agency, the child's teacher, or some other person is present at the meeting, who is knowledgeable about the evaluation procedures used with the child and is familiar with the results of the evaluation (20 U.S.C. 1401(19): 1412 (2)(B), (4), (6): 1414(a)(5).)

Comment. 1. In deciding which teacher will participate in meetings on a child's individualized education program, the agency may wish to consider the following possibilities:

(a) For a handicapped child who is receiving special education, the "teacher" could be the child's special education teacher. If the child's handicap is a speech impairment, the "teacher" could be the speech-language pathologist.

(b) For a handicapped child who is being considered for placement in special education, the "teacher" could be the child's regular teacher, or a teacher qualified to provide education in the type of program in which the child may be placed, or both.

(c) If the child is not in school or has more than one teacher, the agency may designate which teacher will participate in the meeting.

2. Either the teacher or the agency representative should be qualified in the area of the child's suspected disability.

3. For a child whose primary handicap is a speech impairment, the evaluation personnel participating under paragraph (b)(1) of this section would normally be the speech-language pathologist.

13. *For a child with a suspected speech impairment, who represents the evaluation team at the IEP meeting?*

In general, a speech-language pathologist would be the most appropriate person. For many children whose primary handicap is a speech impairment, there may be no other evaluation personnel involved. The comment following Section 121a.532 (Evaluation procedures) states:

Children who have a speech impairment as their primary handicap may not need a complete battery of assessments (e.g., psychological, physical, or adaptive behavior). However, a qualified speech-language pathologist would (1) evaluate each speech impaired child using procedures that are appropriate for the diagnosis and appraisal of speech and language disorders, and (2) where necessary, make referrals for additional assessments needed to make an appropriate placement decision.

§ 121a.345   Parent participation.

(a) Each public agency shall take steps to insure that one or both of the parents of the handicapped child are present at each meeting or are afforded the opportunity to participate, including:

(1) Notifying parents of the meeting early enough to insure that they will have an opportunity to attend; and

(2) Scheduling the meeting at a mutually agreed on time and place.

(b) The notice under paragraph (a) (1) of this section must indicate the purpose, time, and location of the meeting, and who will be in attendance.

(c) If neither parent can attend, the public agency shall use other methods to insure parent participation, including individual or conference telephone calls.

(d) A meeting may be conducted without a parent in attendance if the public agency is unable to convince the parents that they should attend. In this case the public agency must have a record of its attempts to arrange a mutually agreed on time and place such as:

(1) Detailed records of telephone calls made or attempted and the results of those calls.

(2) Copies of correspondence sent to the parents and any responses received, and

(3) Detailed records of visits made to the parent's home or place of employment and the results of those visits.

(e) The public agency shall take whatever action is necessary to insure that the parent understands the proceedings at a meeting, including arranging for an interpreter for parents who are deaf or whose native language is other than English.

(f) The public agency shall give the parent, on request, a copy of the individualized education program.

(20 U.S.C. 1401(19): 1412 (2)(B), (4), (6): 1414(a)(5).)

Comment. The notice in paragraph (a) could also inform parents that they may bring other people to the meeting. As indicated in paragraph (c), the procedure used to notify parents (whether oral or written or both) is left to the discretion of the agency, but the agency must keep a record of its efforts to contact parents.

1. *What is the role of the parents at an IEP meeting?*

Under the law, the parents of a handicapped child are expected to be equal participants, along with school personnel, in developing, reviewing, and revising the child's IEP. This is an active role in which the parents (1) participate in the discussion about the child's special education and related services needs, and (2) join with the other participants in deciding what services the agency will provide to the child. (NOTE: In some instances, parents might elect to bring another participant to the meeting, e.g., a friend or neighbor, someone outside of the agency who knows the law and is familiar with the child's needs, or a specialist who conducted an independent evaluation of the child.)

2. *What is the role of a surrogate parent at the IEP meeting?*

    A surrogate parent is a person appointed to represent the interests of a handicapped child in the educational decision making process when that child has no parent to represent him/her. The surrogate has all of the rights and responsibilities of parents under P.L. 94–142. Thus, the surrogate parent is entitled to (1) participate in the child's IEP meeting, (2) see the child's educational records, and (3) receive notice, grant consent, and invoke due process to resolve differences.

3. *Must the public agency let the parents know who will be at the IEP meeting?*

    Yes. In notifying parents about the meeting, the agency "must indicate the purpose, time, and location of the meeting, and who will be in attendance." (§ 121a.345(b)) In providing such notice, the agency should (a) give the name and position of each person who will be attending, (b) discuss with the parents the appropriateness of the child attending (See question No. 9 under § 121a.344.), and (c) inform the parents of their right to bring other participants to the meeting (See § 121a.344(a)(5).) (NOTE: It is appropriate for the agency to ask whether parents intend to bring a participant to the meeting.)

4. *Are parents required to sign IEPs?*

    Signatures are not required by either the Act or regulations. However, having such signatures is considered by parents and by advocates and agency personnel at all levels (Local, State and National) to be a useful procedure. (NOTE: a National Survey indicates that, in practice, most IEPs *do* have parent's signatures.) The following are some of the purposes for which signed IEPs might be used:

    a. The use of signatures is one way to document who has been in attendance at the meeting. (NOTE: This is useful for monitoring and compliance purposes.) If signatures are not used, the agency must find some other way to provide such documentation.

    b. If the parents sign the IEP, this is a way to indicate that they approve the child's "program." However, if their signatures are used for this purpose, the agency must inform the parents that such approval does not take away the right to request another IEP meeting at any time they feel that a change is needed in the child's IEP. (NOTE: One way of insuring that parents are informed about this right is to include such a statement in the IEP that the parents sign.)

    c. If the agency representative signs the IEP, the parents have a signed record of the services that the agency has agreed to provide. (NOTE: Even if the school personnel do not sign, the agency still must provide, or assure the provision of, the services called for in the IEP.)

5. *If the parents sign the IEP, does this indicate consent for initial placement?*

    The parents' signature approving the IEP could satisfy the consent requirement in the regulations if the IEP includes a statement which meets the definition of consent in Section 121a.500:

> As used in this part, "consent" means that (a) The parent has been fully informed of all information relevant to the activity for which consent is sought ... (b) The parent understands and agrees in writing to the carrying out of the activity ... and the consent describes that activity and lists all records (if any) which will be released and to whom; and (c) The parent understands that the granting of consent is voluntary ... and may be revoked at any time.

NOTE: Because "informed consent" is closely linked to the written prior notice requirement in Section 121a.505, an agency could distribute the notice and explain its contents at the time the IEP is signed and consent is obtained for initial placement.

---

§ 121a.346   Content of individualized education program.
The individualized education program for each child must include:
(a) A statement of the child's
present levels of educational performance;

---

1. *What should be included in the statement of the child's present levels of educational performance?*
   The statement of present levels of educational performance will be different for each handicapped child. Thus, determinations about the content of the statement for an individual child are matters that are left to the discretion of participants in the IEP meetings. However, the following are some points to be taken into account in writing this part of the IEP.
   a. The statement should accurately describe the effect of the child's handicap on his/her performance in any area of education that is affected, including (1) academic areas (reading, math, communication, etc.) and (2) non-academic areas ("daily life activities," mobility, etc.) (NOTE: Labels such as "mentally retarded" or "deaf" could not be used as a substitute for the description of "present levels of educational performance.")
   b. The statement should be presented in terms of objective measurable observations to the extent possible. Data from the child's evaluation would be a good source of such information. Test scores that were

judged pertinent to the child's diagnosis might be included, where appropriate. However, the scores should be self-explanatory (i.e., they can be interpreted by all participants without the use of test manuals or any other aids.) Whatever test results are used should reflect the impact of the handicap on the child's performance. Thus, raw scores would not usually be sufficient.

c. There should be a direct relationship between the present levels of educational performance and the other components of the IEP. Thus, if the statement describes a problem with the child's reading level and points to a deficiency in a specific reading skill, these problems and needs should be addressed under both (1) goals and objectives, and (2) specific special education and related services to be provided to the child.

> § 121a.346 *Content of IEP*—Continued
>   (b) A statement of annual goals, including short term instructional objectives;

2. *Why are goals and objectives required in the IEP?*
   The statutory requirement for including annual goals and short term objectives and for having at least an annual review of a handicapped child's IEP, provides a mechanism for determining (1) whether the anticipated outcomes are being met (i.e., is the child progressing in his/her "program") and (2) whether the placement and services are appropriate to the child's special learning needs.
   In effect, the IEP requirement is designed to insure on-going accountability and to provide protections for handicapped children and their parents. However, the goals and objectives in the IEP are not intended to address the specifics that are traditionally found in daily, weekly, or monthly instructional plans.

3. *What are "annual goals" as used in the IEP Requirement of P.L. 94–142?*
   The annual goals in the IEP are statements which describe what a handicapped child can reasonably be expected to accomplish within one calendar year in his/her special education program. As indicated earlier, there must be a direct relationship between (a) the annual goals and (b) the present levels of educational performance—which are based on the current evaluation of the child.

4. *What does the term "short term instructional objectives" mean as it is used in P.L. 94–142?*
   IEP objectives are measurable, intermediate steps between a handicapped child's present levels of educational performance and the annual goals that are established for the child. The objectives (a) are developed based

on a logical breakdown of the major components of the annual goals, and (b) can serve as "milestones" for indicating progress toward meeting the goals.

The IEP objectives (as well as the goals) are concerned mainly with meeting the special education and related service needs of a handicapped child, and may not necessarily cover other areas of the child's education. Stated another way, the objectives in the IEP should focus on offsetting or reducing the problems resulting from the child's handicap which interfere with his/her learning and educational performance in school.

Thus, for a child with a mild speech impairment, the IEP objectives would focus on improving the child's communication skills, by either (1) correcting the impairment, or (2) minimizing its effect on the child's ability to communicate. However, the child's IEP would not usually include objectives related to other parts of his/her educational program. On the other hand, the goals and objectives for a severely retarded child would be more comprehensive and cover more of the child's school program than if he/she only has a mild handicap.

In some respects, IEP objectives are similar to other educational objectives, especially those used in classroom instructional plans. For example, both kinds of objectives are used (1) to describe what a given child is expected to accomplish in a particular area within some specified time period, and (2) to determine the extent to which the child is progressing toward those accomplishments.

In other respects, however, objectives in IEPs are different from those used in instructional plans. The main difference is in the amount of detail. IEP objectives provide general "benchmarks" for determining progress toward meeting the annual goals. These objectives are usually projected to be accomplished on at least a quarterly or semester basis or for an entire reporting period during the school year. On the other hand, the objectives in instructional plans deal with more specific outcomes that are to be accomplished on a daily, weekly, or monthly basis. The instructional plans themselves usually include details not required in an IEP, such as the specific methods, activities, and materials (e.g., use of flash cards, etc.) that will be used in accomplishing the objectives.

5. *Is there a relationship between the goals and objectives in the IEP and those that are in "instructional plans" of special education personnel?*
Yes. There should be direct relationship between the IEP goals and objectives for a given handicapped child and those that are in the special education "instructional plans" for the child. From a Federal compliance standpoint, the IEP is not intended to be detailed enough to be used as an instructional plan. The IEP, through its goals and objectives, (1) sets the general direction to be taken by "IEP implementers" in working with a child, and (2) serves as the basis for developing a detailed instructional plan for the child.

6. *If a handicapped child is enrolled in both regular and special education classes, should the IEP include the goals and objectives of the regular teacher(s)?*
   In general the answer is no. To meet the Federal requirements, the IEP goals and objectives need only target on offsetting the child's handicap. For example, if a learning disabled child is functioning several grades below his/her indicated ability in reading and has a special problem with word recognition, the IEP goals and objectives would be directed toward (1) closing the gap between the child's indicated ability and current level of functioning, and (2) helping the child to increase his/her ability to use "word attack" skills effectively (or to find some other approach to increase his/her independence in reading).

   The special education teacher might develop a detailed instructional plan based on the child's IEP. However, it would not be necessary for the IEP itself to include the specific "lesson plan" objectives from either the special education teacher or the child's regular teacher(s).

   Since the child's reading problem will likely have an effect on his/her performance in regular education, the child's regular teacher(s) should either be informed about and/or receive a copy of the child's IEP. (NOTE: At the discretion of the agency or the parents, the regular teacher also might attend the IEP meeting. See earlier questions and answers on participants at meetings.) Moreover, the agency should insure that the regular teacher(s) receives on-going assistance throughout the year (e.g., from the special teacher or through inservice training), as necessary, in order to help in minimizing the effect of the child's impairment on his/her participation in the regular program.

7. *When must IEP objectives be written—before placement or after placement?*
   IEP objectives must be written before placement. Once a handicapped child is placed in a special education program, the teacher might develop lesson plans or more detailed objectives *based* on the IEP; however, such plans and objectives are not required and would not be a part of the IEP itself.

8. *Can short term instructional objectives be changed without holding another IEP meeting?*
   The legislative history of the Act makes it clear that the parents of a handicapped child are to be involved throughout the entire process of developing, reviewing, and revising the child's IEP. In some cases—if the parents are involved in the decision—it might be possible to make a change in the short term instructional objectives without holding another IEP meeting. This procedure can only be used under the following conditions:
   a. No change can be made in any other part of the child's IEP (e.g., annual goals and the kind and amount of services).
   b. Prior written notice must be given in accordance with Section 121a.504. The notice must include a statement indicating that the agency will hold an IEP meeting to discuss the proposed change, if

the parents request it. (Through the prior notice provision, parents have the opportunity to accept or reject the proposed change before it is carried out. If they reject it, they would contact the agency and request another meeting.)

NOTE (1) Since the IEP is not an instructional plan with detailed objectives (See questions 4–6, above), the need to make changes in the IEP objectives should not be a common, routine occurrence. If significant changes in the objectives are necessary (e.g., replacing all of the objectives under a particular goal), this would usually require another IEP meeting, and might mean that the child would need to be reevaluated.

NOTE (2) In addition to meeting the written notice requirement, it is recommended that the teacher either call or meet with the parents to discuss the proposed change. If the parents and teacher do meet together, the written notice could be given to the parents at the meeting.

---

§ 121a.346 *Content of IEP*—Continued

(c) A statement of the specific special education and related services to be provided to the child, and the extent to which the child will be able to participate in regular educational programs;

---

9. *Does the IEP list all special education and related services needed or only those available in the public agency?*

Each public agency must provide a free appropriate public education to all handicapped children under its jurisdiction. Therefore, the IEP for an individual handicapped child must include all of the specific special education and related services needed by the child—as determined by the child's current evaluation. This means that the services must be listed in the IEP even if they are not available in the local agency, and must be provided by the agency through contract or other arrangements.

10. *Is the IEP a commitment to provide services—i.e., must a public agency provide the services listed?*

Yes. Each handicapped child's IEP must include all services necessary to meet his/her identified special education and related services needs; and all services in the IEP must be provided in order for the agency to be in compliance with the Act. One of the purposes of the IEP is to set forth in writing a commitment of resources necessary to enable a handicapped child to receive needed special education and related services.

11. *Must the public agency itself provide IEP services directly to a handicapped child?*

The public agency responsible for the education of a handicapped child could provide IEP services to the child (1) directly, through the agency's own staff resources, (2) by contracting with another public or private agency, or (3) through other arrangements. In providing the services, the agency may use whatever State, local, Federal, and private sources of support are available for those purposes. However, the services must be at no cost to the parents; and responsibility for insuring that the IEP services are provided remains with the child's public agency.

12. *Does the IEP include only special education and related services or the total education of the child?*

In general, the IEP is limited to matters concerning the provision of special education and related services. (NOTE: The regulations define (a) "special education" as specially designed instruction to meet the unique needs of a handicapped child, and (b) "related services" as those which are necessary to assist the child to benefit from special education.)

For some handicapped children, the IEP will only address a very limited part of their education (e.g., for a speech impaired child, the IEP would generally be limited to the child's speech impairment). For other children (e.g., those who are profoundly retarded), the IEP may cover their total education. An IEP for a physically impaired child with no mental impairment might consist only of specially designed physical education; however, if the child also has a mental impairment, the IEP might cover most of the child's education.

NOTE: If modifications to the regular education program are required to compensate for the child's handicap, these modifications would be included in the child's IEP (e.g., for hearing impaired child, special seating arrangements, or providing assignments in writing, where necessary).

13. *Must physical education (PE) be included in every handicapped child's IEP?*

In general, the answer is yes. However, the kind and amount of information to be included in the IEP depends upon the physical-motor needs of the individual child and the type of PE program that is to be provided. The following is a description of some of the different kinds of PE program arrangements:

a. *Regular PE with Non-Handicapped Students.* Many learning disabled and speech impaired children participate in the regular PE program with non-handicapped students and without any special provisions. In addition, some children with other handicapping conditions and without any physical-motor problems (e.g., some educable mentally retarded (EMR) children) also participate in the regular PE program.

If a handicapped child is enrolled in the regular PE program without any special adaptations, only minimal information about the PE program is required in the IEP. Section 121a.346(c) requires a statement of "the extent to which the child will be able to participate in regular educational programs." Thus, for an EMR child who is in regular PE, the IEP would only have to indicate that the child is participating in the program (i.e., "regular PE").

Moreover, if a speech impaired child (for example) is (a) enrolled full-time in the regular education program (except for receiving speech-language pathology services), and (b) is treated equally in all respects with non-handicapped students (including participating in the regular PE program), it would not be necessary under the law to refer to PE in the child's IEP. What would be required is a statement indicating that the child is enrolled full-time in the regular education program.

b. *Regular PE with Adaptations.* Some individual children in various disability areas (including those with physical impairments) are able to participate in the regular PE program with non-handicapped students if special adaptations are made for them. For these children, the IEP would (1) include a brief statement of the physical-motor needs which require "adapted PE" (i.e., under "present levels of educational performance"), and (2) describe the special adaptations that are necessary (e.g., when bowling is a part of the curriculum, the use of a bowling rail for the blind, or a bowling ramp for children in wheel chairs, or a spring-handle bowling ball for students with cerebral palsy).

c. *Specially Designed PE.* Sometimes, an individual handicapped child will require specially designed PE that is different from that for non-handicapped children. It might also differ from the kind of PE provided to other children with the same handicapping condition. A child might participate in a special body conditioning or weight-training program, or, depending upon his/her specific needs and abilities, participate in some type of individual skill sport.

For these children, the PE program would be included under all parts of the IEP (e.g., present levels of educational performance, goals and objectives, and specific services to be provided). However, as indicated earlier, the PE goals and objectives, etc., would not have to be presented in any more detail than any other areas included in the IEP.

d. *PE in Special Settings.* Under certain circumstances, some of the handicapped students within a given disability receive their education in a special setting (e.g., a residential school or a separate wing of a regular school building). The PE program for these students is usually based on a State approved curriculum guide; and most of the students participate, as a group, in the same basic PE program.

When a handicapped child in a special setting participates in a basic PE program with the other students and no individual adaptations are made for the child, only minimal information is required in the IEP. For example, the IEP (1) would indicate that the child is participating in the basic PE program, and (2) could make specific reference to the applicable parts of the PE curriculum guide which apply to the individual child.

For children who have physical-motor problems or need specific help in the development of gross motor skills, the IEP would include a statement of (1) the child's special physical needs, and (2) the specific PE program, and any other special education services which will be provided to meet those needs. However, since the IEP is not an instructional plan, the PE program would not have to be described in any more detail than any other areas included in the IEP. To the extent that these students participate, as a group, in a basic PE program under an approved curriculum guide, it is permissible for a child's IEP to cross-reference the applicable parts of the guide which apply to the child.

NOTE: For handicapped children who are educated in special settings, it is assumed that the least restrictive environment provision has been implemented—i.e., that determinations are made about whether an individual child in a residential school (for example) can participate in some part of the regular school program of the local educational agency; and, when indicated, that the child enrolls in that PE program.

14. *Must vocational education services be listed in a child's IEP?*
Yes. Both P.L. 94–142 and P.L. 94–482, the Vocational Education Amendments of 1976, require that vocational education be listed in a child's IEP. In addition, the Vocational Education Data System mandated in P.L. 94–482 requires that local and State agencies providing vocational education to handicapped students use the IEP as a basis for reporting services.

If a handicapped child is in a vocational education program and needs no special modifications to the program to compensate for his/her handicap, then his/her participation in the program need only be noted in the section indicating the extent of the child's participation in vocational education. However, if participation in vocational education is included as a part of a total special education program, or if modifications to the normal vocational education program are required to compensate for the child's handicap, then the vocational education program would have to be addressed in the IEP in the same way as any other area of special education. All efforts should be made to ensure that the providers of the vocational education services participate in the development of the IEP.

15. *Must the IEP specify the extent or amount of services or simply list the services to be provided?*

The extent or amount of services must be stated in the IEP, so that the resource commitment can be clear to parents and other IEP team members. Some general standard of time must be indicated, which (1) is appropriate to the specific service to be provided, and (2) is clear to all IEP participants. For example, in the case of speech-language pathology services, the IEP would indicate the number of sessions per week to be provided and the approximate length per session.

Changes in the amount of services listed in the IEP cannot be made without holding another IEP meeting. However, as long as there is no change in the overall amount, some adjustments in scheduling the services should be possible (based on the professional judgement of the service provider) without holding another IEP meeting. (NOTE: The parents should be notified whenever this occurs.)

---

§ 121a.346 *Content of IEP*—Continued

(d) The projected dates for initiation of services and the anticipated duration of the services; and

(e) Appropriate objective criteria and evaluation procedures and schedules for determining, on at least an annual basis, whether the short term instructional objectives are being achieved.

(20 U.S.C. 1401(19); 1412 (2)(B), (4), (6), 1414(a)(5); Senate Report No. 94–168, p. 11 (1975).)

---

16. *Can the anticipated duration of services be projected for more than one calendar year?*

   In general, the anticipated duration of services would be projected for a period of up to one calendar year. (There is a direct relationship between the anticipated duration of services and the other parts of the IEP (e.g., annual goals and short term objectives); and each part of the IEP would be addressed whenever there is a review of the child's "program.") However, for purposes of communicating that a particular service might be needed for an extended period of time, the anticipated duration of such services could be projected beyond one calendar year, provided that the "duration" is considered whenever a child's IEP is reviewed.

17. *Must the "evaluation procedures and schedules" be included as a separate item in the IEP?*

The evaluation procedures and schedules need not be included as a separate item in the IEP, but they must be presented in a recognizable form and be clearly linked to the short term objectives. (NOTE: In many instances, these components are incorporated directly into the objectives.)

OTHER "CONTENT" QUESTIONS

18. *Is it permissible for an agency to have the IEP completed when the meeting begins?*

    It would not be appropriate for an agency to present a completed IEP to parents for their signature. The Act defines the IEP as a written statement *developed in any meeting* with the agency representative, the teacher, the parent, and the child whenever appropriate.

    It would be appropriate for agency staff to come prepared with evaluation findings, statements of present levels of educational performance, and in some cases, with a recommendation regarding annual goals, short term instructional objectives, and the kind of special education and related services to be provided. However, the agency must make it clear to the parents from the outset of the meeting that the services proposed by the agency are only recommendations for review and discussion with the parents. The legislative history makes it clear that parents must be given the opportunity to be active participants in all major decisions affecting the education of their handicapped children.

19. *Is there a prescribed format or length for IEPs?*

    No. The format and length of IEPs are matters left to the discretion of State and local agencies. The IEP should be as long as necessary to adequately describe a child's program. However, as indicated earlier, the IEP is not intended to be a detailed instructional plan; and, therefore, the Federal IEP requirements can usually be met in a one to three page form. (NOTE: In a national survey on IEPs conducted through a BEH contract, it was found that 47% of the IEPs reviewed were 3 pages or less in length.)

20. *Is it permissible to integrate the IEP requirement under P.L. 94–142 with the individualized service plan requirements under one of the other Federal programs in which such plans are mandated (e.g., Medicaid and Title XX), or must they be maintained as separate, distinct records?*

    In instances when a handicapped child must have both an IEP and an individualized service plan under one of the other Federal programs, it may be possible to develop a single, consolidated document, provided that (1) it contains all required information from both programs, (2) all necessary parties participate in its development, and (3) it includes an assurance that the requirements of each participating agency are met.

Examples of individualized service plans which might be integrated with the IEP are: (a) the Individualized Care Plan (Medicaid), (b) the Individualized Program Plan (Title XX), (c) the Individualized Service Plan (Title XVI, SSA, SSI) and (d) the Individualized written Rehabilitation Plan (Rehabilitation Act of 1973).

21. *Is the IEP subject to the confidentiality requirements under P.L. 94–142?*
Yes. The IEP is subject to the confidentiality requirements of both the Act (Section 617(c)) and regulations (§§ 121a.560–121a.576). In addition, under the Family Educational Rights and Privacy Act (FERPA), the IEP is considered to be an "educational record," and is subject to the same protections as other records relating to the student that are maintained by the public agency. (NOTE: The Act and regulations for P.L. 94–142 both cross reference the FERPA.)

NOTE: Under Section 99.31 of the FERPA regulations, an educational agency may disclose personally identifiable information from the education records of a student without the written consent of the parents "if the disclosure is—(1) To other school officials, including teachers, within the educational institution or local educational agency who have been determined by the agency or institution to have legitimate educational interests."

---

§ 121a.347   Private School placements.

(a) *Developing individualized education programs.* (1) Before a public agency places a handicapped child in, or refers a child to, a private school or facility, the agency shall initiate and conduct a meeting to develop an individualized education program for the child in accordance with § 121a.343.

(2) The agency shall insure that a representative of the private school facility attends the meeting. If the representative cannot attend, the agency shall use other methods to insure participation by the private school or facility, including individual or conference telephone calls.

(3) The public agency shall also develop an individualized educational program for each handicapped child who was placed in a private school or facility by the agency before the effective date of these regulations.

(b) *Reviewing and revising individualized education programs.* (1)

After a handicapped child enters a private school or facility, any meetings to review and revise the child's individualized education program may be initiated and conducted by the private school or facility at the discretion of the public agency.

(2) If the private school or facility initiates and conducts these meetings, the public agency shall insure that the parents and an agency representative:

(i) Are involved in any decision about the child's individualized education program; and

(ii) Agree to any proposed changes in the program before those changes are implemented.

(c) *Responsibility.* Even if a private school or facility implements a child's individualized education program, responsibility for compliance with this part remains with the public agency and the State educational agency.

(20 U.S.C. 1413(a)(4)(B).)

If placement decisions are made at the time the IEP is developed, how can a private school representative be in attendance at the meeting?

Generally, a child who requires placement in either a public or private residential school has already been receiving special education; and the parents and school personnel have often jointly been involved over a prolonged period of time in attempting to find the most appropriate placement for the child. At some point in this process (e.g., at a meeting where the child's current IEP is being reviewed), the possibility of residential school placement might be proposed—by either the parents or school personnel. If both agree, then the matter would be explored with the residential school. A subsequent meeting would then be conducted to finalize the IEP. At the meeting in which the IEP is finalized, the public agency must insure that a representative of the residential school either (1) attends the meeting, or (2) participates through individual or conference telephone calls.

---

§ 121a.348   Handicapped children in parochial or other private schools.

If a handicapped child is enrolled in a parochial or other private school and receives special education or related services from a public agency, the public agency shall:

(a) Initiate and conduct meetings to develop, review, and revise an individualized education program for the child, in accordance with § 121a.343; and

(b) Insure that a representative of the parochial or other private school attends each meeting. If the representative cannot attend, the agency shall use other methods to insure participation by the private school, including individual or conference telephone calls.

(20 U.S.C. 1413(a)(4)(A).)

NOTE: A separate policy clarification paper is being developed concerning the education of handicapped children placed in parochial or other private schools by their parents. Any questions concerning IEPs for this group of children will be addressed in the private school paper.

---

§ 121a.349   Individualized education program—accountability.

Each public agency must provide special education and related services to a handicapped child in accordance with an individualized education program. However, Part B of the Act does not require that any agency, teacher, or other person be held accountable if a child does not achieve the growth projected in the annual goals and objectives.
(20 U.S.C. 1412(2)(B); 1414(a) (5), (6): Cong. Rec. at H 7152 (daily ed., July 21, 1975).)
Comment. This section is intended to relieve concerns that the individualized education program constitutes a guarantee by the public agency and the teacher that a child will progress at a specified rate. However, this section does not relieve agencies and teachers from making good faith efforts to assist the child in achieving the objectives and goals listed in the individualized education program. Further, the section does not limit a parent's right to complain and ask for revisions of the child's program, or to invoke due process procedures, if the parent feels that these efforts are not being made.

Is the IEP a performance contract?
Section 121a.349 (above) was written specifically to address this question. The IEP is *not* a performance contract which can be held against a teacher or public agency if a handicapped child does not meet the IEP objectives. As stated above, the agency must provide special education and related services in accordance with each handicapped child's IEP. However, P.L. 94–142 does not require that the agency, the teacher, or other persons be held accountable if the child does not achieve the growth projected in the written statement.

APPENDIX D

State Education Agency
Special Education Units

If specific contact person is unknown, address inquiries to Director

Alabama
Division of Exceptional Children and Youth
State Department of Education
868 State Office Building
Montgomery, Alabama 36104
(205) 832–3230

Alaska
Section on Exceptional Children and Youth
Division of Instructional Services
State Department of Education
Pouch F
Juneau, Alaska 99801
(907) 465–2970

American Samoa
Division of Special Education
State Department of Education
Pago Pago, American Samoa 96799
(Dial Oper) 633–4789

Arizona
Division of Special Education
State Department of Education
1535 W. Jefferson
Phoenix, Arizona 85007
(602) 271–3183

Arkansas
Division of Instructional Services
State Department of Education
Arch Ford Education Building
Little Rock, Arkansas 72201
(501) 371–2161

California
Special Education Support Unit
State Department of Education
721 Capitol Mall
Sacramento, California 95814
(916) 445–4036

Colorado
Pupil Services Unit
State Department of Education
State Office Building
201 E. Colfax
Denver, Colorado 80203
(303) 839–2727

Connecticut
Bureau of Pupil Personnel & Special Educational Services
State Department of Education
P.O. Box 2219
Hartford, Connecticut 06115
(203) 566–4383

Delaware
State Department of Public Instruction
Townsend Building
Dover, Delaware 19901
(302) 678–5471

District of Columbia
Division of Special Educational Programs
415 12th Street, N.W.
Washington, D.C. 20004
(202) 724–4018

Florida
Bureau of Education for Exceptional Students
State Department of Education
319 Knott Building
Tallahassee, Florida 32304
(904) 488–1570 or 3205

Georgia
Division of Early Childhood and Special Education
State Department of Education
State Office Building
Atlanta, Georgia 30334
(404) 656–2678

Guam
Department of Education
P.O. Box DE
Agana, Guam 96910
(Dial Oper) 772–8300

Hawaii
Special Needs Branch
State Department of Education
Box 2360
Honolulu, Hawaii 96804
(808) 548–6923

Idaho
Special Education Division
State Department of Education
Len Jordan Building
Boise, Idaho 83720
(208) 384–2203

Illinois
Department of Special Educational Services
State Department of Education
100 North First Street
Springfield, Illinois 62777
(217) 782–6601

Indiana
Division of Special Education
State Department of Public Instruction
229 State House
Indianapolis, Indiana 46204
(317) 927–0216

Iowa
Division of Special Education
State Department of Public Instruction
Grimes State Office Building
Des Moines, Iowa 50319
(515) 281–3176

Kansas
Division of Special Education
State Department of Education
120 East Tenth Street
Topeka, Kansas 66612
(913) 296–3866

Kentucky
Bureau of Education for Exceptional Children
State Department of Education
West Frankfort Complex
8th Floor Capital Plaza Tower
Frankfort, Kentucky 40601
(502) 564–4970

Louisiana
Special Educational Services
State Department of Education
Capitol Station
P.O. Box 44064
Baton Rouge, Louisiana 70804
(504) 342–3641

Maine
Division of Special Education
State Department of Educational
   & Cultural Services
Augusta, Maine 04330
(207) 289–3451

Mariana Islands
Division of Special Education
Department of Education Headquarters
Saipan, Mariana Islands 96950

Maryland
Division of Special Education
State Department of Education
P.O. Box 8717, BWI Airport
Baltimore, Maryland 21240
(301) 796–8300 x 256

Massachusetts
Division of Special Education
State Department of Education
31 St. James Avenue
Boston, Massachusetts 02116
(617) 727–6217

Michigan
Special Education Services
State Department of Education
P.O. Box 420
Lansing, Michigan 48902
(517) 373–1695

Minnesota
Special Education Section
State Department of Education
Capitol Square
550 Cedar Street
St. Paul, Minnesota 55101
(612) 296–4163

Mississippi
Division of Special Education
State Department of Education
P.O. Box 771
Jackson, Mississippi 39205
(601) 354-6950

Missouri
Division of Special Education
Department of Elementary and Secondary Education
P.O. Box 480
Jefferson City, Missouri 65101
(314) 751-2965

Montana
Division of Special Education
Office of the Superintendent of Public Instruction
State Capitol
Helena, Montana 59601
(406) 449-5660

Nebraska
Special Education Section
State Department of Education
223 South 10th Street
Lincoln, Nebraska 68508
(402) 471-2471

Nevada
Division of Special Education
State Department of Education
400 W. King St., Capitol Complex
Carson City, Nevada 89701
(702) 885-5700 x 214

New Hampshire
Division of Special Education
State Department of Education
105 Loudon Road, Building #3
Concord, New Hampshire 03301
(603) 271-3741

New Jersey
Division of Special Education
State Department of Education
225 W. State Street
Trenton, New Jersey 08625
(609) 292-7602

New Mexico
Division of Special Education
State Department of Education
State Educational Building
300 Don Gaspar Avenue
Santa Fe, New Mexico 87503
(505) 827–2793

New York
Office for the Education of Children with Handicapping Conditions
State Department of Education
55 Elk Street
Albany, New York 12234
(518) 474–5548

North Carolina
Division for Exceptional Children
State Department of Public Instruction
Raleigh, North Carolina 27611
(919) 733–3921

North Dakota
Division of Special Education
State Department of Public Instruction
State Capitol
Bismarck, North Dakota 58501
(701) 224–2277

Ohio
Division of Special Education
State Department of Education
933 High Street
Worthington, Ohio 43085
(614) 466–2650

Oklahoma
Division of Special Education
State Department of Education
2500 N. Lincoln, Suite 263
Oklahoma City, Oklahoma 73105
(405) 521–3351

Oregon
Division of Special Education
State Department of Education
942 Lancaster Drive, N.E.
Salem, Oregon 97310
(503) 378–3598

Pennsylvania
Bureau of Special and Compensatory Education
State Department of Education
P.O. Box 911
Harrisburg, Pennsylvania 17126
(717) 783–1264

Puerto Rico
Special Education Programs for Handicapped Children
Department of Education
Box 759
Hato Rey, Puerto Rico 00919
(809) 764–1255

Rhode Island
Division of Special Education
State Department of Education
235 Promenade Street
Providence, Rhode Island 02908
(401) 277–3505

South Carolina
Office of Programs for the Handicapped
State Department of Education
Room 309, Rutledge Building
Columbia, South Carolina 29201
(803) 758–7432

South Dakota
Section for Special Education
Division of Elementary & Secondary Education
New State Office Building
Pierre, South Dakota 57501
(605) 773–3678

Tennessee
Division of Education for the Handicapped
State Department of Education
103 Cordell Hull Building
Nashville, Tennessee 37219
(615) 741–2851

Texas
Division of Special Education
Texas Education Agency
201 East 11th Street
Austin, Texas 78701
(512) 475–3501, 3507

Utah
Division of Special Education
Utah State Board of Education
250 E. 5th South
Salt Lake City, Utah 84111
(801) 533–5982

Vermont
Special Educational and Pupil Personnel Services
State Department of Education
Montpelier, Vermont 05602
(802) 828–3141

Virgin Islands
Division of Special Education
Department of Education
P.O. Box 630, Charlotte Amalie
St. Thomas, Virgin Islands 00801
(809) 774–0100 x 213

Virginia
Division of Special Education
State Department of Education
P.O. Box 6Q
Richmond, Virginia 23216
(804) 552–2402

Washington
Special Services Section
State Department of Public Instruction
Old Capitol Building
Olympia, Washington 98504
(206) 753–2563

West Virginia
Division of Special Education
Student Support System
State Department of Education
Capitol Complex, Room B-057
Charleston, West Virginia 25305
(304) 348–2034

Wisconsin
Division for Handicapped Children
State Department of Public Instruction
125 S. Webster
Madison, Wisconsin 53702
(608) 266–1649

Wyoming
Office of Exceptional Children
State Department of Education
Cheyenne, Wyoming 82002
(307) 777-7416

Bureau of Indian Affairs
Department of the Interior
Special Education Division
1951 Constitution Ave. N.W.
Washington, DC 20245
(202) 343-5517

APPENDIX E

National Centers for Information on Education of the Handicapped

Office of Special Education and Rehabilitation Services
U.S. Department of Education
400 Maryland Avenue, S.W.
Washington, DC 20202
(202) 245–9661

Closer Look
Box 1492
Washington, DC 20013
(202) 833–4160

Exceptional Child Education Resources
Reston, Virginia 22091
(800) 336–3728
(Residents of Virginia call collect (703) 620–3660)

The National Committee-Arts for the Handicapped
Washington, DC
(202) 223–8007

Association for the Severely Handicapped
Seattle, Washington
(206) 374–5011

National Learning Disabilities Assistance Project
Andover, Massachusetts
(617) 470–1080

Market Linkage Project for Special Education
Westerville, Ohio
(614) 890–8200

IRUC: Information and Research Utilization Center
for Physical Education and Recreation for the Handicapped
Washington, DC
(202) 833–5547

National Information Center for Special Education
Los Angeles, California
(213) 741–6681

National Association of State Directors of Special Education
Suite 610E
1201 16th St., N. W.
Washington, DC
(202) 833–4193

National Inservice Network
Indiana University
Bloomington, Indiana 47407
(812) 337–2734

APPENDIX F

Newsletters Containing Current Information on Programs for Handicapped Individuals

For subscription information contact the publishers. (Annual subscription rates in effect July 1, 1980.)

Education of the Handicapped (Bi-Weekly, $105)
Capitol Publications, Inc.
2430 Pennsylvania Ave., N.W.
Washington, DC 20037

Liaison Bulletin (Bi-Weekly, $30)
National Association of State Directors
of Special Education, Inc.
1201 Sixteenth St., N.W.
Suite 610 E
Washington, DC 20036

Update (Bi-Monthly, $8) (Contains section entitled Insight which covers governmental affairs and judicial reports.)
The Council for Exceptional Children
1920 Association Drive
Reston, VA 22091

APPENDIX G

Legal Advocacy Organizations

Many of the following organizations may be of assistance to parents, schools, or attorneys seeking information on laws for the handicapped or current and completed litigation.

Children's Defense Fund
1520 New Hampshire Ave., NW
Washington, DC 20036
(202) 483–1470

Commission on the Mentally Disabled
American Bar Association
1800 M St., NW
Washington, DC 20036
(202) 331–2240

Disabilities Rights Center
1346 Connecticut Ave., NW
Suite 1124
Washington, DC 20036
(202) 223–3304

Mental Health Law Project
1220 19th St., NW
Washington, DC 20036
(202) 467–5730

U.S. Department of Justice
Office of Special Litigation
Civil Rights Division
Washington, DC 20530
(202) 633–3430

Public Interest Law Center (PILCOP)
1315 Walnut St.
Philadelphia, PA 19107
(215) 735–7200

South Carolina P&A Training and
T/A Project
P.O. Box 1254
Charleston, SC 20402
(803) 723–2518

EMC Institute
24 Maplewood Mall
Philadelphia, PA 19144
(215) 849–7095

National Center for Law and the Handicapped
The American National Bank Building
211 W. Washington St., Suite 1900
South Bend, IN 46601
(219) 288–4751

Mid-Central Legal Center for the
Developmentally Disabled
University of Kansas Medical Center
Children's Rehabilitation Unit/UAF
39th and Rainbow Sts.
Kansas City, KS 66103
(913) 588–5647

Louisiana Center for the Public Interest
700 Maison Blanche Building
New Orleans, LA 70112
(504) 524–8182

DD Law Project
University of Maryland Law School
500 West Baltimore St.
Baltimore, MD 21201
(301) 528–6307

Boston University Law School
Center for Law and Health Sciences
209 Bay State Rd.
Boston, MA 02215
(617) 353–2904

Central Minnesota Legal Services
222 Grain Exchange Building
323 4th Ave., South
Minneapolis, MN 55415
(612) 338–0968

Education Law Center, Inc.
Suite 800-605 Broad St.
Newark, NJ 07102
(201) 624–1815

Community Services for the Handicapped
Center for Legal Representation
P.O. Box 1269
Los Lunas, NM 87031
(505) 865–9611, ext. 245

Juvenile Rights Project of ACLU Foundation
22 E. 40th St.
New York, NY 10016
(212) 725–1222

Developmental Disabilities Training Institute
#3 Craige Trailer Park-194a
University of North Carolina
Chapel Hill, NC 27514
(919) 966–5463

Index

Date Due